KINGDOMS OF GOLD,
KINGDOMS OF JADE

THE AMERICAS BEFORE COLUMBUS

BRIAN M. FAGAN

KINGDOMS OF GOLD, KINGDOMS OF JADE

THE AMERICAS BEFORE COLUMBUS

with 180 illustrations, 16 in color

THAMES AND HUDSON

To Duane Newhart, in memoriam
Edie Newhart, with love

FRONTISPIECE *Jade mask of a lord from the Classic Maya city of Palenque.*
In the kingdoms of the Maya and ancient Mexico jade was the most
highly valued precious material. In the kingdoms of ancient Peru,
however – the other great hearth of pre-Columbian American civilization –
gold was prized above all else.

First published in the United States in 1991 by
Thames and Hudson Inc., 500 Fifth Avenue
New York, New York 10110

Library of Congress Catalog Card Number 91-65315

Typeset in Monophoto Trump Medieval
Printed and bound in Spain by
Artes Graficas Toledo S.A.
D.L. TO–1136–1991

CONTENTS

THE ENCHANTED VISION

"And when we saw all those towns and villages built in the water, and other great towns on dry land, and that straight and narrow causeway leading to Mexico, we were astounded. These great towns . . . and buildings rising from the water, all made of stone, seemed like an enchanted vision . . . Indeed some of our soldiers asked whether it was not all a dream . . . It was all so wonderful that I do not know how to describe this first glimpse of things never heard of, seen, or dreamed of before . . ." Conquistador Bernal Díaz del Castillo never forgot that memorable day in November 1519, when Hernan Cortés' men gazed down on the great Aztec capital Tenochtitlan. The city shimmered in the clear sunlight of the Mexican highlands, seemingly floating in the shallow waters of Lake Texcoco. Díaz wrote of Tenochtitlan half a century after he wandered through its streets and plazas, through a market that rivaled that of Seville and Constantinople, yet the enchanted vision seemed as clear as the day he first encountered the wonders of Aztec civilization as an impressionable young soldier.

A quarter of a century earlier, on 12 October 1492, Christopher Columbus, Admiral of the Ocean Sea, had landed on San Salvador in the Bahamas, to come in contact with a world of unimaginable complexity. He met simple, naked people "very well made, of very handsome bodies and very good faces." Columbus believed he had landed on islands off the east coast of Asia, so he called his hosts "Indios," Indians. But only seven years after Columbus' death in 1506, Vasco Nuñez de Balboa trekked across mainland Central America and gazed on the waters of the Pacific stretching to the far horizon. The term "Indian" persisted, but it was apparent that these were not Asians. The Indians inhabited what Amerigo Vespucci called "a New World more densely peopled and abounding in animals than Europe, or Asia, or Africa."

The scholarly debates over the American Indian began as soon as Columbus returned to Spain. He paraded some of his strange captives before King Ferdinand and Queen Isabella in Seville. Friar and scholar alike gazed in astonishment. Who were these people? What manner of humans had "no boundaries of kingdoms and princes, and no king?" Were they, indeed, creations of God, human beings, at all? It took the famous Papal Bull of Pope Alexander VI in 1493 to resolve this point officially. *Inter Cetera* proclaimed the Indians were "people well disposed to embrace the Christian faith."

Adventurers, colonists, and missionaries descended on the Indies, decimating Indian populations with imported diseases, forced labor, and genocide.

At first, all Indians were assumed to be simple, unsophisticated people. Then, in 1519, Cortés arrived at the gates of Tenochtitlan and revealed the exotic world of the Aztecs to an astonished Europe. The Spaniards explored an orderly city of more than 200,000 people, ruled by a divine king who lived in magnificent splendor in a palace surrounded by fine gardens and aviaries. Moctezuma's domains stretched from the Pacific to the Gulf of Mexico, from sea level to more than 7,000 ft (2,100 m). His temples towered over the city, stained with the blood of human victims sacrificed to powerful gods. Here was a monarch whose wealth rivaled that of European kings. The polished and worldly Aztec lords were a far cry from Columbus' simple Indians, even if they did engage in human sacrifice.

As the Aztec empire crumbled in the face of the conquistadors, Francisco Pizarro and 168 Spaniards landed on the northern frontiers of the gold-rich Inca empire and marched resolutely into the highlands, toward the legendary Andean capital, Cuzco. They encountered the Supreme Inca Atahualpa at Cajamarca in the northern highlands and slaughtered his entourage to a man. Atahualpa assembled a roomful of gold from his kingdom as ransom, stripping the Temple of the Sun at Cuzco of its gold sheathing in the process. The gold was seized and Atahualpa garrotted. Within weeks, the leaderless Inca empire began to collapse. The Spaniards occupied Cuzco and looked with amazement at stone walls fashioned of blocks so precisely fitted together that a sword blade would not sink between them. The Temple of the Sun boasted a garden with golden flowers. Cuzco's storehouses burst with fine textiles, grain, and all the wealth of an empire that stretched from Lake Titicaca in the south to the Ecuadorian coast in the north, and from the Pacific Ocean to the borders of the Amazon rainforest on the far side of the Andes.

A Clash of Cultures

There is something undeniably romantic and tragic about the Spanish conquest of the Aztecs and the Incas. Romantic, because it was indeed extraordinary that the conquistadors should find and then defeat with so few men two completely unknown civilizations (the only imaginable equivalent in our own day would be if a spaceship from earth were to discover and subdue an alien race on perhaps Mars or Venus). Tragic, because Moctezuma and Atahualpa were so obviously ill-equipped, mentally and technologically, to defend themselves against their ruthless foe. They had neither any psychological understanding of their opponents, nor the weaponry – the horses and the muskets – with which to fight them. The Incas did in fact put up a dogged resistance over many years, and the last independent ruler of a much truncated Inca kingdom did not die until 1572. But both empires were doomed from the start.

RIGHT *Aztec alabaster head, discovered in the recent excavations in the Great Temple of Tenochtitlan.* OVERLEAF: LEFT *The New Fire ceremony, from the Codex Borbonicus, with four priests burning so-called "year bundles."* OVERLEAF: RIGHT *Scene from the Codex Borgia, finest of all Mexican manuscripts.*

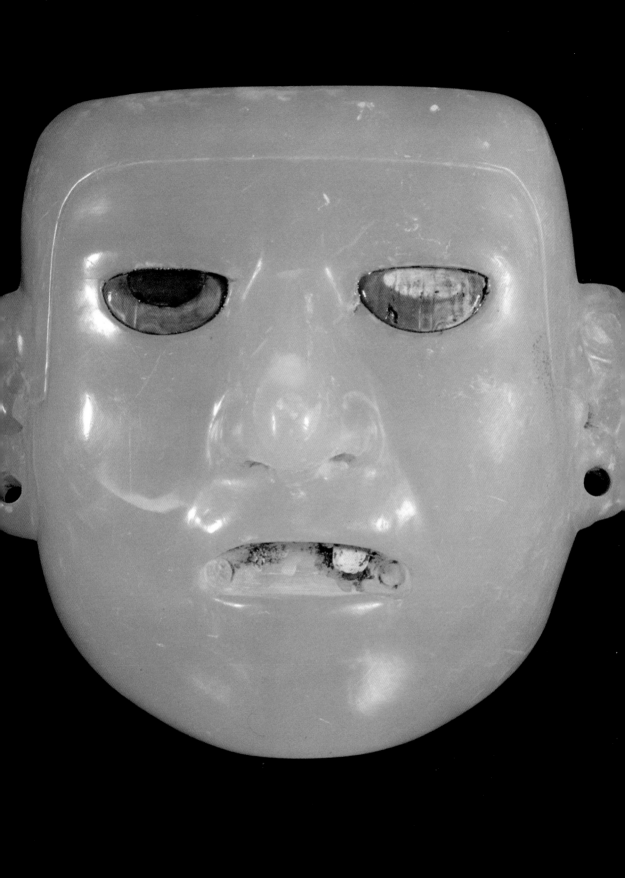

en tieRo d no che q se hazia de el
q un gran cacique q ados conarcaban todos los
pes las cerimonyas y Ritos q enello vsaban

The romance and the tragedy both struck a chord very early on in Spanish hearts, and there are extremely vivid first-hand accounts of their exploits by several conquistadors. One could not, for example, ask for a more dramatic or moving description of the last months of the Aztec empire than Bernal Díaz's *Conquest of New Spain*, completed in the 1570s. This sense of an epic quality has been carried over into more recent evocations of these great events. The American historian William Prescott's *Conquest of Peru*, written in the 1840s, is still the classic romantic narrative of the collapse of the Inca empire.

Inevitably, however, the romantic vision has cast native Americans in the role of inferior players in the clash of European and New World cultures. Five centuries of Western domination have served only to reinforce this belief in the superiority of the colonizing forces. Today American Indians, if their existence is remembered at all, are invariably seen as impoverished peoples on the fringes of modern society – to be pitied, or exploited, but rarely admired. And yet it was their cultures, as we shall see, that produced masterpieces in gold, silver, terracotta, and jade, masterpieces that fetch astronomical prices on the international art market. It was their cultures that created (and still create) some of the most vibrant and colorful textiles ever made. It was their cultures that gave the world over half the food plants we consume today. And it was, above all, their cultures that built great cities and powerful civilizations in tropical jungles and high mountains, regions considered too demanding by white settlers. Even today in Peru – where the capital lies at Spanish Lima on the coast, not where it once was at Inca Cuzco in the Andes – there is a basic failure to understand how the Incas could ever have supported the millions of subjects of their highland civilization. It has been left to archaeologists and indigenous peoples in recent years to rediscover the brilliantly simple agricultural methods that once made the mountains fertile. The modern tragedy is that those methods are still being neglected through arrogance and ignorance on the part of the dominant, colonial culture of the coast.

It is time, therefore, to look again at the history and achievements of pre-Columbian America. The sources for that history are many and various – written records penned by early colonists and explorers, and oral traditions taken down by missionaries and anthropologists. The prime sources of evidence, however, come from archaeology and the surviving artifacts and monuments of the native Americans themselves. In recent decades there have been an unprecedented number of remarkable archaeological discoveries. Excavations in the heart of Mexico City have stripped bare the successive building stages of the Great Temple of the Aztecs, providing fascinating new insights into Aztec cult practices. Farther south, in the Maya heartland of southern Yucatán, Guatemala, and western Honduras, an international team of scholars is even now busy deciphering the Maya hieroglyphs inscribed on stone monuments – thus revealing the history of a great civilization that was lost for over a thousand years. Far from being the peace-loving stargazers

LEFT *Quetzal feather headdress once belonging to the Aztec emperor Moctezuma, and presented by Cortés to the Hapsburg emperor, Charles V.*

previously conceived of, living scattered around semi-populated "ceremonial centers," the ancient Maya are proving to have been every bit as warlike as other civilized peoples, and the builders of fully-fledged, bustling cities in the tropical rainforest.

In Peru, spectacular tomb finds at the site of Sipán, on the desert coast, have uncovered the richest burials ever discovered intact anywhere in the Americas. They are important not only for the magnificent skill in goldworking and other crafts that they reveal, but for the new light they shed on the ancient Moche people, contemporaries of the Maya and like them builders of one of the major civilizations of pre-Columbian America. The Maya had to contend with the humid, tropical jungle, but for the Moche it was the terrible aridity of the Peruvian coast that had to be overcome. They dug vast networks of canals and irrigation channels to water their fields and supply their towns and villages. But the forces of nature were relentless. One of the startling findings of modern archaeology in Peru is the extent to which early civilizations there were vulnerable to adverse climatic changes. As we shall see, there is good evidence to suggest that Moche civilization collapsed as a result of decade-long droughts, followed by devastating earthquakes and catastrophic floods.

The Moche were by no means the earliest of Peru's civilizations. Archaeologists had long puzzled over the mysterious religious cult of the first millennium BC centered on Chavín de Huantar in the highlands. Fresh excavations at that site have indicated the strength there of symbolic and material links with the tropical lowlands to the east and the desert coast to the west. Prominent among the rainforest symbolism of the Chavín cult is the image of the jaguar, the most fearsome and powerful jungle predator in the Americas. Is it a coincidence that the jaguar also dominates the art and imagery of the jungle culture of the Olmecs, the earliest civilization of Mesoamerica* – knowledge of whose existence, like that of Chavín, we owe entirely to archaeology?

Olmec, Maya, Teotihuacan, Zapotec, Toltec, Aztec in Mesoamerica; Chavín, Moche, Nazca, Chimor, Huari, Inca in the Andes – our understanding of all these great pre-Columbian civilizations has been immeasurably enhanced by archaeological fieldwork over the last two or three decades. Perhaps for the first time it is now possible to gain some kind of overview, some broad picture, of what these civilizations were like, of how they arose and how they developed and why each in turn collapsed. The broad brush approach has its limitations: much important detail is undoubtedly lost and certain parts of the picture are inevitably distorted. But by bringing the story

---

* "Mesoamerica" is used by archaeologists to mean central and southern Mexico including the Gulf Coast and Yucatán Peninsula, Guatemala, El Salvador, and part of Honduras, Nicaragua, and northern Costa Rica. This is the general area where the Central American civilizations flourished. For the purposes of this book, the term "Andes" refers to coastal and lowland areas as well as the highlands of western South America.

of all these civilizations together in a single narrative, one can at least begin to perceive certain themes and intriguing parallels that might otherwise remain hidden. The power of natural forces and the pervasive imagery of the jaguar are two themes we have already touched on. Another, as we shall see, is the ubiquitous presence of artificial mounds or pyramids – does this reflect long-distance contacts and influences or simply a universal desire to reach towards the heavens?

The Mesoamerican and Andean civilizations must not, however, be looked at in isolation. What sets them apart from the general run of native American cultures? How indeed can one define the word "civilization" in the context of pre-Columbian America? The problem is to find a definition that accommodates both differences and similarities, the fact, for example, that the Aztecs had writing while the Incas did not. The answer seems to lie in the much greater economic, political, and social complexity of the great states of the Maya and Moche, of Teotihuacan and Chimor. The simple, basically egalitarian village societies of earlier times became part of much larger, more hierarchical societies ruled by a tiny minority in the name of powerful, temperamental gods. These societies were social and economic pyramids, with power held in the hands of an elite who organized the labor not of hundreds, but of thousands of commoners. But how did this complexity arise? When did village priests become powerful chiefs, then kings? The answers to these questions lie deep in prehistoric times, and take us back ultimately to the origins of all native Americans.

America's great civilizations were confined to Mesoamerica and the Andean region. In the North American Southwest, Midwest, and Southeast, there are abundant traces of once powerful societies, where great chiefs presided over imposing settlements like Snaketown in Arizona or Cahokia near St Louis. These centers were not, however, on the same scale as Tenochtitlan or Cuzco, nor, apparently, was their social and political organization ever as hierarchical as that of the Central and South American civilizations. Why did such societies not develop into complex civilizations to rival those of Mesoamerica and the Andes? The answer will emerge out of our discussion of the history of all the American Indian cultures.

There has been a tendency to think of the native American societies of 1492 as frozen in time, as static entities that appeared, dramatically and unexpectedly, on the familiar stage of Western history the moment Christopher Columbus landed in the Indies. This kaleidoscope of initial impressions is, in fact, but one scene of an immensely long archaeological movie that began many millennia ago, in the arctic wastes of the late Ice Age. This book begins, like that movie, with a dramatic climax, in the remarkable worlds of the Aztecs and Incas as Cortés and Pizarro stumbled across them after 1519. From there, our film script calls for a long flashback to the very beginnings of pre-Columbian time, and traces the many and rich strands that together created the Americas of 1492 and beyond.

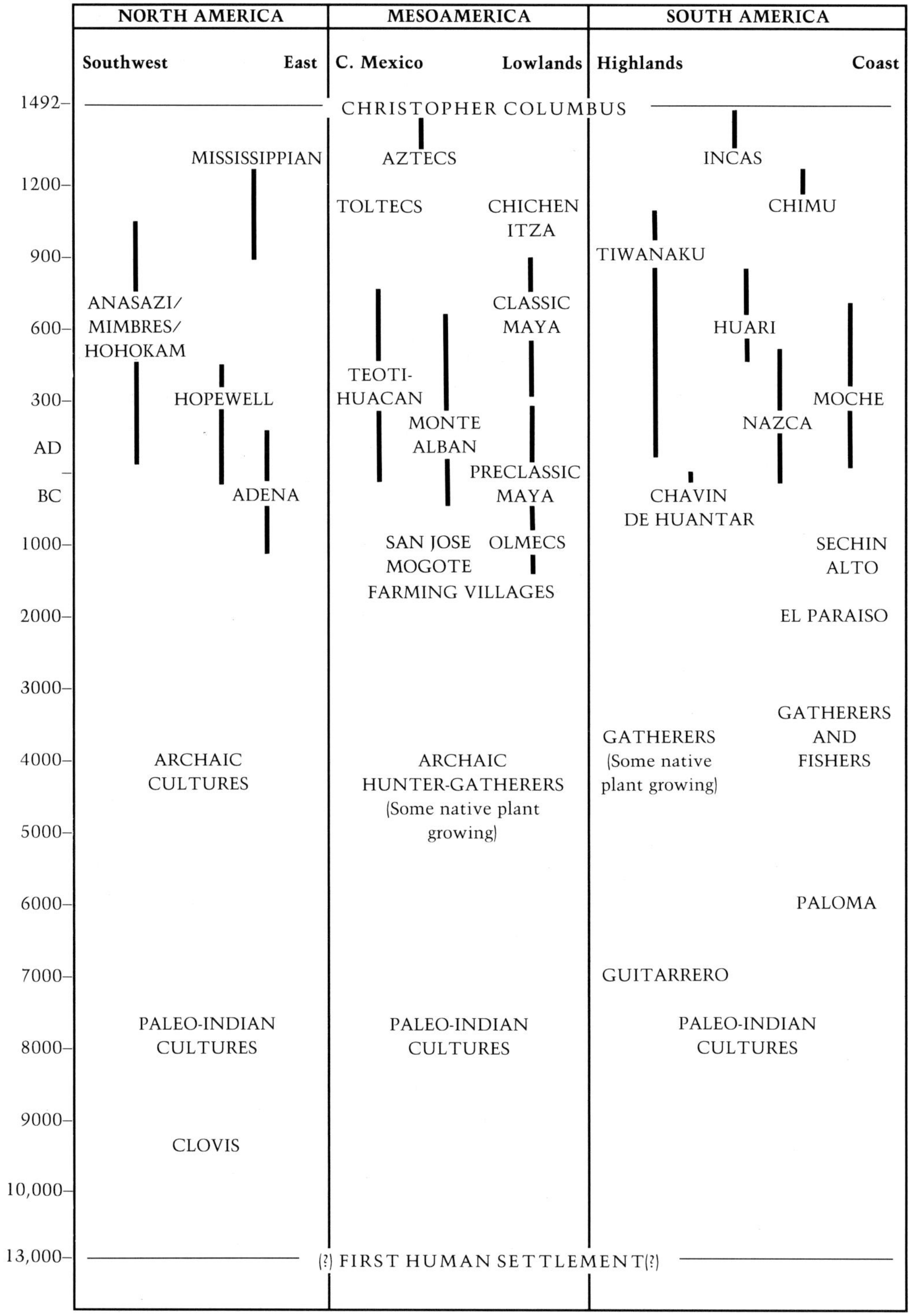

	NORTH AMERICA		MESOAMERICA		SOUTH AMERICA	
	Southwest	East	C. Mexico	Lowlands	Highlands	Coast

1492– CHRISTOPHER COLUMBUS

MISSISSIPPIAN

AZTECS

INCAS

1200–

TOLTECS   CHICHEN ITZA

CHIMU

900–

TIWANAKU

ANASAZI/
MIMBRES/
HOHOKAM

CLASSIC MAYA

600–

HUARI

TEOTI-
HUACAN

MOCHE

300–

HOPEWELL

MONTE ALBAN

NAZCA

AD

PRECLASSIC

BC

ADENA   MAYA

CHAVIN
DE HUANTAR

1000–

SAN JOSE   OLMECS
MOGOTE

SECHIN
ALTO

FARMING VILLAGES

2000–

EL PARAISO

3000–

GATHERERS
AND

GATHERERS
(Some native
plant growing)

FISHERS

4000– ARCHAIC
CULTURES

ARCHAIC
HUNTER-GATHERERS
(Some native plant
growing)

5000–

6000–

PALOMA

7000–

GUITARRERO

PALEO-INDIAN
CULTURES

PALEO-INDIAN
CULTURES

PALEO-INDIAN
CULTURES

8000–

9000–

CLOVIS

10,000–

13,000– (?) FIRST HUMAN SETTLEMENT(?)

PART ONE

THE CIVILIZATIONS OF 1492

"The eight or nine temples in the city were all close to one another within a large enclosure. Within this compound they all stood together, though each had its own staircase, its own special courtyard, its chambers, and its sleeping quarters for the priests of the temples . . . How marvelous it was to gaze upon them . . . All stuccoed, carved, and crowned with different types of merlons, painted with animals [covered] with stone figures . . ."

Diego Duran, *The Aztecs* (1591), quoting a conquistador

Head of the Aztec goddess Coyolxauhqui, part of a giant stone relief found at the foot of the Great Temple stairway in Mexico City.

CHAPTER ONE

THE WORLD OF THE FIFTH SUN
The Aztecs of Mexico

"The dismal drum of [Huitzilopochtli] sounded again, accompanied by conches, horns, and trumpet-like instruments. It was a terrifying sound, and we saw our comrades being dragged up to the steps to be sacrificed. When they had hauled them up to a small platform in front of the shrine where they kept their accursed idols we saw them put plumes on the heads of many of them; and then they made them dance with a sort of fan . . . Then after·they had danced the [priests] laid them on their backs on some narrow stones of sacrifice and, cutting open their chests, drew out their palpitating hearts which they offered to the idols before them. Then they kicked the bodies down the steps, and the Indian butchers who were waiting below cut off their arms and legs and flayed their faces . . ."

Bernal Díaz and his fellow conquistadors were horrified by the Aztec custom of human sacrifice. The priests offered victims to the gods in many ways, by shooting them with arrows, burning or beheading them, by drowning, and, most commonly, by ripping out their hearts. Our gut reaction is still one of abhorrence. The world of the Aztecs may be as close to us in time as the era of Britain's Tudor monarchs or Austria's Hapsburg emperors, but in many ways it seems so different, so alien, that it appears as remote as the centuries of Homer's Trojan War or the heyday of ancient Rome. It was the end result of thousands of years of isolated development in a separate continent. Aztec lords (or Mexica as they called themselves) presided over a city of pyramids and sacred temples that reeked with the blood of human sacrifice. Religious festivals honored such insatiable deities as Huitzilopochtli, the war and sun god, and Xipe Totec, the god of planting. In honor of Xipe Totec young men would don the flayed skin of a sacrificial victim, and wear it until it rotted off. A new, clean youth emerged, a symbolic emergence of a fresh sprout from an old maize husk. The symbolism is startling to us, its physical expression distasteful, but there is an internal coherence to it. The notion of fertility, of rebirth, suffused Aztec art, poetry, and religion. Nor was human sacrifice practiced on the whim of a dictatorial emperor. It stemmed from the profound and ancient belief that the sun god in his passage across the heavens had to be sustained by the nourishment of human hearts. The conquistadors may have felt the practice to be barbaric, yet they themselves were brutal in the extreme in their suppression of the native populations. The truth is that Old and New Worlds were indeed very different in the sixteenth century, but neither side valued human life very highly. And the Aztecs created a civilization – with its capital built on a lake, its organized religion and ritual calendar, its division into social classes, and its brilliantly successful methods of food production – every bit as complex as anything seen in the Old World.

Legendary Origins

In 1519, the Aztec ruler Moctezuma presided over an empire of some five million subjects that extended from the lowlying coast of the Gulf of Mexico to the Pacific, and from northern Mexico to Guatemala. Only two years later, his empire was in tatters. "The queen and mistress of the entire land," as one Spanish historian called the capital Tenochtitlan, was but a ruinfield and memories of the Aztec empire were dimming fast.

In 1529 a Franciscan friar named Bernardino de Sahagún arrived in Mexico. The young missionary was of scholarly bent and soon mastered Nahuatl, the indigenous lingua franca. Sahagún was fascinated by the tales of pre-Conquest days told by the older generation. He enlisted prominent Aztec elders as informants, some of them merchants, others nobles and commoners. Sahagún soon discovered that the Aztecs communicated with the aid of pictorial codices, birchbark books, most of which had been burned in an initial campaign against pagan ways after the Conquest. His informants produced hidden codices and went through them picture by picture, taking Sahagún

The Aztec empire together with the capital Mexico (Tenochtitlan) and modern regions.

back to the world of their ancestors. The codices were not written scripts in the modern sense. They served as *aides-mémoire*, prompt books for the orators who were entrusted with the transmission of oral history and other knowledge to later generations. Trained orators learned the great discourses of the past, delivered court speeches, taught students in school. "It was then that the words of wisdom came forth," remarked the friar's informants. Between 1547 and 1569, Sahagún compiled one of the masterworks of American scholarship, his *General History of the Things of New Spain*, a twelve-volume compendium on Aztec civilization.

The *General History* treats of the "gods worshipped by the natives," of Aztec religion, ritual, and cosmology, of astrology and "Very Curious Things Concerning the Skills of Their Language." Sahagún describes the people themselves, their nobles, the history of their rulers, and "the merchants and artisans of Gold, Precious Stones, and Rich Feathers." There are descriptions of Aztec natural history and medicine, and, in the last volume, a priceless account of the Spanish Conquest through Indian eyes, from which we quoted in the Introduction.

The histories Sahagún and other friars collected are an amalgam of legend and historical fact, a jumble of officially sanctioned genealogies and blatant political propaganda that confuse scholars to this day. They begin on a mythical island in a lake named Aztlan, somewhere northwest of the Valley of Mexico. The original Aztecs were semi-civilized farmers, who may have scraped a living under the rule of the powerful Toltecs, people we shall meet again in a later chapter. Like many other such groups, the Aztecs migrated to the Valley of Mexico from the north in the mid-twelfth century. "The rock is called Chicomoztoc, which has holes on seven sides; and from there came forth the Mexicans, carrying their women . . . that was a fearsome place, for there abounded the countless wild beasts established in the area . . . and it is full of thorns, of sweet agave, and of pastures; and being thus very far-off, no one still knew later where it was."

The legends tell how a heterogeneous group of at least seven Aztec clans wandered in the Valley of Mexico, losing themselves in the "mountains, the woods, and the place of crags." They had entered a morass of shifting alliances and constant warfare between small, competing states. The Aztecs were insignificant players in this political and religious maze, scorned by all, yet ultimately the people who pulled together these warring interests into a single state. How did they achieve this extraordinary transformation in their fortunes?

The Rise of the Aztec State

The Valley of Mexico in the thirteenth and fourteenth centuries has been compared to the constantly quarreling Balkan states in Europe before World War I. Every state, however small, was vying for the role of true heir to the

RIGHT *So-called "chacmool" painted stone and plaster statue, with its receptacle for the hearts of sacrificial victims, found at the entrance to Tlaloc's shrine at the summit of the Great Temple of Tenochtitlan.*

Toltecs. It was during this period, so Aztec legend recounts, that the war god Huitzilopochtli assumed supreme spiritual leadership. Huitzilopochtli, "the humming bird of the south," was probably an amalgam of an ancient tribal hero and a lake god named Opochtli. He had emerged fully grown from his mother Coatlicue's womb, brandishing his weapon, Xiuhcoatl, the Serpent of Fire. This bloodthirsty deity governed the destiny of the Aztecs until the Spanish Conquest. Huitzilopochtli appeared before one of the priest-leaders, ordering him to search for a cactus where a great eagle perched. It was here, he said, that his new capital, Tenochtitlan, was to rise – "the Place of the Prickly Pear Cactus." The priests duly found the cactus and the eagle and recognized the symbolism of the place. The cactus fruits were red, in the shape of the human hearts that the god devoured. And the eagle was the symbol of the sun, of Huitzilopochtli himself. Less than a century and a half later, the greatest city in the Americas lay on this spot.

A more unprepossessing location for a future capital city it would be hard to imagine. Initially Tenochtitlan was little more than a hamlet on a swampy island at the southern end of Lake Texcoco – the lake that once filled much of the Valley of Mexico. But the Aztecs were nothing if not tough and resourceful. By backbreaking labor they dug canals to convert their island swamp into a patchwork quilt of irrigated, extraordinarily fertile raised fields (so-called *chinampas*). And – making the most of their strategic and secure central location in the Valley – they forged clever alliances with whichever group among their neighbors seemed to have the upper hand. At first it was the Tepanecs: the Aztecs became their shock troops, greatly feared throughout the Valley. Then, in 1426, with the accession of their fourth ruler Itzcoatl ("Obsidian Snake"), the Aztecs felt sufficiently powerful to turn on their erstwhile political masters, and they crushed them militarily. They then formed the famous Triple Alliance, consisting of the three lake cities of Tenochtitlan, Texcoco, and Tlacopan, which consolidated the Aztec rise to fortune.

Itzcoatl and his second-in-command Tlacaelel, a man credited with great brilliance and cunning, reshaped Aztec history and society. They burned all the books of their defeated enemies, proclaiming themselves the true heirs of the mighty Toltecs. And they exalted the power of Huitzilopochtli as justification for military conquest. In his name, all political, religious, and economic power was concentrated in the hands of the ruler, all wealth and social privilege in the hands of the nobles and warrior knights. Itzcoatl's successor, Moctezuma Ilhuicamina (1440–1468), proclaimed that war was to be considered the principal occupation of the Aztecs, war designed not only to expand the imperial domains, but to ensure a constant supply of prisoners to satisfy the insatiable Huitzilopochtli. Moctezuma's priests now sacrificed not single victims, but hundreds of people to the war god each year. Meanwhile his warriors pursued a campaign of conquest, particularly to the east among the Huaxtecs.

LEFT *The startling life-size clay sculpture of an Eagle Warrior found inside the precinct of the Eagle Warriors during the recent Great Temple excavations.*

"Masters of the Entire World"

Moctezuma Ilhuicamina's successors inherited not only what was by now a growing capital city, but an empire founded on conquest and dependent on a mounting crescendo of human sacrifice. Two relatively weak rulers were followed by Ahuitzotl (1486–1501), an energetic general. During his reign parts of Guatemala and even El Salvador paid tribute to the mighty Aztecs. When Ahuitzotl's armies put down a rebellion among the Huaxtecs in 1487, Ahuitzotl and his priests celebrated completion of the final phase of the Great Temple in Tenochtitlan with an orgy of lavish gift-giving and human sacrifice that left blood flowing down the temple steps. No less than 20,000 captives were reputedly sacrificed, many brought in long processions from the Huaxtec region, some tied together with ropes through their noses. The dedication ceremonies were "an awesome spectacle: the street, squares, marketplaces and houses were so bursting with people that it looked like an anthill. And all of this was done with the purpose of lifting up the majesty and greatness of

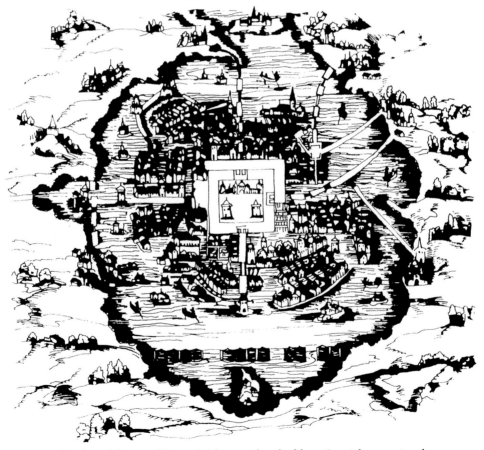

A somewhat fanciful view of Tenochtitlan, as sketched by a Spanish conquistador.

Mexico." Leaders from all over Mesoamerica were entertained and plied with bribes and gifts. Ahuitzotl distributed the equivalent of a year's tribute to his friends and enemies, including no less than 33,000 handfuls of exotic tropical bird feathers. This fantastic royal largesse shows the extent to which wealth and power rested in the hands of one man – the Aztec ruler.

By this time, the Aztec empire was at its peak. But it was locked into a vicious circle of conquest and further conquest. The Aztecs were forced to expand their domains simply to obtain more victims and more tribute. Increasingly, the empire became vulnerable to sedition and rebellion. There are signs in Aztec proverbs and verse that their society was one of growing philosophical ambivalence, between ferocious militarism and human sacrifice on the one hand, and notions of benevolence, humility, and mercy on the other. But the forces of militarism held sway. In the world of the Fifth Sun, nourished by human hearts, no ruler dared put the intemperate Huitzilopochtli on a diet.

In 1502, the Aztec nobles chose Moctezuma Xocoyotzin ("the Younger"), a nephew of Ahuitzotl, as their new ruler. It was his misfortune to preside over the collapse of an empire. By all accounts a brave warrior, he was also dangerously introspective at a time of crisis. Repeatedly, his armies took the field against the powerful city of Tlaxcala and her neighbors in the Puebla-Tlaxcala valley, a rival that had always managed to remain independent of the all-powerful Aztecs. Despite imposing a military blockade, Moctezuma never succeeded in subjugating Tlaxcala, a standoff that cost him dearly when the Tlaxcalans eagerly joined the Spaniards against their hated foes in 1519. Two years later Tenochtitlan had fallen to the foreigners.

The World of the Fifth Sun

For all their ardent militarism, the Aztecs were by no means an unthinking or unfeeling people. For them every deed, however ambitious or prosaic, was imbued with symbolic meaning and governed by ritual. Aztec sacred places commanded reverence. Everyone "whether noble or plebian, removed their sandals in the courtyard before they entered to worship their gods." Like that of earlier Mexican societies, the Aztec world view was partly governed by the lore of the stars and the heavenly bodies, for the words of the gods and the procession of time could be read in the skies.

Aztec priests used charts and poetry to teach people the cycles of years. Each person's destiny was tied to his or her birth date, and to two intermeshing calendars that measured secular and ritual time. As we shall see in later chapters, both calendars were based on day and year counts that had originated among much earlier civilizations.

The secular calendar, measuring the 365-day solar year, served to schedule planting, harvest, and the holding of market days. It consisted of 18 named months of 20 days each, making up a total of 360 days. The remaining 5 days of the solar year were of evil omen and dread significance. Each month had its own special ceremonies reflecting the fundamental division into wet and dry (agricultural and non-agricultural) seasons. The new year began with rites in honor of Tlaloc, the god of rain taken over from the Toltecs, subsequent months commemorating Xipe Totec, the spring deity. The seven months corresponding to September to March in our calendar were associated appropriately enough for a dry season with warfare, hunting, and fire.

The sacred, ritual calendar ran on a cycle of 260 days, consisting of 20 "weeks" of 13 days each. Each week had its own patron deity, as did each day name. For example, the goddess Mayahuel, the deity of intoxicating drink, was the patron of days with the rabbit sign, for the drunkard weaved and strutted about in the same erratic way as the rabbit. The 260-day cycle seems to have been used as a kind of horoscope, to help foretell the future. Certain days were lucky, others unlucky, and the priests were called on to pronounce when corn should be sown, or which days Aztec armies should do battle.

Once every 52 years, the secular and ritual calendrical cycles coincided. At this dread moment, time was believed to expire. All fires in every temple, palace, and house were to be quenched. People broke their possessions and stayed awake in fear until the priests on a sacred mountain near Tenochtitlan rekindled the flame symbolizing the start of the new cycle in the chest cavity of a sacrificial victim. Only then did the Aztec world embark on a new, but again finite, cycle.

This cyclical view of time – in many ways so different from our own linear view, where events unfold in an endless sequence – was, and still is, deeply embedded in the American Indian psyche. Aztec creation legends taught that Four Suns lasting 2028 years had preceded the present world of the Fifth Sun. After the Fourth Sun was destroyed by a great flood, primeval waters covered the darkened earth. The gods gathered at the ancient city of Teotihuacan (whose ruins not far from Tenochtitlan were a place of pilgrimage for the Aztecs), where the gods Nanauatzin and Tecuziztecatl jumped into the sacrificial fire and became the sun and moon. They were immobile, so the wind god Ehécatl "arose and exerted himself fiercely and violently as he blew. At once he could move him [the sun] who thereupon went his way. And when he had already followed his course, only the moon remained there. At the time when the sun came to enter the place where he set, then once more the moon moved."

This new world of the Fifth Sun, the world in which the Aztecs believed they lived, would itself end one day in violent destruction. To postpone this fearful moment the gods demanded sacrificial victims. It was the Aztecs' sacred duty to feed the sun daily with *chalchiuhuatl*, "the precious liquid," a form of nectar found in human blood. To the Aztecs, life was symbolized by the heart, *yollotl*, something that was inconceivable without *yolli*, movement itself. The elaborate sacrificial rites, and the preoccupation with blood, so characteristic not only of the Aztecs, but of much older Mesoamerican

Axxi de março dia de sant
benyto. tlaca xi peualiz tli
es gran fiesta

Blood Sacrifice

TOP _An Aztec Jaguar Warrior armed with a shield and obsidian-bladed club prepares to attack a sacrificial victim, whose club is tipped only with feathers._ ABOVE _Sacrificial victims have their hearts torn out in honor of the war god Huitzilopochtli, whose shrine lies at the summit of the temple-pyramid._

civilizations, were not so much an expression of fear, or even an attempt to placate angry deities. They were the fulfillment of an obligation to return food and energy from society to the earth, the sky, and the waters. The Nahuatl word for sacrifice is *uemmana*, *uentli*, "offering," and *mana*, "to spread out."

Many Spaniards called the Aztecs cannibals, and indeed the nineteenth-century American historian William Prescott embellished the stereotype even more by writing of a "banquet teeming with delicious beverages and delicate viands, prepared with art and attended by both sexes." Despite extravagant claims that human flesh was a vital part of Aztec diet, used to correct protein deficiencies, most experts believe that they only consumed small amounts on important ritual occasions, perhaps as acts of renewal.

Feeding the sun was the warriors' business. Aztec poets spoke of the battlefield with passionate euphemisms, as if battle were a rain of blossoms wherein warriors in all their finery fell and died like tree blossoms in springtime. This was the celebrated "flowery death," the cherished fate of the most elite of Aztec warriors. They, and all the Aztecs, were conditioned to believe that they were the chosen people of the sun, charged with the duty of supplying it with the only food that nourished it – *chalchiuhuatl*. Everywhere, in state-run schools, in public art and poetry, in the design of temples, even in dress codes and daily life, the leaders of the Aztecs proclaimed that their people were engaged on a divine quest – to forge an empire in the name of Huitzilopochtli.

The Great Temple: Symbolic Center of the Universe

The focal point for the rites of human sacrifice was the Great Temple in Tenochtitlan. Until quite recently our knowledge of this hub of the Aztec universe came largely from documentary sources. The Spaniards demolished the final temple at the conquest and built their own cathedral on much the same site. But then in 1978 electricity workers digging a pit came across a gigantic oval stone, over 3.2 m (10 ft 7 in) in diameter, not far from the cathedral. Reliefs carved on the stone depicted the dismembered body of the goddess Coyolxauhqui who, according to myth, had been killed by her brother, Huitzilopochtli. The Mexican authorities quickly realized that this extraordinary find held the key to unlocking the mysteries of the whole site. They established the Great Temple Project under the direction of Eduardo Matos Moctezuma (appropriately named indeed for such an enterprise) and, in the space of five years, he made the most important series of Aztec archaeological discoveries of all time.

Matos Moctezuma and his colleagues unearthed the remains of the Great Temple itself. Little survived of the final building razed by the Spanish, but beneath it lay no less than six earlier phases of the temple, the second dating to about 1390 virtually complete. It transpired that the original building had been a small and crude construction, later enclosed within successively larger

RIGHT *Giant statue of the goddess Coatlicue, mythical mother of Huitzilopochtli, which may once have resided in the war-god's shrine on the Great Temple. Two serpents form her head and she wears a necklace of hands, hearts, and a skull.*

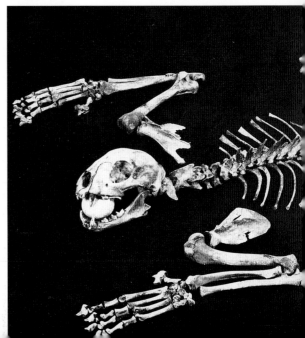

Discoveries from the Great Temple Excavations

MAIN PICTURE *The Great Temple (left) and its ceremonial precinct in an artist's reconstruction.* FAR LEFT *Stone sculpture of the "Old God," Huehueteotl, and below, under excavation by Eduardo Matos Moctezuma.* BOTTOM LEFT *Stone head of the fertility god Xipe Totec, wearing the skin of a sacrificial victim.* BOTTOM CENTER *Jaguar skeleton buried beneath the temple with a greenstone ball in its mouth, perhaps representing the spirit of the deceased.* BOTTOM RIGHT *Stone mask of Tlaloc, the goggle-eyed god of rain.*

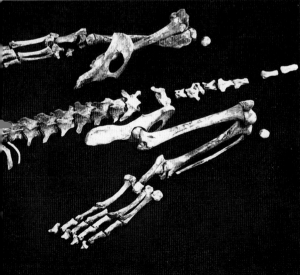

shells, new pyramids each with their own shrines, sculpture, offerings, and other artifacts. In all about 6,000 objects were excavated from 86 separate offering caches – some of them objects of Aztec manufacture, but the great majority clearly tribute or spoils of war from different parts of the empire buried here as a sacred expression of Aztec power and might. They included magnificent artifacts of obsidian, jade, and terracotta – and even ancient stone masks from Teotihuacan, which has led Matos Moctezuma to make the fascinating suggestion that the Aztecs were themselves amateur archaeologists, who dug up the masks at this ruined city.

How did these offerings relate to the layout and purpose of the temple itself? Matos Moctezuma's excavations have shed new light on the Aztec view of the cosmos. According to the Aztecs, the earth lay in the center of the universe, encircled by a ring of water. Above lay the heavens with the gods and beneath lay the Underworld. The terrestrial level of existence had a central point, located at the Great Temple, from which radiated the four directions of the Aztec world. The Great Temple was the symbolic pivotal point, the place where a vertical channel led both to the heavens and to the Underworld. The symbolism went even further, for Tenochtitlan itself lay in the midst of a lake. Indeed it was sometimes called Cemanahuac, ''Place in a circle of water,'' thought of as a turquoise ring. Such, also, was Aztlan, the mythical Aztec island homeland, surrounded by water. Thus, Tenochtitlan was the symbolic center of the universe and the place where the supreme ruler interceded with the gods.

The Great Temple in the heart of Tenochtitlan depicted the Aztec vision of the cosmos. According to Matos Moctezuma, the platform that supported the whole structure of the temple corresponded to the terrestrial level of existence. The four tapering tiers of the pyramid itself rose to the summit and represented the celestial levels. At the summit was the supreme level, with the two shrines to the two supreme gods, Huitzilopochtli and Tlaloc. The Underworld lay beneath the platform, and Matos Moctezuma points out that most of the offerings come from below it. These offerings include a very large number associated with Tlaloc – not just depictions of him, but extraordinary quantities of fish and marine animal bones appropriate for this god of water and rain. Most remarkable of all is the offering of a complete jaguar skeleton: in later chapters we shall have cause to remember the presence here of this ferocious predator, so much at home in watery environments, as we survey its all-pervading influence in older civilizations.

The Imperial State

The Aztec state was, in effect, an oligarchy controlled by the rulers of the Triple Alliance cities, with the ruler of Tenochtitlan supreme among them. Control of potentially rebellious nobles from the provinces was exercised by requiring them to attend court and to supply warriors and foodstuffs in time of war. These lesser lords also had marriages arranged for them with women of the royal "harem," the better to bond together members of the elite with ties of blood-relationship. But what held the empire together was tribute. Where Aztec armies conquered, inevitably the tribute and tax collectors followed.

It is tempting to think of the Aztec empire as a monolithic, centralized state like that of imperial Rome. In fact, it is best described as a patchwork of alliances held together by a tribute machine. Regular supplies were ensured by orchestrated campaigns of taxation, political marriages, and veiled threats of armed force – there being no permanent, standing army. Tax collectors supervised carefully specified tribute payments to be made at regular intervals. Twenty-six towns, for example, had to supply one of the royal palaces with firewood. Indeed by the time of the Spanish Conquest one of Tenochtitlan's three palaces alone was sufficiently well provisioned by tribute to house and feed the entire Spanish and Tlaxcalan army.

Tribute took many other forms – raw materials like gold dust for fine ornaments, tropical bird feathers for ceremonial headdresses and warriors' uniforms, cotton mantles, tree gum, and animal skins were but a few of the demands. Jaguar skins, for example, were at a high premium, symbolizing as they did rulership and indomitable courage. It was no coincidence that Jaguar Knights, caparisoned in jaguar pelts, were among the most powerful warrior elite in Aztec society.

Coupled with tribute went trade. The entire city of Tenochtitlan depended on its professional merchants, the *pochteca*. While family vendors brought foodstuffs from the Valley of Mexico's network of irrigated fields into the city's markets, hundreds of artisans depended on the merchants and on tribute assessments for their exotic raw materials. Cacao beans served as a form of legal tender, the basis of a centuries-old pricing system that used not only cacao beans but cotton cloths, and even small pieces of copper, as price tokens. Cacao was also a prized luxury, for it made a variety of chocolate drinks that were the privilege of the nobility. Servants prepared frothy potions of this precious elixir with honey, spices, or chili. In moderation, chocolate "gladdens one, refreshes one, consoles one, invigorates one," said Sahagún's informants. Excessive consumption was said to make one dizzy, even deranged.

Long-distance traders had been active in the region for thousands of years, and the merchants followed in the tradition. They traveled on foot everywhere, learned local languages, and prepared the way for their master's armies. They traded valuables on these expeditions, valuables like "golden mountain-shaped miters, like royal crowns; and golden forehead rosettes, and golden necklaces of radiating pendants," also "the things used by common folk . . . obsidian ear plugs . . . and razors with leather handles, and pointed obsidian blades." The highly organized guilds of the *pochteca* were the eyes and ears of the Aztec ruler and the state. They would cement their social positions within their guild by throwing elaborate feasts. Sometimes wealthy

Feather Regalia

ABOVE LEFT, ABOVE RIGHT *Details from two pages of the Codex Mendoza illustrating Aztec warriors' costumes (right: feather headgear, quilted cotton tunics, and shields itemized in a list of tribute; left: as worn by captains and generals).* LEFT *Fan of bamboo and multi-colored feathers, showing a butterfly in the center.* NEAR RIGHT *Ceremonial featherwork shield, sent to Europe by Cortés, with a coyote, a version of the Aztec fire god, shown outlined in flames.* FAR RIGHT *Dyeing (above) and fixing the feathers.*

pochteca would purchase a slave and sacrifice him to Huitzilopochtli, hand out gifts, and feast their colleagues on tamales, chocolate, and hallucinogenic mushrooms. "He who eats many of them sees many things which make him afraid, or make him laugh . . .," remembered one of Sahagún's mushroom takers.

The merchants' activities centered on the great market at Tenochtitlan's satellite city, Tlatelolco, surely the greatest emporium in pre-Columbian America. Thousands of merchants and farmers displayed their wares in an open plaza that assaulted the visitor with bright sounds and peculiar smells. Dark-watered canals brought dozens of small canoes to the heart of the marketplace. Let conquistador Bernal Díaz take up the description:

"Let us begin with the dealers in gold, silver, and precious stones, feathers, cloaks, and embroidered goods, and male and female slaves who are also sold there . . . Next there were those who sold coarser cloth, and cotton goods and fabrics made of twisted thread, and there were chocolate merchants with their chocolate. In this way you could see every kind of merchandise to be found anywhere in New Spain . . . There were those who sold sisal cloth and ropes and the sandals they wear on their feet, which are made from the same plant. All three were kept in one part of the market, in the place assigned to them, and in another part were the skins of tigers and lions, otters, jackals, and deer, badgers, mountain cats, and other wild animals, some tanned and some untanned, and other classes of merchandise . . ."

Bernal Díaz walked through the great market the day after Hernan Cortés entered the Aztec capital in 1519. "We were astounded at the great number of people and the quantities of merchandise, and at the orderliness and good arrangements that prevailed," he wrote. "The murmur and hum of their voices and the words that they used could be heard more than a league off." Tenochtitlan's market was a hub of the Aztec world, an emporium so vast that one Spanish chronicler estimated that 20,000 to 25,000 people visited it a day, and nearly 50,000 on scheduled market days. But it was not to last.

The Spanish Conquest

The campaigns against Tlaxcala were at their height when Moctezuma Xocoyotzin began to receive ominous portents of new and momentous events. Coastal Indians reported seeing mountains moving on the sea. "An omen of evil fire [a comet] appeared in the heavens. It was like a tongue of fire, like a flame, like the light of dawn . . ." Moctezuma's uneasiness deepened when confidential messengers brought reports of white-bearded strangers to Maya country in distant Yucatán, strangers from over the eastern horizon who fought with the local people. A year later a tax collector named Pinotl hurried from the Gulf Coast with tales of winged towers bearing white-faced, long-bearded men. He had traded gold for their green glass beads. These were the ships of Juan de Grijalva, who had crossed from Cuba to explore the newly discovered mainland in 1517.

Moctezuma and his priests puzzled over these inexplicable events. Their imaginations reached back into their mythical history. Like the Aztecs themselves, the strangers appeared to have arrived after a long journey from a place veiled in mystery. The newcomers came across the wide ocean, home of the primordial mother, from the east, the direction of authority in Mesoamerican belief. The east was the direction of the rising sun, of renewal and fertility, linked to the power of the feathered serpent, the symbol of the powerful winds that brought summer rain. This was the ancient god Quetzalcoatl, a mingling of the iridescent green feathers of the quetzal bird, associated with royalty, and *coatl*, the serpent with his sinuous, flowing movement. And, by strange historical coincidence, Hernan Cortés landed in Mexico in the year "One Reed" in the Aztec calendar, a year associated with plumed serpents. Thus, Moctezuma became convinced that this was the returning Toltec god "Topiltzin Quetzalcoatl who had come to land. For it was in their hearts that he would come to land, just to find his mat, his seat."

Two years later, Hernan Cortés was astounded when Moctezuma's emissaries greeted him like a god. "They put him into the turquoise serpent mask with which went the quetzal feather head fan . . . And they put the necklace on him . . ." The bedecked Cortés bound the ambassadors in irons, fired off a large cannon, then released them after challenging them to a fight. When Moctezuma heard that Cortés had accepted the god's regalia he caused two prisoners to be sacrificed in the emissaries' presence for "they had gone to . . . look into the faces, the heads of the gods had verily spoken to them." As for Cortés, he cultivated Moctezuma's dissatisfied allies and advanced relentlessly on the waiting capital. The conquistadors paused to wonder at the great city glistening in the morning light, a sight they would remember for the rest of their lives. "But today all that I then saw is overthrown and destroyed: nothing is left standing," wrote Bernal Díaz many years later. Moctezuma's uneasy empire collapsed around his ears in 1521 in the face of an army of some 600 hardened Spanish soldiers armed with crude muskets, horses, and huge dogs, and a large force of Indian warriors.

The world of the Fifth Sun was built on a cyclical vision of history, a vision as ancient as civilization itself in Mexico. The fatalistic Aztecs believed Cortés was a returning god almost to the bitter end. One can hardly blame them, for their world view and their ideology came from vastly different roots from those of their conquerors. The beliefs that sustained this stoic civilization fashioned the relationships between rulers and their subjects in deeply religious terms. When the divine ruler faltered, so did his subjects, and the beliefs that underpinned them. Civilization collapsed, as it had so often done in Mexico before. The aggressive, individualistic newcomers brought not the divine benevolence of Quetzalcoatl, but suffering, death, exotic disease, and slavery.

CHAPTER TWO

LAND OF THE FOUR QUARTERS
The Incas of Peru

"It was not long before sunset, when the van of the royal procession entered the gates of the city . . . Elevated high above his vassals came the Inca Atahualpa, borne on a sedan or open litter, on which was a sort of throne made of massive gold of inestimable value. The palanquin was lined with the richly colored plumes of tropical birds, and studded with shining plates of gold and silver . . . Round his neck was suspended a collar of emeralds of uncommon size and brilliancy. His short hair was decorated with golden ornaments . . . The bearing of the Inca was sedate and dignified; and from his lofty station he looked down on the multitudes below with an air of composure, like one accustomed to command."

Drawing on eyewitness Spanish accounts, the nineteenth-century historian William Prescott vividly recreated Inca Atahualpa's entrance into the city of Cajamarca, Peru, on the evening of 16 November 1532. Here the Spaniards under Pizarro sprang their trap: "Pizarro saw that the hour had come. He waved a white scarf in the air, the appointed signal. The fatal gun was fired from the fortress . . . Rushing from the avenues of the great halls in which they were concealed, [the Spaniards] poured into the *plaza*, horse and foot, each in his own dark column, and threw themselves into the midst of the Indian crowd." Soon Atahualpa and his entourage were overcome. In the months that followed, Inca bearers brought an enormous ransom of gold and silver artifacts to Cajamarca, where it was melted down into bullion by the Spanish. But Atahualpa's captors showed no mercy: on 26 July 1533, they killed him.

Soon the Spaniards marched south and laid waste to the imperial capital Cuzco. Conquistador Mancio Serra de Leguicamo received the gold disc from the Temple of the Sun as his share of the loot. Half a century later he recalled on his deathbed how "we found these lands in such a state that there was not even a robber or a vicious or idle man, or adulterous or immoral woman." But now, he reflected sadly, "this great kingdom has fallen into such disorder . . . it has passed from one extreme to another." The Inca empire, the last of the magnificent pre-Columbian civilizations, had passed into oblivion.

As Leguicamo lay dying, Garcilaso de la Vega, "El Inca," born of Spanish and Inca nobility, began work on "the most genuinely American book that has ever been written." *The Royal Commentaries of the Inca* set out to

RIGHT *Gold sacrificial knife or "tumi" from Peru's north coast, c. 1100–1300, inlaid with turquoise and indicative of the kind of superb metalwork produced in Inca times, but largely melted down by the Spanish. About 15 in (39 cm) tall.*

describe the birth, expansion, and fall of the Inca empire from its legendary origins until the execution of the last independent Inca ruler in 1572. Vega drew on his "ties with both nations" to paint a picture of an orderly, conforming society, where the rights of the individual were subordinated to those of the community. El Inca quoted his uncle, who told him how, in the earliest mythical days, "The prince went northwards, and the princess south. They spoke to all the men and women they found in that wilderness and said that their father the Sun had sent them from the sky to be teachers and benefactors to the dwellers in all that land, delivering them from the wild lives they led . . ." Like the Aztecs, the Inca prided themselves on their rags-to-riches history.

Land of the Four Quarters

The Incas called their empire *Tawantinsuyu*, "Land of the Four Quarters." Four highways from Cuzco's central plaza divided the kingdom into the four *suyu* (quarters), which were themselves linked to the four quarters of the Inca heavens. The empire measured some 2,700 miles (4,300 km) from end to end, extending from the southern borders of modern Colombia down the highlands and coastal regions of Ecuador and Peru, across highland Bolivia into northwestern Argentina, and far south into central Chile. It was the largest empire of antiquity ever to arise south of the equator, and quite possibly the largest in existence on earth at the time of the Spanish Conquest. Some ten million people were living within the Inca realm when the empire was at its height.

Tawantinsuyu was a land of dramatic environmental contrasts, of high mountains and lowlying coastal deserts, encompassing tropical rainforest and some of the driest landscapes on earth. The Inca homeland lay to the south, high in the central Andes and northwest of Lake Titicaca, in a small area around Cuzco. The flat basin around Lake Titicaca is known today as the Altiplano, in Inca times a productive area of potato fields and extensive pastureland where domesticated llamas provided wool and carried loads. Far to the north, the arid Pacific coastal plain, intersected by a series of relatively short river valleys, supported huge irrigation schemes that turned both river floodplains and intervening desert areas into rich and populous agricultural landscapes. These were the two poles of Andean civilization, the southern highlands and the northern coastal lowlands, for the densest populations lived at opposite ends of Tawantinsuyu, a cultural and demographic polarity that had been a reality in Andean life for thousands of years. The Incas were the first people to join the two centers of Andean civilization into a single empire, this unification achieved using a technology based on simple bronze, copper, and stone. For all its great size, its superb road network, and its apparent splendor, the Incas' Land of the Four Quarters lasted for little longer than a century.

LEFT *Sacsahuaman, the great fortress of the Inca capital Cuzco, built after 1438 by the Inca ruler Pachakuti.*

The Emergence of the Incas

The Incas emerge into recorded history during the fourteenth century, a period of political turbulence, not on the north coast where the kingdom of Chimor was all-powerful, but in the southern mountains. Here, neighbor was pitted against neighbor in a state of constant antagonism, competing for control of the rich Altiplano. This was the region once controlled by the mighty state of Tiwanaku that had flourished on the eastern shores of Lake Titicaca until about AD 1000 or 1100. Much later, the Incas sought legitimacy by claiming that they were descended from the rulers of Tiwanaku, but archaeology tells us this is untrue. In fact, the Incas were just one of many local farming cultures in the southern highlands.

   The official Inca histories taken down by Spanish chroniclers speak of at least eight rulers between AD 1200 and 1438, but these records are hardly reliable. The earliest Inca leaders were little more than successful warrior chiefs, based at the growing village of Cuzco. The eighth ruler, however, Viracocha Inca, was more ambitious. Previous chiefs had contented themselves with merely raiding neighboring communities without actually

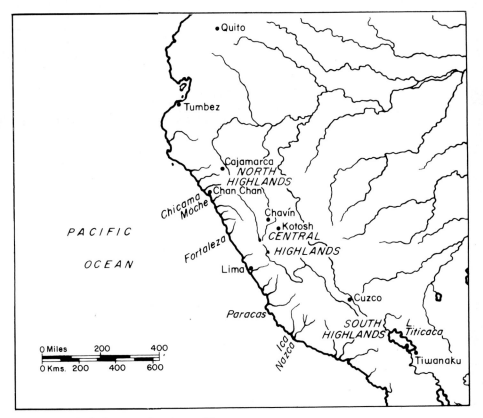

ABOVE *Principal places and regions of Peru.*

RIGHT *The solemn, dignified face of a Quechua Indian, modern descendant of the Incas.*

subjugating them. Viracocha Inca went much further. He conquered the area around Cuzco, and held on to the new territories. By forging new alliances, Viracocha Inca was able to patch together a larger sphere of influence for what may now be called his small kingdom.

Then, in about 1438, Viracocha Inca's domain came under attack from the powerful Chanca people to the north. The Chanca laid siege to Cuzco. The aged Viracocha Inca retreated to the hills, leaving the defence of his capital to one of his sons, Yupanqui. In an epic struggle, the young man routed and conquered the Chanca. He became supreme ruler, and adopted the name Pachakuti, "He who remakes the World." Pachakuti did indeed restructure the Inca world. He is said to have rebuilt Cuzco in the form of a puma, the great fortress of Sacsahuaman forming the head. "He [Pachakuti] ordered twenty thousand men in from the provinces, and that the villages supply them with food . . . Four thousand of them quarried and cut the stones; six thousand hauled them with great cables of leather and hemp; the others dug the ditch and laid the foundations, while still others cut poles and beams for the timbers," wrote Pedro de Cieza de León, a sixteenth-century Spanish chronicler of the Incas. Pachakuti also created a state religion based around the sun god, Inti, and a cult of royal ancestor worship.

Pachakuti's reforms and new ideology had an immediate and dramatic effect on the Incas. By 1450, his armies controlled the rich northern Titicaca Basin. This was just the beginning, for the Inca juggernaut rolled on. In a series of brilliant campaigns Pachakuti's successor Topa Inca (1471–1493) extended the empire into Ecuador, northern Argentina, parts of Bolivia, and Chile – truly the exploits of an Alexander the Great of the continent, as archaeologist Michael Moseley dubs him. Topa Inca's armies also conquered the Chimú state on the northern coast. The next king, Wayna Capac (1493–1525), pushed the empire deeper into Ecuador. As Hernan Cortés was toppling the distant Aztec civilization in Mexico, Tawantinsuyu reached its zenith, even if effective Inca rule was confined to Peru, Ecuador, and highland Bolivia. Many of the Incas' southern conquests may never have been fully integrated into the empire.

Cuzco: Capital of an Empire

At the time of the Spanish Conquest, Cuzco was a city of single-story houses with steeply pitched, thatched roofs. Pachakuti and his successors had laid out the town on a cruciform plan with narrow, paved streets. A stone-lined channel for fast-flowing water down the middle of each street provided very efficient sanitation – far better than anything known in Europe at the time. The water was so clean in the two small rivers running through the city that the Incas bathed there.

One of the rivers passed through the huge central plaza, dividing it into two parts. To the west lay Cusipata, where the people celebrated their festivals with great entertainments. Aucaypata to the east was larger and surrounded on three sides by the closely fitted granite walls of the Incas' palaces and ceremonial buildings. Pizarro himself occupied Pachakuti's palace, the Casana, remarkable for its enormous hall, said by Garcilaso de la Vega to be capable of holding 4,000 people. A later ruler, Wayna Capac, had lived in a palace with a gateway of red, white, and multicolored stone and "two towers of fine appearance."

The Temple of the Sun, the Coricancha, lay a few hundred yards south of the central plaza, at least six one-roomed buildings with gold-clad walls grouped around an open courtyard. The magnificent masonry enclosure wall stood at least 15 ft (4.5 m) high. Inside, the conquistadors found "many golden llamas, women, pitchers, jars, and other objects." There was a garden of golden plants, adorned with replicas of maize with silver stems and ears of gold. This lay in the center of the temple, in front of the room that contained a golden image, "an image of the sun of great size, made of gold, beautifully wrought and set with many precious stones."

The masonry for all these public buildings was remarkable, great blocks joined together perfectly without mortar. The builders were so expert that it is practically impossible to insert a knife blade between the fitted stones. How did the Incas manage to quarry, transport, and fit these blocks? University of California architect Jean-Pierre Protzen has studied Inca stonemasonry and visited the remote quarries where the red granite for the Sun Temple came from. He believes the Incas searched for stone blocks that had fractured naturally from the quarry cliffs, but often removed and rough-shaped them with river cobbles of different weights. The rough, or sometimes shaped, blocks were then dragged along a network of roads to Cuzco, where they were dressed and fitted. Protzen noticed that the blocks in dismantled Inca walls displayed concave depressions on their upper surfaces. He believes the stonemasons hammered out these depressions to fit the overlying boulder in the next course. Protzen took his dressed block, placed it on a larger stone, and traced the outline. Then he pounded out a depression in the underlying boulder, using the fine dust from his work to see where the fit was still inaccurate. With trial and error, he achieved a snug match, using the same technique to prepare the lateral joints that appeared on the front and back of his "wall." In this case, however, the join was only a few centimeters thick and the depression behind could be filled with fine rubble.

All of this stonework required thousands of hours of laborious pounding and fitting, but time and labor were of no consideration to rulers with abundant manpower and no Western notions of time. The result was some remarkable, and highly durable, buildings.

Cuzco was far more than a royal capital and spiritual center. It was a storehouse as well. The Incas kept their supplies in rows of identical fieldstone sheds, storehouses "full of cloaks, wool, weapons, metal, cloth, and all other goods that are grown in this country. There were weapons and

Masterbuilders in Stone

RIGHT AND FAR RIGHT *The alpaca (agate miniature, right) and the llama – the only draught animals in the Americas – could carry loads of up to 100 lbs (45 kg), but it was mostly human labor that shifted the great stone blocks used in Inca buildings.* BELOW LEFT *Ancient and modern: Spanish colonial masonry rests on Inca foundations in this Cuzco building, the Coca-Cola sign recalling the modern use for a pre-Columbian drug, the coca leaf.* BELOW CENTER *Machu Picchu, most remote and romantic of all Inca sites.* BELOW RIGHT *The magnificent masonry of an Inca building in Cuzco, with cruder Spanish-period infilling of the doorway.*

thousands of tiny, colored hummingbird feathers used to adorn the clothing of the nobility.'' There were even cloaks covered with dense layers of gold and silver counters that looked almost like chain mail. Cuzco was the hub of a vast and well-supplied empire.

The Sun God and the Cult of the Royal Mummies

The monolithic gateway at the ancient city of Tiwanaku near Lake Titicaca bears the image of what is often called the "Gateway God." He was an ancient sky god, the creator and weather god, a primeval deity. The Inca version of the sky god had three important roles (among many others). He was Viracocha, the universal creator, Inti the Sun God, and Illapa, the deity associated with thunderstorms and weather generally. The new ideology promoted by Pachakuti elevated Inti, the Sun God, to national patron of the Incas. In time, the people came to believe they were under Inti's protection, and that their leaders were descended from this deity. Inca religion linked the ideas of universal creation, national patronage, and divine ancestry of rulers.

It was but a short step from this to the belief that the divine Inca himself should not die, and that his spirit should be kept alive by worship of his royal mummy. Thus grew up the strange cult of royal ancestor worship – a cult that ensured that each new ruler would seek new land and thereby expand the empire. For when an Inca ruler died, one of his sons now inherited his powers as ruler, his rights to govern, to wage war, and to levy taxes. But the new leader received no material goods whatsoever from his father. All his predecessor's land, buildings, chattels, and servants were still considered to be the deceased's property and were entrusted to his *panaqa*, the deceased leader's other descendants in the male line. *Panaqa* members served the departed king, acted as his courtiers, maintained his mummy, and were fed by his perceived generosity. An Inca ruler was never considered dead, and maintained a lavish court in the hands of his descendants. "It was customary for the dead rulers to visit one another, and they held great dances and revelries. Sometimes the dead went to the houses of the living, and sometimes the living visited them,'' wrote Pedro Pizarro in 1571.

The royal mummies sat in special wall niches in the Coricancha temple in Cuzco during important ceremonies, alongside images of the Sun God. "The bodies of the kings and lords were venerated by the people as a whole, and not just by their own descendants, because they were convinced that . . . in heaven their souls played a great role in helping the people and looking after their needs,'' recorded chronicler Bernabé Cobo. The mummies attended every major ceremony, sitting in Cuzco's plaza in order of seniority. "In front of the mummies they lit a fire of a certain kind of wood . . . In the fire they burned the food they had set before the mummies to eat . . . The dead toasted one another, and they drank to the living, and vice versa; this was done by the ministers in their names.''

Meanwhile, the living ruler inherited power and prestige, but no material possessions or land to support him or to endow his own *panaqa*. It was up to him to acquire new wealth, especially in the form of land and compulsory labor. Inca law required every male head-of-household to contribute labor to the state each year, the so-called *mit'a* tax. Inca subjects paid the tax by cultivating state-owned lands, by serving in the army, or by laboring on public projects such as road building. In return the state provided produce from its lands to feed the laboring taxpayer. Thus a new Inca needed both new labor and new land if he were to prosper. This meant conquest of outlying territories which were then annexed to the empire. No Inca ruler could reign without land that enabled him to reciprocate generously, to build support.

The fundamental changes in Inca society after Pachakuti's reign were due in large part to the elaboration of royal mummy worship. In earlier times, each local kin group (*ayllu*) had set aside some land for the support of all ancestors. The institution of split inheritance for the rulers now meant that there were many more material demands on the people. As time went on, more and more land was owned by the dead and unavailable to the living rulers of an ever more complex state.

What advantages did the mummy cult bring Inca society? At the material level it seems largely designed to keep in check the power of the nobles, who were members of the *panaqas*. Their political prestige and power was second only to that of the supreme Inca himself, and their ambitions could be contained by membership of the wealthy *panaqas*. Every noble's son attended school in Cuzco, learning not only military skills, but Inca history and philosophy, the basic values that linked the ruler's ambitions with those of his subjects. A loyal and hardworking noble was rewarded with gifts of land, servants, and other privileges. So were valiant lesser nobles and soldiers, for, as in Aztec society, prowess on the battlefield was the key to upward mobility.

Holding Together an Empire

Control and conformity – these were the foundations of the Inca empire. The ruler, *Sapa Inca*, "the unique Inca," was at the apex of a rigid social hierarchy effectively controlled by the royal family. The nobility held all key government posts in the military, the priesthood, and the bureaucracy. Many were of royal blood, others were Incas by privilege through marriage or political alliance, entitled to wear the headbands and ear plugs of nobility.

The Incas ruled distant lands indirectly, somewhat in the manner the British governed parts of Africa in colonial times. The conquerors would appoint a hereditary *curaca*, a governor, usually of local birth, to preside over a population of about 100 people or more, while Inca nobles held the more important posts. Commoners were forbidden to own luxury goods such as gold objects, indeed anything excess to their household's immediate needs. The harsh laws that regulated property ownership were designed to curb stealing, and, by all indications, were remarkably successful in doing so.

Once new territories were conquered, the Incas would send in a small army of specially trained officials, who were the "scribes" of the empire. They were masters of the *quipu*, the knotted string. These functionaries would inventory everything on their knotted tallies – populations, villages, animals, grain stocks, plots of land, even household artifacts. The *quipu* substituted for the clay tablet and the papyrus roll in Inca society. The Incas had no writing. Like most pre-Columbian societies, they relied on human speech and memory to transmit lore from one generation to the next, for carrying royal decisions from one province to the next. But unlike the Aztec codex, the *quipu* was purely a way of storing precise information, a pre-Columbian computer memory, if you will.

We can only marvel at the ability of the Sapa Inca to control his vast domains, separated as they were not only by long distances, but by dramatic changes in altitude. Inca engineers developed a massive road system over some of the most rugged terrain on earth, a lattice of highways and tracks that covered a staggering 19,000 miles (30,000 km). The Inca empire could never have been created without this communication system that carried important officials, government correspondence, entire armies, and all manner of commodities and trade goods. Road-building started long before Inca times, for earlier states like Chimor on the coast also needed to connect dense concentrations of farmers in widely separated valleys. But the Incas vastly extended the network. The resulting lattice was a conceptual framework for the *quipu* makers, who used the sequences of sites on the roads to relate different areas to one another. Anthropologist John Murra has called these roads the "flag" of the Inca state, for they were a highly visible link between the individual and the remote central government. The same lattice of communication helped define symbolic alignments, link sacred shrines to the Temple of the Sun in Cuzco, and even separate different groups of people living near the capital.

Early Spanish chroniclers repeatedly praised Inca roads and described them as superior to European highways of the day. Cieza de León wrote of the route from Cuzco to Quito in Ecuador: "I believe there is no account of a road as great as this, running through deep valleys, high mountains, banks of snow, torrents of water, living rock, and wild rivers. Through some places it went through flat and paved; it was excavated into precipices and cut through rock in the mountains; it passed with walls along rivers, and had steps and resting spots in the snows. In all places it was clean and swept free of refuse, with lodgings, storehouses, Sun temples, and posts along the route . . . Oh! Can any thing similar be claimed for . . . any of the powerful kings who ruled the world that they were able to build such a road or provide the supplies found on it?"

The Inca and his officials used runners to administer the empire. The government built way stations alongside major roads about a mile and a half

Roads, Runners, and Record-keeping

An obscure Inca-Spaniard, Guamán Poma, spent nearly forty years recording these and other scenes of Inca life in the late sixteenth century. MAIN PICTURE *A runner with his conch shell horn and knotted string or "quipu" for conveying messages.* TOP LEFT TO BOTTOM RIGHT *Inca official in front of a bridge; fighting at one of the forts along the road network; roads eased the transport of the harvest from fields to storehouses; the Inca ruler checks food stores with a quipu official at one of the warehouses along the road system.*

(2.5 km) apart. Here runners waited to carry messages, so that royal commands could be relayed quickly from one end of the empire to the other. The Inca communication system was highly efficient, and operated at the limits that such a system could achieve. A team of official runners could carry an important message 125 to 150 miles (200–250 km) in a day. A message and its reply could be sent from Cuzco to Quito and back in 10 to 12 days. The same roads moved tribute on llama and human backs over enormous distances, and also served to deploy armies rapidly. The llama can carry only about 100 lbs (45 kg), slightly more than a man. It was the only draught animal used in the Americas. Both Mesoamerican and Andean civilizations were built very largely on people's backs.

Offshore, large balsawood rafts with rectangular sails plied the Pacific coast, carrying gold, silver, and other valuable cargoes that were traded with coastal communities far to the north. Francisco Pizarro's navigator Bartolomé Ruiz encountered an Inca raft with cotton sails in 1527, the first European contact with Inca civilization. "They were carrying many pieces of silver and gold as personal ornaments . . . including crowns and diadems, belts and bracelets . . . They were carrying many wool and cotton mantles and Moorish tunics . . . and many other pieces of clothing colored with cochineal, crimson, blue, yellow, and all other colors, and worked with different types of ornate embroidery . . . They were taking all this to trade for fish shells from which they make counters, colored scarlet and white," Ruiz reported to Charles I of Spain.

By the 1520s, the Incas controlled the lives of millions of people living in scattered villages and larger religious and political centers. At Cuzco, and other major communities, expert artisans labored to produce magnificent gold and silver ornaments, models of llamas and other animals, earrings and masks, cups, even golden maize, all for the ruler and the nobility. One of the great tragedies of history is that nearly all these artifacts and prized heirlooms were melted down immediately after the Spanish Conquest. We know more about Inca metalworking from artifacts found in pre-Inca cemeteries than we do from their own artifacts. In later chapters we describe that technology and the brilliant Andean mastery of textiles.

Tawantinsuyu Vanquished

The seeds of the Incas' destruction were sown as Tawantinsuyu expanded. As early as the reign of Pachakuti's son Topa Inca, the Incas ran out of open terrain to conquer. Their armies were adapted to campaigns conducted in settled, cultivated lands, in open environments where the tactics of massed warriors using long-range weapons were effective. The soldiers fought hand-to-hand, but always in situations where there was good visibility and ample ground to arrange one's forces. As successive rulers found no more open country to conquer, they turned their attention to the heavily vegetated slopes of the eastern Andes and the tropical rainforest of the Amazon Basin.

LEFT *This magnificent Chimú gold pectoral, or chest ornament, gives us a glimpse of the artistry and brilliance of Inca-period metalwork melted down by the Spanish.*

Here they encountered Vietnam-like problems. Their enemies attacked suddenly and without warning, melting into the trees before a counterattack could be mounted. The Incas suffered greatly from the heat and humidity. Decimated by fever, their armies retreated in disorder, leaving thousands of casualties behind them. The Inca eventually gave up campaigning in the forests and referred contemptuously to their enemies there as savages who mated with animals.

Successive Inca rulers tried various measures to modify the policy of continuous growth. When a new land was conquered, they would resettle some of its inhabitants in other areas to discourage rebellion, then bring in colonists from the Cuzco region. The use of such colonists was a shift away from the millennia-old policy of village self-sufficiency and kin ties as the way of organizing society, for the newcomers strengthened state control. So did another policy change that put the care of royal estates and *panaqa* lands in the hands not of transitory *mit'a* taxpayers but of permanent retainers. But ultimately the state proved vulnerable at the very top.

In 1525, Pachakuti's grandson Huayna Capac died while campaigning in Ecuador. His unexpected demise triggered a bitter power struggle between two of his sons, half-brothers Huascar and Atahualpa. Huascar was a legal heir, while Atahualpa was the progeny of a secondary marriage of Huayna Capac and unqualified for the succession. Reform-minded Huascar succeeded to the throne of an empire overextended by its ancestors. He proposed the abolition of the royal mummy cult and annexation of *panaqa* lands. This so infuriated the nobility that they plotted his downfall. Civil war broke out in 1529 or 1530 and lasted for three years. The fragile unity of Tawantinsuyu disintegrated as Atahualpa's more expert armies slowly pulverized Huascar's forces. In 1532, Atahualpa's generals captured Cuzco and Huascar and the civil war was over. But by an extraordinary chance of history the victorious leader met Francisco Pizarro and his band of 168 Spaniards while on his way to Cuzco for his coronation. It was then that the protectors of the Inca, their own ancestors, turned against their descendants and brought them down.

Both the Aztec and Inca empires collapsed in a matter of months, although spirited resistance continued in Peru for many years. Both empires had foundations rooted in a quicksand of uneasy alliances and unwilling tribute states. The Aztec empire had probably reached its zenith before Cortés arrived, and would, quite possibly, have entered a cycle of rapid decline within a few generations. The Incas' ancestors were driving their empire inexorably toward collapse. We should hardly be surprised at the rapid demise of both kingdoms, for cycles of quick ascent to power, glorious climax, and sudden decline were a common feature of both Mesoamerican and Andean history for several thousand years.

We must now turn back to trace the course of that history, back to the very beginnings of ancient America, to the world of the late Ice Age, to which the first Americans belonged.

PART TWO

THE FIRST AMERICANS

*"Long ago there were no stars, no moon, no sun. There was only darkness
and water. A raft floated on the water, and on the raft sat a turtle. Then
from the sky, a spirit came down and sat on the raft . . . Then the spirit
said that something else was needed, and he made people. He took earth
and mixed it with water and made two figures, a man and a woman. The
first man was called Kuksu, and the first woman was called Morning Star,
and by and by there were many people on the earth . . ."*

Maidu creation myth from central California

Arikara chief Sitting Bear, heir to over 12,000 years of American Indian history.

▲▲

CHAPTER THREE

THE BIG-GAME HUNTERS
Clovis and the Bison Hunters

The early summer wind sloughs across the undulating plains, raising clouds of dust. The bison-hide tents of the Clovis hunters cling to the ground, offering little resistance to the chill breeze, thin wisps of smoke rising toward the light blue sky. The sun has just risen. Two men bundled in skin cloaks crawl out of a tent and shiver in the cool of dawn. They keep low as they gaze intently across the small stream that winds through a row of willow trees below them. The hunters watch as a small mammoth herd moves sluggishly towards the swamp ground just downstream. The families have camped at this favored location for days, waiting for the lumbering beasts. The older man nods with satisfaction and turns to summon the men. It is time to stampede the unsuspecting herd, to move in for the kill.

The two Clovis families in the camp have lived by themselves for months, last summer's rendezvous with their neighbors just a memory. They know of other hunters in nearby valleys, of others further upstream, but there are no signs of human life on the endless, grass-covered plains that stretch to the far horizon. Their world is one of harsh winters and long, dry summers where life is hard, where game is always on the move. It is a world inhabited by mythical spirits and powerful animal-beings known only to the medicine man, who tells tales and recites myths on long winter nights.

These hunters lived on the Great Plains some 12,000 years ago. They were the primordial ancestors of the Aztecs, Incas, and other myriad societies that inhabited the Americas in 1492. But where did they come from and how long ago did they first settle in the New World?

Roots

It was a Jesuit missionary, José de Acosta, who first argued that the native Americans came from Asia. It was entirely possible, he wrote in 1589, that American Indians had followed the exotic beasts across Asia to the New World at least 2,000 years before Cortés gazed on Tenochtitlan. There were, he said, ''only short stretches of navigation,'' a remarkable statement considering that the Bering Strait was only discovered in 1725. Today, every serious student of pre-Columbian culture agrees that the native Americans came from Siberia. The open-water crossings across the Pacific Ocean in more southerly latitudes were simply too vast for people with only simple coastal craft. The arts of offshore navigation, of reading star transits out of sight of land, were unknown in Pacific waters until about 4,000 years ago, long after humans crossed into the New World by land. Despite agreement about the overland route, the manner and date of this first colonization remain the subject of intense and unrelenting controversy. The most vigorous debate surrounds the date of first settlement. When did the first settlers arrive: 50,000 years ago, 25,000 years ago, or after 15,000 years ago, at the very end of the Great Ice Age?

We can narrow the search immediately, for no fossil bones from archaic human beings such as the Neanderthals or other early people have been found in the Americas. This means that anatomically modern humans, *Homo sapiens sapiens*, were the colonizers of the New World, and they had not settled in Siberia until within, at the most, the past 35,000 years. But what evidence is there that the American Indians are, in fact, descended from northern Asians? Can we detect distinct waves of migration into the Americas?

A team of physical anthropologists from all over the United States has collaborated on a study of genetic markers in American Indian populations. They studied the variants (called Gm allotypes) of a particular protein found in the fluid portion of the blood, the serum. All proteins "drift," or produce variants, over the generations. Members of an interbreeding human population will share a set of such variants. Thus by comparing the Gm allotypes of two different populations one can work out their genetic "distance," which can be calibrated to give an indication of the length of time since these populations last interbred. The geneticists studied thousands of samples from human populations all over the Americas. Most of them formed a single genetic grouping, common to peoples living in all parts of the New World. Only the Athabaskans and Eskimo-Aleut populations of the far north displayed genetic differences. Thus this evidence indicates that there are three genetically distinct populations of native Americans, suggesting that there were three separate waves of migration in prehistory.

More recently, geneticist Douglas Wallace of Emory University has studied the genetics of mitochondria, small, energy-producing bodies found in each human cell. By charting similarities and differences among mitochondrial genes in cells from widely separated Indian groups in Arizona, the Yucatán, and the Amazon Basin, Wallace has been able to chronicle genetic links between these peoples and show they shared common ancestors, perhaps 15,000 to 30,000 years ago. Wallace believes that his Indian groups, and more than 95 percent of all native Americans, are descended from these people, perhaps a single band who crossed the Bering Strait in the late Ice Age.

Arizona State University physical anthropologist Christy Turner has approached the problem from another perspective, that of dental morphology. He is an expert on the changing physical characteristics of teeth, for their crowns and roots give clues as to the degrees of relationship between prehistoric populations. Crowns and roots have a high genetic component that minimizes the effects of environmental differences, sexual dimorphism, and age variations. Turner has shown that the teeth of both modern and prehistoric native Americans display fewer variations in their dental morphology than do eastern Asians. Their crown- and root-trait frequencies are similar to those of northern Asians. He calls these characteristics "Sinodonty," patterns of tooth features that include scooped out edges on incisors, and triple-rooted lower molars, among other features. Traveling far and wide in Europe and Asia, Turner has been able to show that Sinodonty, which he believes evolved some 20,000 years ago, occurs only in northern and eastern Asia and the Americas, whereas another characteristic pattern, "Sundadonty," is typical of prehistoric populations in the western USSR, southeast Asia, and eastern Asia.* Turner argues that there was an initial migration out of northeast Asia at the end of the Ice Age, followed – again on dental evidence – by two further migrations later in prehistory.

Joseph Greenberg is a linguist at Stanford University, who has devoted much of his career to a comprehensive survey of American Indian languages. Back in 1956, he proposed that most North American and all South American languages were part of one large "Amerind" family. This was the earliest group of languages spoken in the Americas. There were only two other groups, "Aleut-Eskimo" and "Na-Dene," both of them confined to North America. Greenberg spent years compiling a huge database of the vocabulary and grammar of native American languages, defining the differences between his three groups. So great are they that there is little chance they come from a single linguistic stock. By no means every linguist agrees with Greenberg's three groups, for there are some who hypothesize that there were numerous stocks. But it is striking that Greenberg's classification with its three broad groups coincides well with Christy Turner's dental information, and with the genetic data. If Turner is right in dating the appearance of Sinodonty in northern China to about 20,000 years ago, then first colonization must have been at the very end of the Ice Age, perhaps even after 15,000 years ago.

Ancestors

What, then, is the archaeological evidence for the ancestral Americans in northeast Asia? Anyone living in this vast region needed tailored clothing to survive nine-month winters, and specialized bone and antler technology for the chase. There would never have been many of them, for this bitterly cold

---

* Readers interested in the complex story of modern human origins are referred to the author's *The Journey from Eden* (Thames and Hudson, London and New York 1990), which recounts the intricate controversies surrounding the subject. For the debates over the first settlement of the Americas, see his *The Great Journey* (Thames and Hudson, London and New York 1987).

land could support far less than a person per square mile. Searching for these people is like looking for an archaeological needle in a haystack.

Only a handful of Soviet excavations record the presence of these hardy people, notably in the Kamchatka Peninsula and in the Middle Aldan River Valley, sites dating to after 14,000 years ago, perhaps a little earlier. Their small flint tools somewhat resemble hunting weapons made in northern China after 25,000 years ago. Perhaps, then, the ultimate homeland of the first Americans lies in northern China. Whatever the homeland, the first human settlement of these harsh latitudes took many centuries, part of a natural expansion of growing hunter-gatherer populations searching for dispersed game herds and sparse marine and plant foods. In more favored areas, the hunters may have camped astride migration routes of reindeer, mammoth, and other animals. Others congregated along lakes and rivers, perhaps along sea shores where sea mammals could be clubbed and taken from the ice. Everywhere, however, the ancestors of the first Americans were mobile and armed with light spears for taking game on the run in open country. In due time, some of them penetrated the heart of a now-sunken continent, Beringia, that was once the gateway to the Americas.

Beringia: The Lost Continent

For much of the past three-quarters-of-a-million years, the world's sea levels have been far lower than today, for vast ice sheets locked up much of the water from the ocean. Only 18,000 years ago, the Atlantic and the Pacific lapped coasts more than 300 ft (90 m) below modern levels. We must imagine a world where vast areas of lowlying continental shelf lay open to human settlement, joining island southeast Asia to the mainland, Britain to continental Europe, and Siberia to Alaska. The heart of a now-sunken continent, known to geologists as Beringia, joined Asia and North America for much of the past 100,000 years. This land bridge was only at its maximum extent at the intense climaxes of Ice Age glaciation, the last times about 50,000 years ago, and again around 18,000 years ago. But in the interim the shoreline still lay on average about 130 ft (40 m) below modern contours, enough to join Siberia and Alaska with an ice-free shelf. The land bridge did not finally vanish under rising seas until about 12,000 years ago. Theoretically, Ice Age groups could have traversed central Beringia any time between 50,000 and 15,000 years ago without using watercraft. What was this lost continent like? Could it have supported human life?

We must imagine a landscape of arid steppe-tundra, covered with a patchwork of grasses, sedges, and clumps of wormwood. Broad rivers flowed across floodplains that were swampy and marshy in the warm months, supporting lush grasses, willow brush, and other feed ideal for large Ice Age herbivores. The extinct woolly mammoth flourished in Beringia, a squat elephant with enormous padded feet, high massive head, and thick hair and

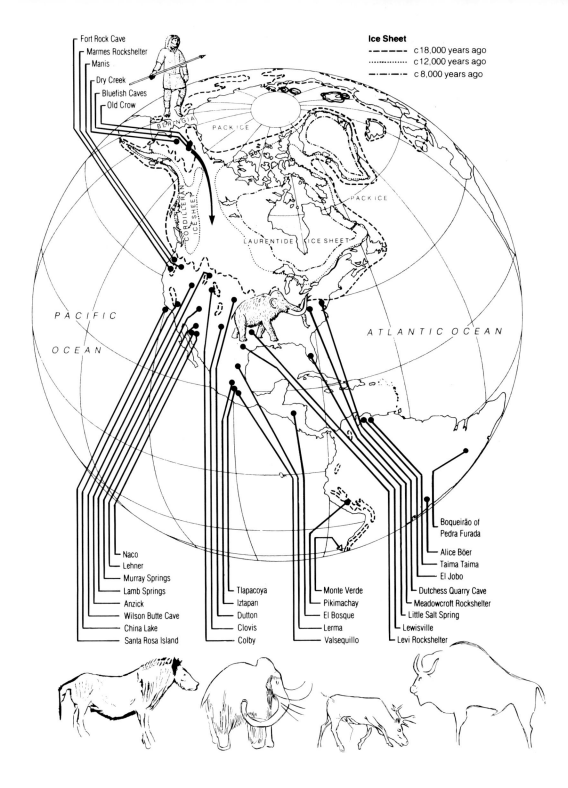

Ice Sheet
- - - - - c 18,000 years ago
········· c 12,000 years ago
-·-·-·- c 8,000 years ago

Fort Rock Cave
Marmes Rockshelter
Manis
Dry Creek
Bluefish Caves
Old Crow

BERINGIA

PACK ICE

CORDILLERAN ICE SHEET

LAURENTIDE ICE SHEET

PACK ICE

PACIFIC OCEAN

ATLANTIC OCEAN

Naco
Lehner
Murray Springs
Lamb Springs
Anzick
Wilson Butte Cave
China Lake
Santa Rosa Island

Tlapacoya
Iztapan
Dutton
Clovis
Colby

Monte Verde
Pikimachay
El Bosque
Lerma
Valsequillo

Boqueirão of Pedra Furada
Alice Böer
Taima Taima
El Jobo
Dutchess Quarry Cave
Meadowcroft Rockshelter
Little Salt Spring
Lewisville
Levi Rockshelter

TOP *Major early archaeological sites and other locations in the Americas during the last stages of the Ice Age, when human colonization took place. The routes that humans used to move south are still uncertain. One much discussed and controversial route is shown here: the widening corridor between the Cordilleran and Laurentian ice sheets.* ABOVE *Part of the Ice Age bestiary hunted by the first Americans – wild horse, woolly mammoth, reindeer/caribou, and steppe bison – seen here as depicted by cave artists in France.*

underwool. So did the now-vanished steppe bison, heavily built with enormous horns, and a coat as much as 30 in (76 cm) deep to protect it against arctic cold. There were many other big-game animals that lived on the steppe-tundra, including wild horse, reindeer/caribou, fast-running saiga antelope, and arctic fox. As we shall see, much of the Beringian fauna became extinct soon after the Ice Age, resulting in major adjustments in Indian lifeways.

One plausible scenario for first settlement is as follows. By about 15,000 years ago, a few hundred hunter-gatherer bands lived widely scattered in northeast Asia. The endless rhythm of late Ice Age life continued, just as it had for thousands of years. Band split off from band, as a result of quarrels, or when food became short, or perhaps when hunters ventured far afield in search of new prey. In time, a few families moved on to the land bridge to the east, exploiting herds of mammoth, bison, and other game. And in due course some of their descendants pursued these creatures onto the higher ground east of the land bridge. They may have moved into Alaska as rapid global warming began some 14,000 years ago, a warming vastly greater than anything experienced in our own time. Summer and winter temperatures rose, ice sheets shrank over Scandinavia, the Alps, and North America, and world sea levels rose inexorably, flooding lowlying continental shelves and isolating Siberia from Alaska. At first, the change would have been imperceptible, but within a couple of millennia the land bridge was shrinking rapidly. Eventually, a shallow but stormy strait separated two vast continents – and the human beings living in them.

At most, the population of Alaska probably numbered a few hundred in those remote days, but from these isolated bands evolved all the incredible diversity and brilliance of native American culture in 1492. Their archaeological footsteps have almost eluded us, for they stayed but a few days or weeks in most places. At Bluefish Caves, within sight of the desolate Keele Range in the western Yukon, Jacques Cinq-Mars of the Archaeological Survey of Canada has recovered a handful of small stone tools, dating to between 15,000 and 12,000 years ago, that had been used to kill mammoth, horse, bison, and caribou. Cinq-Mars believes the caves were visited around 12,000 years ago, perhaps a thousand years before some other hunters camped at Dry Creek in the Nenana Valley in the northern foothills of the Alaska Range. It is not until after about 9,000 years ago that traces of human occupation become more common in Alaska. But far to the south archaeologists have discovered other early sites – some of them dated controversially so early that they hint at colonization of the Americas well before 15,000 years ago. How reliable is this evidence and what are we to make of it?

A Question of Chronology

A few experts believe that human beings penetrated deep into South America very much earlier, long before the end of the Ice Age. But the sites they claim as evidence for such settlement are all problematical. Perhaps the best known of these locations is a rockshelter named Boqueirão of Pedra Furada in northeastern Brazil, a site from a region well known for its later prehistoric rock paintings. Pedra Furada lies on the steep bank of a sandstone cliff above a small river valley and has been shown to have been occupied by prehistoric hunters about 8,000 years ago. French archaeologist Niède Guidon probed much deeper into the sandy levels of the shelter, reaching bedrock at a depth of about 10 ft (3 m). "Traces of human occupations succeed one another throughout the stratigraphic sequence," she wrote in a report on the excavations. According to Guidon, these deep, sandy layers contain "hearths," heavy concentrations of ash and charcoal, also simple stone artifacts made on pebbles as well as more elaborate tools. The earliest dates for human occupation at Pedra Furada were first reported at about 32,000 years ago, but are now claimed to be as early as 47,000 years before the present, this early reading said to be associated with an ash-filled hearth ringed with a circle of stones.

Pedra Furada has raised violent archaeological passions, for a minority of archaeologists firmly believe that this remote site, which is hard of access, contains definite evidence for very early human settlement indeed. Opponents, who readily admit that they have been unable to visit the shelter, wonder whether the hearths were the result of natural forest fires. They worry whether rain runoff from the cliffs caused mixing in the deposits, or whether the stone "tools" were formed by rock falls from the cliffs above. Even the most enthusiastic outsiders seem to be no more than 80 percent certain that Guidon and her colleagues are correct. There are concerns, too, about the documentation of the still largely unpublished excavations.

Most scholars still have serious reservations about this interesting site, and about other claims for very early human presence in South America. There are reports of 20,000-year-old occupation at Pikimachay Cave high in the Peruvian Andes, and of 30,000-year-old settlement at Monte Verde in Chile. It is only fair to say that none of these, or other shadowy claims from Brazil or Argentina, have yet stood up to detailed, long-term scientific scrutiny. The earliest indisputable evidence for human settlement is much later, after 15,000 years ago.

Ice Sheets, Continental Shelves, and Corridors

The landscape of North America was very different only 15,000 years ago. In the far northwest, Alaska was largely ice free and formed part of Beringia. Two enormous ice sheets covered the rest of the arctic. The Laurentian was centered on Labrador and the Keewatin area of Canada, a complex glacial mass made up of many glaciers fused into a single, frozen wilderness. Glaciologists have traced the rubble of its boundaries from the Atlantic seaboard across the southern shores of the Great Lakes into southeastern Alberta. The glacial margins advanced and retreated with great rapidity, sometimes as much as 3,250 ft (990 m) a year, reaching their maximum extent between about 22,000 and 17,000 years ago. To the west, the Cordilleran complex of mountain glaciers mantled the ranges of southern Alaska and British Columbia, and extended as far south as Seattle by about 14,500 years ago. The Cordilleran ice extended down to the Pacific and flowed over the eastern foothills of the Rockies, where it neared the boundaries of the Laurentian glaciers.

For years, archaeologists thought an "ice-free corridor" separated the two ice sheets, even at the height of the late Ice Age. "Doubtless it was a formidable place," wrote Thomas Canby of the National Geographic Society in 1979, "an ice-walled valley of frigid winds, fierce snows, and clinging fogs . . . yet grazing animals would have entered, and behind them would have come a rivulet of human hunters." Unfortunately, this appealing picture has not stood the test of more recent scientific scrutiny, for Canadian geologists are by no means certain that the corridor ever existed. Even if it did, there is a real question as to whether it would have supported plant, animal, and human life.

If there was no ice-free corridor, would it have been possible for people to pass south into the heart of the continent along the continental shelf that bordered much of the western coast of Alaska and British Columbia? Could people have coasted from inlet to inlet along the rugged, bitterly cold coastline, living off sea mammals and fish? Although it is entirely possible that some late Ice Age Beringian groups were fisherfolk and sea mammal hunters, they would have had to expand a very long way southward along ice-bound, inhospitable coasts before penetrating more benign terrain in what is now Washington and Oregon.

Most likely, the first Americans did not move southward until the ice sheets were in full retreat and there was a large area of open, at least sparsely vegetated country, where familiar big-game species like the mammoth, caribou, and musk-ox flourished. Under this scenario, it would seem unlikely that any humans settled in the heart of the continent and south of the ice sheets until the great thaw began.

The Paleo-Indians

All the experts agree that after about 12,000 years ago there was a veritable explosion of hunter-gatherers into the virgin expanses south of the ice sheets. The earliest of these settlers left but a transitory archaeological signature behind them, mere scatters of stone tools and some broken animal bones, most of them preserved in the lower levels of natural rockshelters. Do these few traces throw any light on the mystery of first settlement?

Meadowcroft Rockshelter lies in a shallow Pennsylvania valley, a favored location visited by prehistoric hunters for more than 12,000 years. The lowest levels of this meticulously investigated site contain a scatter of stone artifacts, which may date to as early as 14,000 years ago. Far to the south in northern Chile, the Monte Verde site lies on the margins of a small creek. Here, some hunter-gatherers camped on low, sandy knolls near a stream some 12,000 to 14,000 years ago. They were mammoth hunters and lived off forest foods, using the simplest stone and wood artifacts, and living in wooden huts with shallow, clay-lined hearths. These two sites are the best proof of some human settlement at the very end of the Ice Age.

Then, between 11,500 and 11,000 years ago, the highly distinctive Clovis culture appears throughout continental North America and parts of Central America. It is at this moment that we emerge from the shadows into historical sunlight, with the appearance of native American peoples who were the ultimate ancestors of the many and diverse societies encountered by Europeans thousands of years later. The Clovis people are best known for their superbly crafted stone projectile points, first identified at a site near the small town of Clovis, New Mexico, after which they are named. These same points, among the finest ever made, have long fascinated not only professional scholars but thousands of amateur collectors all over the United States. Many acquired this enthusiasm while growing up on rural farms, where Clovis points could be picked up on freshly plowed land. As a result, Clovis points have been found all over North America.

We know most about Clovis from the Great Plains. Here, 11,500 years ago, spring and early summer rains nourished dry grasslands in the rainshadow of the western mountains of North America. The plains supported not only big-game species like mammoth, and its near-relative the mastodon, but bison and other large Ice Age animals. They were also home to sparse, mobile bands of Clovis people. Within a few centuries, these hunters had spread to both North American coasts and as far south as Guadalajara, Mexico. Each band's territory was of considerable size, much of it exploited seasonally, perhaps when fruit were in season, or when hunters went in search of toolmaking stone from known outcrops at some distance. In Central and South America, isolated Paleo-Indian points occur in forests and open country, in highlands and lowlands, some of them associated with mastodon and other game animals, including the giant sloth. Some Paleo-Indians lived in Fell's Cave in Patagonia, at the southern tip of mainland South America, by about 11,000 years ago.

Projectile Points and Fluted Bases

We know very little of the ways in which the early Paleo-Indians lived. At Murray Springs in Arizona, Clovis people killed and butchered mammoth and bison on separate occasions, camping nearby. Eleven bison died, enough meat to support 50 to 100 people, perhaps fewer. Not that they always took large animals, for they were opportunists, who hunted species large and small and

RIGHT *Eight superbly made Clovis projectile points, all found in the carcass of a single mammoth at Naco, Arizona.*

collected wild plants during spring, summer, and fall. Hunting plains animals on foot requires remarkable powers of observation and tenacity, and an intimate knowledge of one's prey. The hunters may have followed elephant and bison herds for months, picking off solitary animals, perhaps driving small herds into swamps and over cliffs when the opportunity arose. By using both a spear propelled by a throwing stick and a simple thrusting spear, a team of hunters would try to wound an animal, then pursue it until it weakened.

Wherever they hunted and foraged, the first Americans relied on a portable, lightweight toolkit that was adapted to a life spent covering long distances. Clovis stoneworkers struck off flakes from large lumps, or cores, of fine-grained rock, then shaped the flakes on both sides, fabricating "bifaces" in archaeological parlance. They carried the cores with them wherever they went, and knocked off flakes when needing a scraper, a projectile point, or a knife. In a sense, the bifaces were a form of "savings bank" upon which the hunters drew when they needed new tools.

Clovis stoneworkers were experts at their craft, carefully selecting the finest of fine-grained rocks from which to fashion beautiful projectile points, sometimes thinned with a longitudinal "fluting" flake at the base for ease of hafting. The points were mounted in wooden foreshafts that worked loose from the main shaft once the head penetrated the quarry.

When agricultural worker Moisie Aguirre found six Clovis points while laying irrigation pipe for an apple orchard near East Wenatchee, Washington, in 1987, a thrill went through the small community of Paleo-Indian experts and passed through the collecting world as well. Peter Mehringer and an archaeological team from Washington State University uncovered a dense concentration of Clovis points, bifaces, and a decorated bone tool in an area of only 21.5 sq. ft (1.9 sq. m). A cluster of Clovis points included two magnificent matched heads in translucent chalcedony, the finest ever recorded. Mehringer used volcanic ash adhering to some of the stone tools to date them to about 11,250 years ago, but the site, like so many other Clovis locations, remains an enigma. "Was it a single tool cache," he wondered, "a habitation, the last resting place of a Clovis chief, a flint knapper's hut, a hunting shrine, even a shaman's tent?" Future excavations may resolve the enigma.

The Big-Game Vanishes

By 11,000 years ago, the human population of the Americas had grown from a few hunting bands into many thousands, scattered in small groups between the far north and the frontiers of Tierra del Fuego at the southern tip of South America. But, just as human numbers rose, the Ice Age "megafauna," the big-game animals, abruptly vanished within a few centuries. Therein lies one of the major controversies of American Indian history. Was this cause and effect? Why did the mammoth, the mastodon, the wild horse, and dozens of other species die out so rapidly?

The effect on Paleo-Indian life must have been devastating, for only a handful of species like the bison survived the mass extinction. The extraordinary range of animals that vanished dwarfs even the rates of humanly-caused extinctions in recent centuries. Every human group, even those living on the bison-rich North American Plains, had to adjust to a new world where animals were smaller and other food sources like plants, fish, birds, and sea mammals were the new staples. But why did the megafauna disappear? Was it the result of major climatic change, or from overhunting?

Paul Martin of the University of Arizona believes the Paleo-Indians were the villains, spreading rapidly over the Americas, slaughtering big-game along the way. They killed mammoth and mastodon, native horses (not reintroduced until the Spanish Conquest), tapirs, camels, ground sloths, giant armadillos, peccaries, cheetahs, and saber-toothed cats. The rapidly expanding humans soon depleted the slow-breeding mammoth and mastodon herds, and other large animals. Martin estimates that a 30 percent removal rate of the megafaunal biomass would have exceeded normal reproduction replacement rates for all extinct late Ice Age mammals. This was devastating overkill so fast-paced that dozens of big-game species were hunted into extinction by the newcomers. The entire blitzkrieg took but five or six centuries to complete.

Martin's dramatic hunting carnival may be part of the answer, but we need to consider a remarkable fact. The end of the Ice Age saw a dramatic loss of big-game species not only in the Americas, but in many other parts of the world. Europe and Eurasia lost the mammoth, woolly rhinoceros, cave bear, and numerous other cold-loving species. In Australia, many species of giant kangaroo and wombats also died out. "We live in a zoologically impoverished world from which all the hugest, and fiercest, and strange forms have recently disappeared," wrote the famous biologist Alfred Wallace in 1876. Yet there had been mass extinctions at the end of earlier geological epochs and Ice Age glaciations, and these had affected small mammal and other animal populations as well. This time amphibians, reptiles, and freshwater and ocean fish populations remained relatively unchanged. Perhaps the larger animals, already vulnerable at a period of profound climatic change, were pushed into extinction by human hunters during the first great wave of world colonization by modern humans at the end of the Ice Age, when whole continents – Australia and North America in particular – were peopled for the first time. Most likely, a complicated set of circumstances sounded the death-knell of the American megafauna. And when the game was gone, human predators had to adjust to a new, even more demanding post-Ice Age world.

The successors of the first Americans adapted to every kind of environment imaginable, from sea level deserts to high altitude grasslands and humid tropical rainforests. A new diversity of native American societies evolved over thousands of years. As a Maidu creation myth from California puts it: "For a long time everyone spoke the same language, but suddenly people began to speak in different tongues. Kulsu [the Creator], however, could speak all languages, so he called his people together and told them the names of the animals in their own language, taught them to get food, and gave them their laws and rituals. Then he sent each tribe to a different place to live. . . .'' There can be no question that the great diversity of American Indian society dates back to the period between 11,000 and 6,000 years ago, when the world's climate finally achieved its modern configuration.

The megafaunal extinctions wiped out almost all the American big-game animals – but not quite. The bison (better known in historical times as the buffalo) survived, and still survives, despite 11,000 years of human predation.

The Bison Hunters

''The new people asked Inkomi what they should eat. Inkomi created buffalo . . . He taught men how to kill the buffalo, and how to skin the animals . . . He showed people how to butcher the buffalo and what parts could be eaten . . .'' As late as the nineteenth century, some North American Plains Indians still hunted bison on foot. Fur trader Alexander Henry watched expert Assiniboine hunters in 1776. ''They were dressed in ox-skins, with the hair and horns. Their faces were covered, and their gestures so closely resembled those of the animals themselves, that had I not been in on the secret, I would have been as much deceived as the oxen,'' Henry wrote. The decoys slowly lured the beasts toward the corral. They bellowed like bison as the herd fed about half a mile away. The animals moved on. The decoys fell back until the leaders were inside the pound. Then the hunters pounced. The slaughter continued until evening, ensuring ample meat supplies for the winter months ahead.

Bison were the largest and most plentiful of Ice Age animals to survive the great extinction. They succeeded where other animals failed because they adapted to become short-grass feeders, as this type of grassland expanded in post-glacial times. A vast tract of arid, short grassland now extended from the frontiers of Alaska to the shores of the Gulf of Mexico. This was the ''Great Bison Belt,'' which lay in the rainshadow of the western mountains. From 11,000 years ago right up to modern times, Plains hunters lived off an unpredictable prey, following herds whose distributions varied greatly from year to year. There was probably some pattern to the hunters' seasonal movements. For much of the year, the bands would disperse over the open landscape. For a few weeks during the summer, neighboring groups would come together at a time when food was more plentiful. They may have organized cooperative bison drives, using their combined manpower to butcher as many animals as possible. These summer get-togethers were an important feature of hunter-gatherer life everywhere. It was then that marriages were arranged, rituals and dances held, and people exchanged tool-making stone and other valuables.

Sometimes their butchery was on a large scale. Over several fall days about 8,500 years ago, a group of Paleo-Indians living southeast of Kit Carson,

Colorado, stalked a large bison herd. The hunters stayed downwind, slowly and subtly moving the unsuspecting animals into a strategic position at right angles to a dry gulch. Then they stampeded them headlong toward the gully. The leaders hesitated, but were swept on by their charging companions. They were trampled to death in the ensuing confusion, pinned with their heads down and rumps up. Then the hunters moved in with nimble spears.

Thanks to meticulous excavations by archaeologist Joe Ben Wheat at this locale, now known as the Olsen-Chubbock site, we have learned a great deal about the highly organized butchery that followed. Wheat excavated the bone bed in the gully like a giant jigsaw puzzle and reconstructed the ways in which the people cut up the dead beasts. They moved as many carcasses as possible to the edge of the arroyo where they could be cut up in the open. Bison wedged at the bottom were dismembered where they lay. The butchers worked in teams, on several animals at once. They rolled the animals on their bellies, slit the hide down the back, and pulled it down the flanks to form a carpet for the meat. Then they removed the blanket of prime flesh on the back, the forelimbs, shoulder blades, hump meat, and rib cage. They probably ate the tongues and some internal organs as they went along, piling the bones in the gully. Wheat used bone measurements and animal weight estimates to calculate that the hunters killed a staggering 152 bison, butchering about 75 percent of them. The meat from this hunt would have sustained over 100 people for a month or more.

Judging from later Plains practice, these Paleo-Indians would have dried large quantities of the bison meat to make a mixture of dried meat and fat known by its Indian name as pemmican (*pemmi* – meat, *kon* – fat). The nineteenth-century artist Paul Kane saw Plains people make pemmican many times. "The thin slices of dried meat are pounded between two stones until the fibers separate," he wrote. "About 50 lbs. of this are put in a bag of buffalo skin, with about 40 lbs. of melted fat, and mixed together while hot, and

Shamanistic rituals: detail of a Mandan "okipa," or buffalo dance, depicted in the 1830s by the Swiss artist Karl Bodmer. This ceremony acted out creation myths and celebrated the coming of the bison. The final stages saw initiation rites, ordeals that hardened warriors for extreme trials of endurance.

sewed up, forming a hard and compact mass." Pemmican was a good way of storing food for use on the march and during the winter. Bison drives were as important for their pemmican potential as for fresh meat.

By at least 4,500 years ago, some Plains hunters were driving bison into skillfully contrived artificial corrals. At the Ruby site in Wyoming, the hunters built a corral in a lowlying stream bed in such a way that the stampeding animals did not see the enclosure until the last minute. The hunters used natural topographic features like ridges and arroyo banks to funnel their quarry toward the pen. The corral itself consisted of pairs of stout posts separated by horizontal timbers wedged between them. Archaeologists found the downslope side of the corral filled with bison bones to a depth of over a foot (0.3 m), so many animals were killed there. Nearby stood a strongly constructed ceremonial structure formed by the intersection of two arcs of timbers. Eight male bison skulls lay at the southern end of the partially roofed building, which may have been the place where the shaman who supervised the building of the corral and the hunt sat and smoked to invoke spirit helpers.

"Masters of the Threshold"

The word "shaman" comes from the Tungus people of northeast Asia ("shaman" loosely means a sorcerer). Shamans were, and still are, far more than magicians, healers, or mystics. Often called "medicine men," they were the masters of the intangible threshold between the living and the spiritual worlds. It was shamans who recited magic songs in drug-induced trances, who recounted creation legends, and interceded with the ancestors. It was shamans who entered the spirit world of the animal kingdom and ensured success in the hunt. And it was shamans who resolved disputes in close-knit hunter-gatherer societies.

To become a shaman was to receive a form of call, perhaps by surviving a serious illness, where one believed one had cured oneself. Then began a long process of initiation, which could last up to a year. During months of fasting and physical ordeals, the novice acquired the power to rise into the sky. His soul departed from his body, he learned special songs that enabled his spirit to cast off earthly shackles and to fly away from earth. Once this authority had been validated in a public seance, the shaman was an individual apart, someone who had mastered death.

The compelling powers of the shaman lay at the heart of native American society for more than 10,000 years, particularly on the Plains, where the lives of hunters and bison became ever more entwined as hunting intensified with the introduction of the bow and arrow after AD 500, and the horse and the rifle in the late seventeenth century. But ultimately it was elsewhere in the Americas, in regions where people learned to harvest the natural bounty of the sea and the humanly induced bounty of crops on the land, that American Indian societies reached their greatest social and religious complexity.

CHAPTER FOUR

▲▲

THE FISHERFOLK
Coastal Peoples of the
Far West and North

The evening sky is grey, the air dank with chilly Pacific fog. Day after day, the greyness persists, casting the coastal desert in monotonous colors. This is one of the driest places on earth, for the lowlying coast of Peru receives little rainfall. Occasional rivers bring seasonal runoff from the snow-covered Andes far inland, but never enough moisture to support large game. The low reed huts of the hunters' encampment crouch by one such river, a little inland from the Pacific and high enough above the river bed to escape the occasional flash flood. People have lived in this settlement as long as anyone can remember. On this chill evening, everyone is down at water's edge, watching the Pacific rollers closely, for the anchovy are spawning. A woman shouts suddenly, and entire families rush forward into the sea, gathering the incoming fish into baskets. They carry their silvery loads back inland. Some they roast at once on hot stones. But thousands more are laid on racks and dried slowly, for anchovy will be a staple food for months to come.

Even today, the Peruvian Coast is one of the richest fishing grounds in the world. Few other areas of the Americas offered such maritime bounty. But – as we shall explore in this chapter – wherever fish and sea mammals abounded, the native Americans became expert fisherfolk and hunters of seals, walrus, whales, and other marine game. On the southern California coast, in the Pacific Northwest, and along the shores of the Bering Strait, as well as in Peru, hunter-gatherer societies achieved levels of social complexity unimaginable in areas less well favored with natural food stocks. It is no coincidence that some of the most vivid and enduring mythology in all the Americas surrounded the elusive creatures of coast and shore. The Kwakiutl fisherman of the Northwest Coast would pray as he clubbed the first salmon:

> "We have come to meet alive, Swimmer,
> do not feel wrong about what I have done to you,
> friend Swimmer,
> for that is the reason why you came,
> that I may spear you,
> that I may eat you,
> Supernatural One, you, Long-Life-Giver, you, Swimmer.
> Now protect us, me and my wife . . ."

Fisherfolk of the Andean Coast

The desert that mantles the Peruvian and northern Chilean coastline encompasses some of the most arid landscape on earth – a distinctly unpromising environment for human settlers by any measure. Why, then, did it support not only large coastal fishing villages for thousands of years, but eventually some of America's most complex civilizations as well? The answer is that the Pacific made permanent settlement in a desert a viable proposition. The high Andes mountains deflect the strong daily winds off the ocean and cause the ocean to flow strongly northward along the coast, creating the Humboldt Current. This sucks water up from the ocean floor, propelling cold, but nutrient-rich waters to the surface. Here trillions of phytoplankton flourish, microscopic plants that are the prime food of small fish such as anchovy, which are themselves preyed on by larger fish, sea mammals, and birds. Thus, the waters close offshore teem with a bounty of marine life.

The band of cold surface water off Peru and northern Chile creates a stable temperature inversion layer between about 1,000 ft (300 m) and 1,650 ft (500 m) above sea level. Evaporated water does not condense as rain, leading to the intense aridity of the coastal deserts. But fogs are prevalent, especially during the winter months. The fog is blocked below the inversion layer and this moisture supports occasional lush patches of vegetation, known locally as *lomas*. The fog band fingers out rapidly inland, sometimes blocked by the steep slopes of the Andes, sometimes by intense radiation, so there is a distinct ecological zone along the coast where fisherfolk and foragers could flourish for thousands of years.

The history of fishing begins early on the Peruvian coast. So bountiful were the resources that people were able to live in relatively large year-round coastal settlements as early as 7600 BC, and perhaps even earlier. At one site in Peru's Moquegua Valley, the inhabitants lived almost entirely off fish and sea mammals. Their simple huts encircled a depressed area of midden that may have been a central plaza. By 7700 BC, the inhabitants of Quebrada Las Conchas in northern Chile were using fiber fishing nets, hunting inland, and eating sea foods. Some 2,000 years later, their "Chonchorros" successors, unlike hunter-gatherers inland actually living in one place for all their lives, were already perpetuating one of the great and abiding themes of Andean life – reverence for the ancestors.

As we saw in Chapter Two, the cult of the royal mummies was at the center of Inca life, a cult based on ancient traditions of ancestor worship. The belief that the spirits of the dead played an active role in the world of the living was deeply ingrained in Andean psyche. From the very earliest times, each local kin group venerated its ancestors, the protectors of the clan in the spiritual realm. On the coast and in the highlands, the bodies of the ancestors were treated as sacred objects. The living made sacrifices to them, sometimes repeated funeral rites, or renewed precious grave offerings. The origins of this

RIGHT *Boy on a reed craft off the Peruvian coast – part of a tradition of boating and fishing that dates back at least 10,000 years in the Andean region.*

profound belief are linked directly to the development of the ancient art of mummification.

Mummification, the preservation of dead bodies through drying, was practiced by the Chonchorros people and other coastal groups long before it was introduced thousands of miles away in ancient Egypt. Doubtless, as in Egypt, the practice came into being when people observed how bodies could become naturally mummified in the arid local climate. From there, it was but a short step to deliberate preservation of the dead, as sacred objects to be protected and revered. Over more than three millennia, the Andeans perfected their skills at dismembering bodies and removing the brain and viscera. They would treat the corpse to prevent deterioration, a process aided by the hot, dry sun. They became masters at reassembling body parts, using cane or wood to support the vertebral column, arms, and legs. Clay, feathers, and fiber filled out body cavities. Chonchorros morticians coated the deceased's face with clay, then sculpted and painted facial features, replacing hair with wigs or human hair embedded in clay. By no means everyone was mummified, but the rite extended to both men and women, adults and children, with some corpses receiving more elaborate treatment than others. Many families cared for their mummified dead for some time before placing them underground.

Mummification was not unique to northern Chile. The inhabitants of the Paloma site in the Chilca River valley on the central Peruvian coast used salt to arrest decomposition of the dead at least as early as 6000 BC. Paloma lies in a fog oasis where rich *loma* patches once flourished and was occupied for much of the year. This sprawling complex of discolored soil, fish meal, middens, and long-abandoned, semi-subterranean houses yielded more than 200 burials from 55 excavated houses. The people lived off fish, sea mammals and molluscs, the latter collected from the rocky Pacific shore less than 3 miles (4.5 km) away. Huge anchovy schools could be netted from rafts close to shore or collected as they swam ashore to breed, just as they are to this day. The archaeologists who dug Paloma witnessed anchovy runs on two occasions and watched the local people net thousands of fish in a few hours. The fishermen promptly used many of them as bait to catch the voracious jurel, a mackerel-like species that swarms after the anchovies close offshore.

Ancient Paloma's entire existence revolved around the ocean and local plant foods, but life was never easy. Pathologists who examined the Paloma skeletons found that the earliest inhabitants displayed considerable signs of stress, whereas the health of the later Palomans improved considerably. Interestingly, many of the male Palomans exhibited a benign bone growth in the inner ear known as auditory osteomas, a condition that often results from repeated diving in cold water. Palomans did not always die peacefully, for fishing could be hazardous. Tell-tale teeth marks and bone fractures reveal the story of a tragic accident: one man had died when his left leg was bitten off by a shark.

Paloma's burials are a mine of information on early coastal fishing society. Each family buried the dead under a house floor, in a flexed position, the cadaver tied with ropes. The first burial was at the western side of the dwelling. Then others were added around the perimeter, an adult male usually lying in the center. Archaeologist Jeffrey Quilter believes the central burial may have been that of the head-of-household, as if the social system of the living was replicated in death. Judging from the surviving grave goods, the Palomans lived in a relatively egalitarian society. People were buried in animal skins or mats, occasionally accompanied by bone or shell beads. Two adult males, both buried in the same grave in a close embrace, may have been shamans, for a calcite crystal and a wooden staff accompanied them, both important symbols of shamanism today.

Paloma was abandoned in about 2500 BC at a time of rising coastal populations, when many communities shifted inland to live by cultivated fields.

The remarkable evidence for mummification among the sedentary Chinchorros and Paloma people reveals just how deep the roots of Andean religious beliefs went. Strong ties of kinship held people together, and bound them to the ancestral fishing grounds that fed them. In time, kin group leaders may have assumed a special status in society. They and their families were respected in life, then mummified and carefully preserved in death. They were symbols of corporate identity, of group ancestry, of an on-going relationship between people and the territory they occupied.

Fishing communities always flourished along the Peruvian coast, but by 2000 BC they had come under the sway of powerful agricultural states close inland. Fisherfolk are always fiercely independent, so the Andean fishermen remained a distinctive sub-culture of coastal society as late as 1492. Elsewhere, highly sophisticated and complex coastal hunter-gatherers prospered right up to the Spanish Conquest, especially in western North America.

"The Entire Day is a Continuous Meal:" California Fisherfolk

Some of the world's most productive fisheries lay close along the western coasts of the Americas, not only in Peru, but off southern California and throughout the archipelagos of the Pacific Northwest. In many respects the environmental situation in the Santa Barbara Channel region of California parallels that of the coastal Andes. Here, too, the upwelling of cold water from a depth of several hundred feet constantly replenishes the surface layers of the Pacific with nutrients. Here, too, the result is an incredible bounty of marine life. In spring, billions of spawning sardines feed on the nutrients and zooplankton that lie near the surface, moving inshore during the summer. Pelicans and larger fish like albacore and tuna feed on the sardines and other species. Inshore, dense kelp beds protect the southern coast and greatly enrich the shallow water. Even today, the Santa Barbara Channel is a paradise for fishermen.

So rich and diverse were the foods available to the Chumash Indians of the Santa Barbara region and their prehistoric ancestors that they could live in the same villages for many generations, unlike hunter-gatherers inland. "It may be said that for them, the entire day is a continuous meal," wrote one Spanish missionary. California archaeologists estimate that some 15,000 Chumash dwelt in the region in the sixteenth century, with a population density as high as 10 people per square mile, a figure that contrasts sharply with the 0.5 person per square mile typical of much inland desert. It was as if the Chumash farmed the land, and such a close relationship fostered great social complexity. The prerequisite for more complex society was not the way in which one lived, but a permanent, sedentary relationship with the land where one obtained food.

When did the Chumash way of life arise? All the evidence suggests that fishing expertise developed hand in hand with a gradual growth in population in the millennia after 6000 BC. By 2,000 years ago the bones of seals, dolphins, whales, and sharks appear in coastal refuse dumps or middens, perhaps indicating the use of offshore watercraft such as plank canoes for the first time. In historical times these canoes were an important feature of Chumash fishing technology, each craft about 25 ft (7.6 m) long, paddled by four or five men, with planks carefully shaped using stone and shell tools and sewn together with vegetable fiber. Not that the Chumash depended solely on fish and sea mammals. From early times they collected shellfish like the abalone, today such a favored delicacy among California epicures that it lies beyond most restaurantgoers' pockets. And onshore they gathered plant foods, particularly acorns during the rich annual harvest.

Despite the widespread natural bounty, there were still marked local and seasonal variations in food supplies. The Chumash found a simple, and to us very modern, solution: they used shell beads as a kind of money to redistribute resources from an area of plenty to an area of need. Archaeologist Chester King has established that this practice is thousands of years old in the Santa Barbara region. Other kinds of beads, often more difficult to manufacture and therefore of higher value, were worn as ornaments of status, limited to those allowed to obtain them. For a characteristic of Chumash society was its division into classes, with the chief at the pinnacle of the social pyramid, and lower down elite office holders, shamans, and commoners.

The hereditary chief (wot) ruled over each Chumash village. Wots served as war leaders and patrons of ceremonial village feasts. Once during the fall and at the winter solstice, outlying communities near and far flocked to major settlements for rich ceremonies that honored the earth and the sun. Chumash chiefs were constantly bickering over food supplies and territory. Disputes over wives, social insults to chiefs, such as not attending a feast, and blood feuds were all excuses for warfare.

Chumash Life and Art

TOP LEFT TO RIGHT *Scenes of Chumash life from a nineteenth-century California report: gathering acorns, gathering seeds, and cooking food.* ABOVE *Reconstruction by Travis Hudson and Peter Howorth of a Chumash plank canoe.* RIGHT *Chumash rock art at the San Emigdio pictograph site.*

North America after the Ice Age: fisherfolk of the far west and north evolved
contemporaneously with the hunters and farmers of the Southwest and Eastern
Woodlands (Chapter Thirteen).

  Chumash shamans not only maintained relationships with tribal ancestors,
but conducted important ceremonies at the solstices, for in this society as in
so many others, the endless cycle of the seasons was all-important. They
painted the walls of remote inland caves and rockshelters with abstract
patterns and representations of the sun, stars, human beings, birds, fish, and
reptiles – superb works of art that are reckoned to be the finest of any north of
Mexico. The supernatural world manifested itself in the form of a spirit
helper, which appeared in a dream or in a hallucinogenic vision induced by
datura or tobacco. The spirit helper would speak to the dreamer, offer power
and protection, and give a talisman: "The talisman is a thing like a hawk's
head or an eagle's head worn round the neck or around the waist . . . In your
dream a person talks to you – no person in this world talks to you – and gives
you the talisman and when you wake up you have it," recalled one of

anthropologist John Harrington's informants. A dream helper might be an animal spirit, one of the "first people" who had turned into animals at the end of mythic time and lived in the uppermost of the three superimposed worlds of the Chumash cosmos, the "other world."

Sea Mammal Hunters and Fisherfolk on the Northwest Coast

"The performer appeared in a mask which was made of wood . . . Over his body was thrown a fine, large wolfe Skin with Hair outwards and a neat border worked around its edges; thus accoutred he jumped up and down in his canoe with his arms extended, he moved his head in different ways and shaked his fingers briskly . . . all the other Indians sat down in their canoes and sung in concert and struck the sides of their canoes with the butt end of their Paddles keeping exact time . . ." When Captain James Cook sailed into Nootka Sound on Vancouver Island in 1778, he was greeted by masked dancers in canoes, who serenaded the strange visitors. Expert fishermen and whalers, the Nootka enjoyed one of the most complex hunter-gatherer cultures on earth.

At the end of the Ice Age, the rugged Northwest Coast of North America became a strip of green, forested landscape that stretched from the Copper River in Alaska to the Klamath River in northern California. Here vast stands of spruce, cedar, hemlock, and Douglas fir covered the coast. The Pacific and the rivers that flowed into it teemed with sea mammals and dozens of fish species, including halibut that could weigh up to a quarter of a ton. No less than five salmon species appeared in inshore waters each year, jamming rivers as they crowded upstream to spawn. The rich and diverse coastal environment provided over 300 edible animal species alone.

Cook and his successors found the Northwesterners concentrated on river banks or on the islands and shores of the deeply indented coast, especially north of the Columbia River. Their lives followed the rhythm of the seasons. During the summer months, people hunted, foraged, and fished, drying, smoking, and packing perishable foods in oil for the long winter. When the autumn rains came, everyone drew together into more permanent settlements of large planked houses. The winter was the season of feasts and entertainments, when guests came and were honored with speeches and many gifts. Costumed dancers moved through intricate steps, genealogies were recited, family histories told, as honor was paid to the living and to the dead.

The damp, oceanic forests of the Northwest Coast bred prehistoric America's finest carpenters. They worked with tough polished rocks, shell or antler blades in their adzes and chisels, splitting, cutting, and bending cedar, fir, and straight-grained spruce with effortless skill. Experts thought nothing of splitting 100-ft (30-m) long trees for house planks. They fashioned boxes from steamed and scored planks, carved oil bowls and stools, and fabricated ingenious handles for tools of all kinds. Skilled boatbuilders crafted war and

Mastercarvers of the
Northwest Coast

FAR LEFT *Tsimshian totem pole, c. 1870, showing a wolf biting the entrails of a grizzly bear, and twelve human figures around an open hole.* ABOVE AND ABOVE RIGHT *Tlingit clan house, and Haida carved box, both incorporating the stylized eyes and faces characteristic of Northwest Coast art.* RIGHT *Nineteenth-century Tsimshian carved basalt burial mask.* LEFT *Archaeologist Richard Daugherty examines the carved cedarwood representation of a whale's dorsal fin from the Ozette site, Washington. This extraordinary piece, inlaid with over 700 sea otter teeth, is one of 50,000 objects excavated at Ozette, a Makah Indian whale hunting village that was buried under a massive mudslide one rainy night in AD 1750.*

heavy load-carrying canoes from specially felled tree trunks. Working as they did continually with wood, it was only natural that Northwest artisans began to decorate their handiwork as well. They incised and painted designs on the sides of boxes, carved tools and utensils in the likenesses of the animals they saw around them – bears, beavers, birds, seals, whales, and wolves, and in the forms of supernatural beings and mythical ancestors.

When Spanish and English explorers arrived on the Northwest Coast in the eighteenth century, they were amazed to find not only large planked houses, but elaborately carved columns and posts adorning even small villages. They were among people obsessed with the acquisition of privilege and wealth, a society where genealogy and status counted for everything. The Haida people of British Columbia's Queen Charlotte Islands painted and carved heraldic devices on their houses, carvings of animals and mythical beings that were tied to the stories, songs, and privileges of the owner. These crest carvings also adorned mortuary structures commemorating important burials, and the famous genealogical totem poles that rose like artificial forests around settlements. These were intricate ideogram-like depictions of genealogy and family history carved with a carefully coded symbolism that often died with the owner.

This elaborate and long-lived cultural tradition goes back to at least as early as 3500 BC, to a time when the world's sea levels had stabilized at their modern levels. By 450 BC, specialized woodworking tools appear throughout the coast and there are signs of a new preoccupation with status and wealth, and with ceremonial, reflected in new art traditions that include animal motifs that became prestigious crests in later times. All these centuries of increasing elaboration culminated after AD 500, when populations rose sharply and there was an increasing emphasis on whale and sea mammal hunting, and salmon fishing. Successful exploitation of spring and summer fisheries, and of salmon runs, required careful organization, to coordinate the actual fishing with drying and storage of enormous numbers of fish. It was socially prominent individuals who undertook this task, deploying large workforces of extended families and associates, then redistributing the resulting food throughout the community.

These were intensely competitive people, who vied with one another ruthlessly for prestige, wealth, and status. All of them guarded their titles, kin ties, even their special chants and dances, jealously, behaving toward one another with great formal protocol. The greatest wealth and rank accrued to those who oversaw access to the best fisheries, for it was they who controlled the distribution of foodstuffs and prestigious goods such as blankets throughout each community. The most powerful Northwest Coast chiefs were very often individuals with exceptional entrepreneurial and leadership powers. Their authority depended on their ability to attract followers and to retain their loyalty. They did so not only by diplomacy, but by throwing lavish feasts and distributing generous gifts. These *potlatches* were important and solemn occasions where guests came dressed in their ceremonial regalia, to be greeted with formal speeches.

Every potlatch was surrounded by elaborate etiquette. The host would await his guests in the warmth of his planked house, the great central hearth burning red-hot, thick smoke drifting to the rafters. His family and relatives crowded around the walls as the guests arrived, bringing a gust of chill rain with them. They wore tightly woven rain hats and capes, their heraldic devices on their chests. The host greeted each guest formally, seating them in order. He introduced his wives and his son, and delivered an oration in honor of his dead father, whose title he had now inherited. The guests would watch closely as the host displayed gifts he was about to distribute – piles of otter skins, sheet copper ornaments of great value, blankets, war clothing, fine boxes and axes. Step by formal step, the potlatch unfolded deep into the night, as masked dancers performed in honor of the host, commemorating his revered ancestors and his deceased father.

Today, the word potlatch is synonymous with conspicuous displays of wealth and lavish entertainment. In fact, the ancient potlatch was a solemn occasion, where the guests were expected to reciprocate in the future. The potlatch also had the important function, not only of confirming authority, but of distributing wealth through society as a whole. Northwest groups spent much time accumulating wealth and social prestige, just as modern-day Americans do. But there the resemblance ends, for the people regarded all wealth as the property of local kin groups, a means of enhancing the prestige of a group among its neighbors. The display and consumption of this wealth was a major objective of Northwest ceremonial life, for here, as elsewhere, human society functioned not as a result of individualism, but for the common good.

Hunters of the Northern Ice

When European explorers first reached the shores of the Bering Strait and sought an open water passage through the desolate islands of the Canadian Arctic, they were astounded to find human beings flourishing in this remote, unimaginably severe part of the world. Here, winters lasted more than nine months a year and the temperature stayed far below zero for weeks on end. The seas were icebound. When summer came, the land thawed into inhospitable swamp. Swarms of voracious mosquitoes plagued animals and humans alike. How could people live, indeed prosper, under such conditions? As Norwegian explorer Vilhjalmur Stefansson pointed out in the early years of this century, the Arctic is in fact a land abounding in fish, sea mammals, and other game, a bounty that prehistoric hunter-gatherers exploited with great skill for many thousands of years. From the Bering Strait in the west to Labrador in the east, Thule peoples (pronounced the Danish way – Tuleh) spanned more than 6,000 miles (9,650 km) of arctic coastline in 1492.

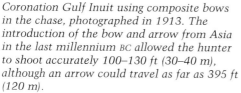

Coronation Gulf Inuit using composite bows in the chase, photographed in 1913. The introduction of the bow and arrow from Asia in the last millennium BC allowed the hunter to shoot accurately 100–130 ft (30–40 m), although an arrow could travel as far as 395 ft (120 m).

Until about 2000 BC, human settlement was confined to Alaskan shores, but then tiny groups of musk-ox hunters moved eastward along the Arctic Ocean shore deep into the myriad islands of the Canadian archipelago. Without stone lamps or any means of heating sea mammal oil, they kept their fires alight with driftwood and fatty musk-ox bones. In the dark of winter, each family would stay inside, semi-somnolent, hunkered down in their musk-ox hide tents, snuggled together under thick skins, with food and fuel within easy reach. One marvels at the ability of people to survive under such conditions, armed with only simple barbed spears and harpoons, not even with bows and arrows, and without dog sleds or large boats.

The revolution, it was nothing less, in arctic living, began along the shores of the Bering Strait in about 700 BC. It was then that the people living on St Lawrence Island and other islands in the Bering Strait developed a highly specialized culture based entirely on the ocean. Up to this time, arctic peoples had had limited success as sea hunters. Now, venturing into open water in small skin kayaks and larger umiaks, hide boats, they became expert whalers, working in teams. They scouted out whale pods from ice floes, followed them through ice leads in kayaks. Then the harpooners would move in using umiaks. This was a time of great innovation that saw the introduction of the bow and arrow, and the development of an entire technology specifically designed for taking whales, walruses, and other maritime prey. Principal among these new hunting weapons was the so-called toggling harpoon.

For thousands of years, local hunters had caught seals using simple barbed harpoons, hoping that the point would remain impaled in the prey as it fought against the line. The toggling harpoon had a hinged head which angled between the skin and blubber so that it could not be dislodged by the animal's movement or by ice. Such weapons proved deadly even against large mammals like the whale, especially when combined with a razor-sharp slate blade, another innovation of the day. So successful was the new technology that many Bering Strait communities could settle permanently in large villages over many generations.

Not that life was ever easy, for these were hazardous seas and disaster might strike at any time. The truth of this came home to archaeologist Albert Dekin, when he excavated a five-centuries-old tragedy at the village of Utqiagvik near Point Barrow. The settlement of driftwood and sod houses lay close to a bluff edge overlooking the pack ice. Inside one house two women, one in her forties, the other in her twenties, slept near a teenage boy and two young girls as a violent storm raged outside. Suddenly, a violent ice surge careened over the bluff and tumbled onto the roof of the tiny house. The roof and ridge pole struck the older woman, then the other inhabitants as they lay asleep on a raised platform at the back of the house. Everyone died in seconds. Next morning the lifeless house was shrouded in thick ice. Only the entrance and kitchen area remained intact.

Five centuries later, some local relic hunters uncovered the frozen house. Fortunately for science, Dekin and a team of experts were called in to investigate. They recovered the frozen bodies and the equipment lying in the collapsed dwelling and, with the local community's permission, sent the human remains to Fairbanks for autopsy. The doctors told them that the women had died instantly from the roof fall, and that they had been in reasonably good health. But both had suffered from anthracosis, the black lung disease that afflicts coal miners caused by inhaling smoke and oil lamp fumes at close quarters. They also suffered from atherosclerosis, narrowing of the arteries caused by deposits of cholesterol and fat, the result of eating much fatty whale and seal blubber. Both women had experienced periods of poor nutrition and ill heath. What impressed the archaeologists was the neatness and order found in the house. Space inside the dwelling was so limited that its owners stacked their summer fishing nets and weapons in alcoves along the entrance tunnel, while snow goggles, ice picks, harpoons, and other winter artifacts lay in skin bags, free of frost in the passage, ready for instant use.

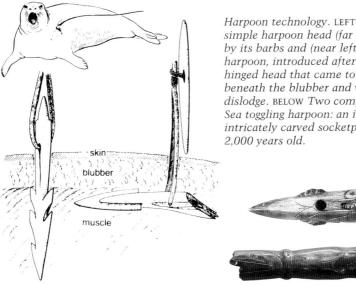

Harpoon technology. LEFT *The traditional simple harpoon head (far left) that held prey by its barbs and (near left) the toggling harpoon, introduced after 700 BC, with a hinged head that came to rest at an angle beneath the blubber and was more difficult to dislodge.* BELOW *Two components of a Bering Sea toggling harpoon: an ivory head and an intricately carved socketpiece, both about 2,000 years old.*

Eskimo Artists and Artisans

ABOVE *The skillful use of kayaks in sea hunting, seen here in a painting of 1872, evolved over a 2,000-year period in arctic waters.* RIGHT *A Copper Eskimo craftsman, photographed in 1916, manipulates a bow drill, one of many Eskimo technological innovations.* BELOW *This tiny ivory mask from Sugluk, Quebec – about 2,500 years old and only 1¼ in (3.3 cm) high – may once have belonged to a Dorset Eskimo shaman.*

Inevitably, the new technologies and hunting methods spread eastward across the far north, in the hands of the Thule people. By AD 1200, they had settled throughout the coasts of the Canadian Arctic and Greenland, absorbing and perhaps pushing aside indigenous folk known to archaeologists as "Dorset" people – today particularly renowned for their life-like portraits fashioned in antler, bone, and ivory of shamans, polar bears, and tiny seals. These were centuries when the southern boundary of northern pack ice had retreated northward, so kayaks and umiaks could range far and wide, following migrating bowhead whales into hitherto inaccessible waters. They were also centuries when a handful of Europeans made the first abortive attempt to settle in the Americas. As early as 982, Norseman Eirik Thorvaldsson the Red sailed from Iceland to explore the mysterious lands to the west. Four years later, he founded a series of tiny settlements on the west coast of Greenland. From these footholds, restless Norsemen ventured far north to the arctic ice and west, across the Davis Strait and into the Canadian archipelago. There they encountered the Thule people, whom they called "Skraelings," "barbarians," people who "possess no iron, but use walrus tusk for missiles and sharpened stones instead of knives." For generations, Norsemen and Thule traded iron tools for walrus ivory, a trade that brought a scattering of Norse artifacts to remote settlements to be excavated by archaeologists centuries later. Then, just as Columbus landed in the Indies, the Norse settlements collapsed in the face of advancing pack ice and quite possibly attacks by Thule people. Europeans did not settle permanently in the Thule homeland until the late nineteenth century.

Along many parts of the western shores of America bountiful seas and rivers thus made it possible for native Americans to lead sedentary lives from very early times – far earlier than in most inland areas. From the coasts of Peru right up to the Arctic, human energies were channeled over the millennia into perfecting ways of exploiting the rich maritime harvest. It is no coincidence that American Indian boatbuilding skills reached their apogee in these coastal regions. Indeed the brilliantly effective Eskimo kayak has given its name to a whole class of watercraft of similar design now in universal use and familiar to watersports enthusiasts everywhere.

Sedentary, settled life gave rise to great cultural complexity – whether the use of mummification in Peruvian burial rites, the Chumash introduction of shell-bead "money," or the potlatch of the Northwest Coast. Throughout these areas there was an emphasis on the community, on communality and the common good, which characterizes all native American societies and sets them apart from the European tradition that lays stress on individuality. The very success of the coastal cultures, however, led them on a different evolutionary path from their counterparts inland. Ultimately it was the skill of American Indians in exploiting the fruits of the land rather than the sea that gave birth to the great American civilizations.

▲▲

CHAPTER FIVE

THE FARMERS
The Story of the Miracle Crops

"Oh Viracocha, ancient Viracocha,
skilled creator,
who makes and establishes,
'on the earth below
may they eat
may they drink'
you say;
for those you have established
those you have made
may food be plentiful.
'Potatoes, maize, all kinds of food
may there be' . . ."

This Andean ritual chant commemorates the very essence of pre-Columbian society – a brilliant expertise with all kinds of native plants. For thousands of years, native Americans collected and manipulated fruits, roots, and seeds, and built up an extraordinary knowledge of their hallucinogenic and medical properties. By 1492, American Indians had domesticated at least 300 grasses, fruits, and root species, far more than any society in the Old World. They were, without question, the world's greatest plant breeders of the day. Maize from Mexico, the potato from the Andes, these in particular were the miracle crops that eventually transformed European diet. In Pizarro's time, the Andeans grew at least 3,000 different varieties of potatoes. And chocolate, quinine, and tobacco are but a few of the drugs and exotic products that native Americans gave to the world. It is hardly surprising that the cycles of planting, growth, and harvest were at the very core of American Indian life, in a continent that lacked potentially domesticable animals as sturdy and versatile as the wild goat, horse, ox, or sheep. Only a handful of indigenous animals were tamable – the alpaca, llama, and turkey among them – and none were suitable for the laborious tasks of heavy load carrying or plowing. American civilization was built by intensive human labor and on highly sophisticated agronomy. How, then, did this expertise come about? Where and when did the prehistoric Americans turn from hunting, foraging, and fishing to farming?

From Forager to Farmer

Farming did not start overnight, at a sudden, dramatic moment when thousands of bands suddenly decided to abandon hunting and foraging and settle down to cultivate their food. Plants were always a valuable part of Stone Age diet, especially in spring, summer and fall, when fruit ripened, nuts matured, and wild stands of edible native grasses like goosefoot in the Midwest or teosinte in Mexico could be harvested by knocking the ripe seed against a basket or uprooting entire plants. Nor was the *idea* of plant cultivation one brilliant individual's brainchild. As long ago as 1883, the great English anthropologist Edward Tylor pointed out that any hunter, "skilled as he is in the habits of the food-plants he gathers, must know full well enough that if seeds or roots are put in a proper place in the ground they will grow." Tending plants in small plots or fields is a laborious business, and one moreover that severely restricts the group's ability to move on if times get hard – traditionally the mobile hunter-gatherer's means to ensure survival. Initially seeds and roots were probably sown and tended as a supplementary food, and to even out inevitable variations in the availability of wild plants. This was not, in itself, a major revolution. The revolution came when these supplements became staples as populations grew and demand for wild plants outstripped supply. Eventually increasingly sophisticated agricultural methods enabled farmers in Mexico and the Andes to support not only their own families, but thousands of non-farmers as well. It was no coincidence that civilization arose first in these areas, where intensive cultivation of maize, potatoes, and other staples was first developed.

First Farmers in the Andes

The archaeologist will never find the first potato or the first bean plant. All the excavator can hope for is to achieve a general understanding of the circumstances under which cultivation began. Such a scenario comes from Guitarrero Cave, a long-occupied cavern overlooking the narrow floodplain of the Rio Santa in the central Andes, about 8,500 ft (2,500 m) above sea level. Cornell University archaeologist Tom Lynch excavated Guitarrero Cave over many months, uncovering a detailed chronicle of life in this remote mountain valley as early as 8000 BC. The Guitarrero people were deer and rabbit hunters, but they relied heavily on plants for food, bedding, clothing, containers, shelter, and weapons. Lynch was fascinated by the many plant foods in the cave, among them local fruit and tubers like oca and ulluco that were vital sources of carbohydrates. But the common beans, lima beans, and chile peppers found in the same occupation levels were certainly not indigenous forms. They could only have come from the eastern slopes of the Andes, transplanted across the mountains to Guitarrero. All three plants were sturdy enough to be planted in small plots of cleared land near the river, and then to be left to fend for themselves while the people hunted and foraged elsewhere, as their ancestors had done for thousands of years. These are the earliest known domesticated plants from anywhere in the Americas.

Undoubtedly, this kind of casual plant tending was commonplace throughout much of the Andes at the time. Traces of potato and ulluco tubers, also gourd fragments, have come from other, broadly contemporary sites in the highlands, all of them in environments where the key to survival was to reduce the risk of starvation by deliberate expansion of the food supply. This commonsense strategy was successful. In time, domesticated plants became staples instead of secondary foods in the Andes, a weapon in a perennial struggle that balanced the forces of population growth against the harsh realities of the mountains.

Eventually the Andeans managed to develop different forms of potato for most types of soil. They prized botanical diversity, even forms that were too bitter for humans, but ideal as animal fodder. Some potatoes needed a great deal of water, others required little. Some forms grew fast, making them best for short growing seasons. Others stored easily, others were consumed at once. The farmers also perfected a unique way of freeze-drying their crops. They would leave the potatoes out in the night frost, allowing the sun to warm them by day. The family would walk over their tubers, pressing out the moisture until, after several nights, the potato became a light, white chunk. The desiccated potatoes could be stored for five or six years, easily carried in bulk, and simply reconstituted by soaking in water. *Ch'uno*, dried potatoes, are still a staple of Andean diet. Thousands of years of experimentation allowed Andean societies to support surprisingly dense populations in mountain valleys, a prerequisite for civilization.

The Story of Maize

"The breaths of the corn maidens blew rain-clouds from their homes in the Summer-land, and when the rains had passed away green corn plants grew everywhere the grains had been planted. And when the plants had grown tall and blossomed, they were laden with ears of corn, yellow, blue, white, speckled, and black." This annual cycle of planting and harvesting maize commemorated by the Zuni of the Southwest lay at the very core of American Indian life in 1492. Maize, sometimes called Indian corn, was a staple food for American Indians in Columbus' day, all the way from Argentina to southern Canada, and from sea level high into the Andes. Corn held center stage in Indian mythology. The Aztecs believed that Quetzalcoatl, the revered Feathered Serpent himself, had turned himself into an ant to steal maize as a gift for humans.

Zea mays is a tropical cultigen, but what is its ancestor? Botanists argue passionately over the issue. Many believe that the original ancestor was not a wild form of maize itself, but a little known grass, teosinte, *Zea mexicana*.

Teosinte grows over much of Central America and has been successfully crossbred with domesticated maize. Its dry seeds can be cracked with even a simple grindstone, or be softened before eating by soaking water. *Zea mexicana* can be "popped" by being placed in a fire, on a hot rock, or in heated sand, just like the popcorn we consume at the movies today. The botanist George Beadle believes that "a teosinte of some 8,000 to 15,000 years ago was the direct ancestor of maize and was transformed into a primitive corn through human selection." The transformation into maize may have taken place simultaneously in many areas of Central America or further south and may have occurred within a very short time, perhaps only a century. Other experts argue, with equal passion, that maize evolved from another wild plant – pod corn. The debate is unresolved.

Unlike goosefoot, or, say, squash, domesticated maize is a demanding crop. It requires not only careful planting but constant weeding, sometimes watering, and protection from birds and other predators. Anyone who became dependent on maize faced many days of laborious brush clearing to prepare large garden plots just to grow enough corn to feed a family for a year. Unlike the casual cultivator, the maize farmer was tied to his fields, had less time to hunt and forage, and lived a life dominated by the realities of land clearance, planting, weeding, and harvest.

It was some time before maize became a staple rather than a supplementary food, for it suffers from a major disadvantage: it lacks one of the vital amino-acids needed to make protein. Thus, maize did not become a staple food until grown in combination with other crops like beans or squash that provide the necessary protein ingredients for a maize-based diet. Almost certainly, it was domesticated at about the same time as beans in Mexico.

Guila Naquitz and Tehuacan. How and when did maize agriculture begin? Maize experts such as Walter Galinat believe that the first maize-like forms of teosinte originated at many locations in southern Mexico, at the same time as people were experimenting with other native plants. Finding the archaeological proof is a formidable task, involving long seasons of excavation in remote, dry caves, where ancient beans, maize cobs, and other plants have survived in arid occupation layers.

University of Michigan archaeologist Kent Flannery has worked on early farming settlements in the Valley of Oaxaca in Mexico for many years. As part of this fieldwork, he excavated Guila Naquitz Cave, occupied sporadically by a tiny band of hunters and foragers over a few thousand years after 8750 BC. It was here that he reconstructed the life of hunters and foragers in Mexico just before maize and bean agriculture began.

Flannery used the seemingly unspectacular finds of stone artifacts, animal bones, and seeds from the cave to conjure up a fascinating portrait of life in a high-risk environment. By using computer simulations, his research team pitted what they knew about the people's lifeway against environmental and climatic data. Like the Andeans, the Guila Naquitz people were constantly at risk of starvation because of drought. Their response was not only to exploit natural resources more effectively, but to take advantage of wetter years to try extending wild plant stands by deliberately sowing additional bean seeds and perhaps teosinte. Apparently this strategy was successful, because Flannery found that 2,000 years later Guila Naquitz was used for longer periods. For weeks on end in late fall, even in dry years, a few families camped in the cave. Every day the men left at dawn to hunt deer and other game. Meanwhile, the women scraped and cleared off the dry brush on small plots near the wild bean stands in the valley. They planted bean seeds in the brown soil as soon as the rains came, watching over the land as the first shoots poked through. Eventually, the families moved away, but not too far, for the women returned regularly to weed the growing beans, harvesting them in spring when nearby wild strains were also mature. The people themselves probably thought nothing of this gradual changeover to plant cultivation, for it was simply a natural extension of foraging strategies they had used for generations. With their plant expertise, hunter-gatherer groups throughout the Americas were preadapted to growing their own food.

Guila Naquitz was a tiny prehistoric settlement, often little more than a casual stopping point within a large hunting territory, and one can be certain that the experiments there were duplicated at many other, still unexcavated, locations. Veteran archaeologist Richard MacNeish came to the Tehuacan Valley in southern highland Mexico in the 1960s to search for early maize with brilliant success. His excavations in dry caves and small villages went back as early as 10,000 BC, when hunters took now-extinct wild horses and deer in the valley. The megafauna vanished and the Tehuacanos turned more and more to wild plants. As populations rose, they experimented with easily storable amaranth, beans, gourds, and teosinte, planting them at the beginning of the rainy season and returning months later to harvest the crops, intended originally purely as a supplement to their normal diet. Within a remarkably short time, perhaps only a few centuries, new domesticated strains of maize, beans, and squash developed. Soon the Tehuacanos moved into larger and more permanent settlements and became farmers rather than foragers.

The Spread of Maize

Even in the earliest centuries, constant experimentation with maize led to the development of many strains of corn, all of them adapted to local conditions, some to greater aridity, others to higher temperatures, others to wet, rainforest environments. By 2500 BC, maize was commonplace throughout Mesoamerica and in almost universal use in thousands of small highland and lowland villages. These were the cultures where the deep roots of Mesoamerican civilization were forged. From Central America, maize seems to have

Maize, the staff of life in the Americas. TOP *Scenes of Aztec maize cultivation from the Codex Florentino; left to right, planting using a digging stick, hoeing, and harvesting.* ABOVE *Guamán Poma's illustrations of Inca agriculture; left to right, maize planting, guarding the young shoots from birds and animals, and harvesting.*

spread east and south toward the Amazon Basin and into the Andes. It was grown in the Andean highlands before 2000 BC and in irrigated fields in Peru's coastal desert by 1800 BC. As we shall see, maize, beans, and potatoes soon became staples of powerful coastal states and highland kingdoms in Peru.

When Europeans first explored the Amazon Basin, they discovered a fertile Atlantic floodplain inhabited by large numbers of farmers. "Inland from the river there could be seen some very large cities that glistened white . . . the land is as good, as fertile . . . as our Spain." The conquistadors found thousands of people living in populous villages amidst fields of maize and other crops. One village "stretched for five leagues without there intervening any space from house to house, which was a marvelous thing to behold." During the first millennium AD, the Marajoara culture flourished in the same region, a network of towns and villages built on large earthworks and ruled by powerful, warlike chiefs. This remarkable society of more than 100,000 people was descended from much earlier, and simpler farming cultures in the region. There can be no doubt that its prosperity was due in considerable part to highly productive maize agriculture on the fertile, easily flooded soils of the Amazon floodplain.

Far to the north, maize reached the North American Southwest somewhat later, by at least 1200 BC. Here, corn was at the northern limits of its range, for it was intolerant of short growing seasons, weak soils, inadequate rainfall, and strong, cold winds. Southwestern farmers soon became experts at selecting the right soils for cultivation, those with good moisture-retaining properties on slopes that received relatively little hot sun. They would divert water from streams and springs, use rainfall runoff to irrigate their lands, disperse their gardens widely to minimize the effects of local droughts and floods. As we shall see in a later chapter, their efforts supported not only thousands of tiny villages but elaborate pueblos, small towns that are now among the most famous archaeological sites in the Americas.

Maize spread last into eastern North America, probably from the Southwest, and perhaps as early as the fifth century AD. At first it was merely a supplementary crop, until higher yielding corn and domesticated beans arrived by about AD 1000. By the time Europeans arrived, maize farmers flourished as far north as the Gaspe Peninsula on the banks of the St Lawrence River. And the fertile river valleys of the Midwest and Southeast supported powerful chiefdoms, described in Chapter Thirteen. Wherever it spread, maize agriculture transformed not only native American society, but the very beliefs that lay at its roots.

As maize assumed ever-greater importance in American life, so a vast mythology developed around the themes of fertility in plants and humans, for the fertility of women symbolized the annual rebirth of young corn. Ritual was, in a real sense, a part of the very act of agriculture. The Pueblo Indians marked, and still mark, every stage of corn growing with elaborate ceremonies, commemorated in poetry and song.

''Five things alone are necessary to the sustenance and comfort of the 'dark ones' [Indians] among the children of earth.
> The sun, who is the Father of all.
> The earth, who is Mother of men.
> The water, who is the Grandfather.
> The fire, who is the Grandmother.
> Our brothers and sisters the Corn, and seeds of growing
> things . . .''

In the mythic geography of American Indian society, it was the shaman who read the heavens, set the time of planting and first-fruit rituals, who presided over fertility rites and initiation ceremonies. And, in time, as the village societies of Mesoamerica and the Andes transformed themselves into great civilizations, the descendants of these individuals became mighty lords and priest-kings living in imposing palaces and presiding over elaborate public ceremonies atop high pyramids. But the roots of these civilizations lay in a myriad small communities where a close, mythic link between life and fertility formed the very essence of human existence.

PART THREE

CIVILIZATIONS OF ANCIENT MESOAMERICA

"And then they got up and came to the Citadel of Rotten Cane, as the name is spoken by the Quichés. The Lords Cotuha and Plumed Serpent came along, together with all the other lords. There had been five changes and five generations of people since the origin of light, the origin of continuity, the origin of life and of humankind.
And they built many houses there.
And they also built houses for the gods, putting these in the center of the highest part of the citadel. They came and they stayed.
After that their domain grew larger; they were more numerous and more crowded . . ."

From *Popol Vuh*, translated by Dennis Tedlock (1985)

A Maya hieroglyph at the city of Tikal carved in stone relief.

CHAPTER SIX

▲▲▲

THE JAGUAR AND THE SHAMAN
Olmecs of the Gulf Coast

In November 1839, two adventurers, American John Lloyd Stephens and British artist Frederick Catherwood, stumbled through thick undergrowth, through "half-buried fragments, to fourteen monuments . . . some in workmanship equal to the finest monuments of the Egyptians." They found themselves in the center of the ruined city of Copán that sprawled for miles through the Central American jungle in what is now Honduras. "It lay before us like a shattered bark in the midst of the ocean, her masts gone, her name effaced, her crew perished, and none to tell whence she came," wrote Stephens in a memorable passage of archaeological writing. "The only sounds . . . were the noise of monkeys moving among the tops of the trees, and the crackling of dry branches broken by their weight." While Stephens explored a maze of plazas and pyramids, Catherwood spent days deciphering intricate hieroglyphs ankle-deep in mud, working in gloves because of the mosquitoes.

Who were the mysterious builders of these vast ruins with their exotic sculptures and complex picture writing? It was Stephens himself who answered the question two years later, after further lengthy explorations at Palenque, Uxmal, Chichén Itzá, and other ruins in the Yucatán. "These cities . . . are not the works of people who have passed away," he wrote in 1843, "but of the same great race which . . . still clings around their ruins." They had been built by the ancestors of the modern Maya Indians.

More than a century of field research has shown that John Lloyd Stephens was correct. But where did the Maya themselves come from? What were the origins of the remarkable Maya civilization that had once flourished in the Central American lowlands? What manner of kings ruled over their great cities, and where did they come from? Scholars have grappled with these questions ever since.

Olmec: The Mother Culture?

A vast chasm separates the thousands of farming villages scattered through Central America in 2000 BC and the sophisticated civilizations that arose with dramatic suddenness only 1,500 years later. It is this chasm that fascinates archaeologists as they search for the origins of the Maya and other Mesoamerican civilizations. Was there one ancestral culture that gave rise to later states of even greater complexity, or did these civilizations emerge from many cultural roots? One candidate may be the mysterious Olmec people of Mexico's Veracruz lowlands.

In 1925, Danish archaeologist Frans Blom and ethnographer Oliver La Farge stumbled on an overgrown, 82-ft (25-m) high earthen mound that stood on swampy La Venta island in the drainage of the Tonala River in lowland Veracruz, Mexico. Their guides showed them distinctive throne-like monuments nearby, one of which was "a large square block of stone . . . We calculated the mass of this block to be at least 9 cubic meters. On its north side is an incised ornament along the upper rim of the table, and under this is a deep niche in which sits a human figure, legs crossed Turkish fashion." Although the island sculptures were unusual, Blom and La Farge assumed that La Venta was the work of Maya lords.

Few experts took much notice of the exotic feline figures from the swampy island, but German scholar Hermann Bayer remarked that they were of "Olmec" origin, for they came from Olman, the ancient Aztec "Rubber Country." Soon, distinctive Olmec vessels and jade artifacts appeared from sites in the Valley of Mexico in the distant highlands, as if the lowland people had traded with other societies over a wide area. Most people assumed the Olmec were a later manifestation of Maya culture until Matthew Stirling of the Smithsonian Institution excavated at Tres Zapotes in southern Veracruz

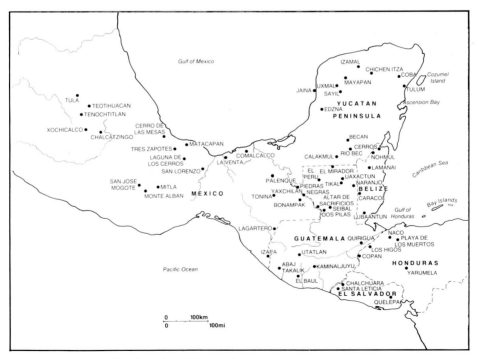

Principal regions and archaeological sites of Mesoamerica.

on the margins of the Maya heartland in 1938. There he discovered a remarkable stela, Stela C, with an Olmec jaguar face on one side and a Maya "Long Count" date of 31 BC on the other. Stirling's discovery caused a storm of controversy, for he argued that the Olmec, far from being an appendage to Maya history were, in fact, much earlier. He turned his attention to La Venta, where he recovered not only four colossal stone heads, but more thrones adorned with half-human and half-feline figures. At La Venta Stirling traced the outlines of a large ceremonial center of pyramids, temples, and open plazas that had once been lined with impressive stone sculptures. It was soon after these discoveries that Mexican scholar Alfonso Caso proclaimed the Olmec civilization the "mother culture" of all Mexican civilization – of Teotihuacan, Monte Albán, the Maya, Toltecs, and Aztecs.

If the Olmec civilization was indeed the mother culture of Mexican civilization, when had it flourished? Stirling worked before the days of radiocarbon dating. It was not until 1955 that his theories were vindicated by charcoal samples that dated La Venta to the centuries between 1100 and 600 BC. The Olmec civilization was at least 3,000 years old and far older than Classic Maya civilization. But the Olmec remained an enigma, vividly summed up by the Mexican art historian Miguel Covarrubias. They were, he said, a "great and mysterious race of artists . . . Everywhere there are archaeological treasures that lie hidden in the jungles and under the rich soil of southern Veracruz, burial mounds and pyramids, masterfully carved colossal monuments of basalt, splendid statuettes of precious jade, and sensitively modeled figures of clay, all of an unprecedented, high artistic quality." Covarrubias painted the Olmec in somewhat romantic terms, as a mother culture marked by an art style centered on a mysterious half-jaguar, half-human figure.

San Lorenzo

Today, few archaeologists would go so far as to describe the Olmec as the mother culture, even if their art, ideology, and lowland adaptation were important catalysts in the development of Mesoamerican civilization. Our knowledge of the Olmec comes almost entirely from two sites: San Lorenzo and La Venta.

San Lorenzo lies about 37 miles (60 km) southwest of La Venta on the lowlying Coatzacoalcos River. Small village settlements flourished in this region for many centuries before the first artificial gravel platforms appeared at San Lorenzo in about 1500 BC. Over the next three centuries, the population rose considerably. Imported materials like basalt, greenstone, and obsidian (volcanic glass) from as far afield as Teotihuacan in the Mexican highlands became more common. This trade may have been in the hands of a newly emerging elite, who were also associated with the new ideologies taking hold in Olmec country.

By 1250 BC, highly distinctive kaolin figurines, ceramics, and monumental stone carving appear, all of them cultural traditions with no earlier history in the region. A century later, San Lorenzo entered its heyday. Now carved and incised Olmec pottery occurs not only in the homeland but in the highlands as well, in the Valleys of Mexico and Oaxaca, and at Chalcatzingo, an important trading center in the state of Morelos. Clearly, San Lorenzo was now something different, the focus of a culture with far-flung trading connections.

San Lorenzo itself was an imposing center, built on a largely artificial platform rising some 164 ft (50 m) above the surrounding river basin. Perhaps, as the site's excavator Michael Coe has argued, San Lorenzo was built in the form of a huge, stylized bird of prey flying eastward. But the vast enterprise was never finished. A grouping of mounds, small pyramid-like structures, and a rectangular courtyard lies along a north-south axis on the summit of the platform, including what Coe believes to be the earliest ballcourt in Mexico. (Ceremonial ball-games, usually involving small teams of players, sometimes sacrificial victims, played an important part in Maya and other later Mesoamerican civilizations. The players attempted to knock a rubber ball – another native American innovation – through a stone hoop in the side walls of a ceremonial ballcourt.)

Undoubtedly, San Lorenzo was an important ceremonial center, for it has yielded eight colossal stone heads and several of the throne-like stone monuments, many of them hewn from basalt quarries nearly 50 miles (80 km) away. Between 900 and 700 BC, San Lorenzo went into rapid decline. The monumental heads and other carvings were deliberately defaced, perhaps as the result of a violent takeover of the site by newcomers. Some of the elite may have moved to the other major Olmec center, La Venta, which continued to flourish for another three centuries.

La Venta

By 1000 BC La Venta had become a major center of Olmec culture. It was then that construction began on the mounds and plazas first studied by Stirling. In the following centuries, La Venta's rulers conducted public rituals in their new temples, burying important people in elaborate tombs and depositing extravagant offerings of precious objects in the ceremonial precincts.

Four colossal stone heads weighing between 11 and 24 tons once dominated the central plaza. Each wears a close-fitting skull-cap, somewhat like the helmets worn by American football players. Each headdress bears a distinctive emblem, which may represent a ruler's name, and perhaps his lineage. The serene, yet faintly intimidating, faces gaze out impassively over the plaza. Archaeologist David Grove believes the heads are actual portrait carvings of Olmec rulers and that we are likely to find additional portraits of them at other locations. Unfortunately, most Olmec portrait carvings have been severely mutilated, but Grove has managed to pair the helmeted, buck-toothed Head 4

Olmec Sculptors, Olmec Lords

ABOVE *Monument known as Altar 4, but probably once a royal throne, from La Venta. An Olmec lord sits beneath a schematic jaguar pelt, and emerges from a niche or cave holding a rope that binds captives carved on the sides of the throne.* BELOW LEFT *Basalt figure called the Wrestler, 26 in (66 cm) tall, found near Minatitlan, Veracruz, and described by the art historian Mary Ellen Miller as "among the most powerful three-dimensional portraits of the ancient New World."* BELOW RIGHT *Colossal head number 1 found at La Venta.* RIGHT *Colossal head number 2 from San Lorenzo, with bird (probably parrot) symbols in the headdress that archaeologist David Grove believes are the identifying glyph of the Olmec lord portrayed in the sculpture.*

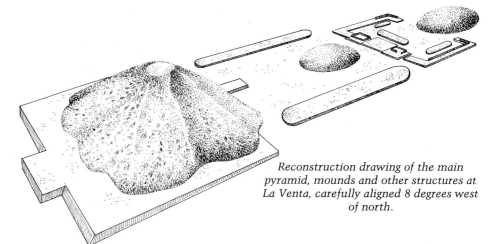

Reconstruction drawing of the main pyramid, mounds and other structures at La Venta, carefully aligned 8 degrees west of north.

at La Venta with a similarly buck-toothed individual (joined with a cord to a seated ruler) depicted on one of the throne-like monuments at San Lorenzo. Perhaps this pairing commemorates a kinship tie between the rulers of these two great Olmec centers. Alternatively, it may mean that San Lorenzo captured this particular La Venta lord in war, a sign not of political unity but of competition and constant rivalry.

Certainly the symbolism of the cord or rope joining two individuals is one that is found on La Venta's throne-like blocks as well. Five of the blocks depict a seated figure, perhaps a ruler, emerging from a deep niche carved into the monument. He leans slightly forward with arms extended to grasp thick, coiled ropes that run along the base to seated figures on the sides, perhaps relatives bound to him by a symbolic kin cord. In several cases, the ruler holds a supernatural, dwarf-like infant in his arms. The sides also bear stylized depictions of jaguars and other themes. If the monoliths served as rulers' thrones, they may have symbolized the mythical jaguar origins of the incumbent, shown seated at the dark cave entrance that led to the underworld. Later Maya lords also sat on jaguar thrones.

Even more remarkable are the many ceremonial caches that come from north of the La Venta pyramid and the vicinity of the plaza. They include offerings of small jade jaguar masks, serpentine and jade axes, and numerous ornaments, often in large numbers. One offering contained a carefully arranged group of sixteen beautifully carved and red painted figurines in jade, serpentine, and one in red volcanic tuff. All are carved in the same style, with bald heads, slanted eyes, and the drooping mouth so characteristic of Olmec art. The figures are well weathered, as if they had been long revered before they were buried. Even more exotic is a mosaic of serpentine blocks thought to depict a conventionalized jaguar mask laid in a layer of olive-colored clay. A headless, kneeling basalt human figure with clasped hands sat at one corner of the mosaic. No less than twenty-eight levels of serpentine blocks lay in further layers of olive and blue clays under this complex mosaic, blocks with a total weight of more than 1000 tons, brought from some distance.

La Venta went into a rapid decline between 450 and 325 BC, when building activity ceased, and many of its monuments were defaced or destroyed.

Olmec Conquerors or Traders?

San Lorenzo and La Venta were far from unique. Large Olmec heads and mounds come from such little explored sites as Tres Zapotes near the Tuxtla mountains and Laguna de los Cerros to the southeast, where some 95 mounds cover more than 100 acres (161 ha). The hinterland of Tres Zapotes alone has yielded no less than eight other unexplored Olmec sites.

This shadowy, precocious society has provoked generations of controversy among archaeologists. Were the Olmec great conquerors, the first to carve out an enormous empire over lowlands and highlands? Current scholarly thinking plays down the imperial theme. Olmec society grew wealthy enough, so the argument goes, to trade with other areas, particularly in the highlands, for raw materials unavailable in the lowland Olmec heartland. Olmec religious beliefs and art styles then spread pervasively along these trade routes.

The swampy Olmec homeland provided fine pottery clays and hematite, but such precious and exotic commodities as jade, serpentine, and schist were vital to Olmec rituals and only found at a distance. Obsidian, too, was a much sought after raw material. Detailed studies of obsidian sources tell us that this dark, lustrous volcanic glass, much prized for mirrors and ceremonial knives, reached Olmec country from many outcrops, some a mere 60 miles (100 km) away, but others from as far afield as Teotihuacan in the Valley of Mexico. Olmec-style artifacts occur sporadically throughout Mexico, into Guatemala, San Salvador, and Honduras. The countless inter-village paths and trade routes that carried tropical foods, animal pelts, and feathers to the highlands had come into being centuries before the Olmec. Along the same paths, too, flowed gifts between neighboring rulers – and complex ideologies and motifs.

The total number of Olmec artifacts is generally very small in outlying areas, except at the remarkable and strategic Chalcatzingo site in Morelos. Chalcatzingo is near rich deposits of white kaolin clay, which was widely used for pottery and figurine making by the Olmec. It was also a convenient halfway location, for it lies near obsidian and greenstone-rich mountains in nearby Guerrero and could have become a major center for the redistribution of local raw materials into Olmec country.

Chalcatzingo displays strong Olmec influence, not only in its artifacts, but in the enormous bas-reliefs carved into rock faces overlooking the site. One shows an important individual seated inside the mouth of a cave or a stylized jaguar mouth. Clouds or rain in the form of spirals emanate from the cave mouth – perhaps the breath of the jaguar-god bringing rain. All the figures at Chalcatzingo are alive with jaguar motifs. Olmec human and jaguar figures

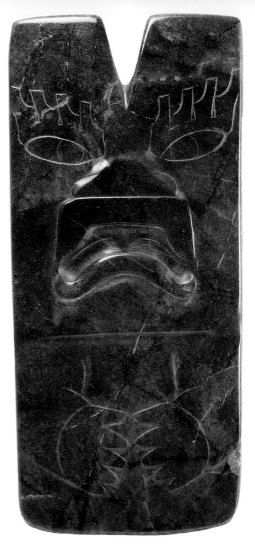

Jaguars, Were-Jaguars, and Babyface Figurines

The strength and supreme hunting ability of the jaguar, particularly in watery environments, gave rise to the pervasive Olmec symbolism that linked this jungle predator with the rain deity and royal power and might. CLOCKWISE FROM TOP FAR LEFT *An adult figure carries a jaguar-baby, detail of Altar 5, probably a throne, from La Venta; two ceremonial stone axes depict the typical Olmec half-human, half-jaguar "were-jaguar," with cleft head, flaming eyebrows, and down-turned snarling mouth; the jaguar's face (top) is also believed to be the inspiration behind the extraordinary mosaic of serpentine blocks (above), nearly 15 ft (4.5 m) across, found at La Venta; there is no doubting the feline – probably jaguar – symbolism of the animal attacking a human figure (left), seen in a rock carving at Chalcatzingo, Morelos; another indication of the long reach of the Olmec style is this greenstone babyface figurine (far left), 7 in (18 cm) tall, from central Mexico.*

An Olmec ruler (perhaps female, given the skirt the figure wears) sits within a cave or stylized jaguar mouth in this giant bas-relief rock carving at Chalcatzingo, Morelos. Clouds or rain, symbols of fertility, billow from the cave mouth.

appear in deep caves in the Guerrero mountains, too, close to the sources of greenstone so greatly valued by the lowland people.

Ceremonial centers and colossal sculptures, fine pottery, intricate figurines made in jadeite and other materials, an ideology based on a relationship between humans and jaguars – what are we to make of Olmec civilization? Everything points to a highly stratified, tautly organized society governed by divine rulers. Such a society is a far cry from the simpler village communities that flourished throughout Central America before 1500 BC.

The Rise of the Olmec Elite

In the final analysis, the power of Olmec rulers was based on their ability to feed their numerous subjects. By studying modern agricultural techniques near San Lorenzo, Michael Coe and Richard Diehl have shown that Olmec agriculture was much more complex than that of the modern inhabitants. They farmed two landscapes. The first was the low uplands around the settlement, which yielded maize and manioc crops twice a year, in both the wet and dry seasons. Even more important were the fertile gardens located on the natural levees of the rivers, which were inundated and refertilized by summer rains. When planted in fall, they would provide exceptionally high yields year after year. San Lorenzo lay in an area of great agricultural potential.

Coe and Diehl believe that this mosaic of gardens played a critical role in the emergence of a much more hierarchical society in Olmec country. Originally, village land was owned communally, by large kin groups. Increasingly, over many generations, certain families probably acquired control of the most fertile levee gardens, over prime fishing and waterfowl hunting preserves. They became a dominant elite in Olmec society.

To give symbolic and ritual expression to their new-found power, the elite built awe-inspiring architectural complexes. Artificial mountains and strategically arranged open spaces were designed to give an impression of overwhelming might, to provide the backdrop for carefully staged public rituals and displays that confirmed supreme authority. Those who ruled over these settings adorned their precincts with colossal statues of themselves.

These, and other public art works, symbolized their prestige and their unique, personal relationship to the gods.

Jaguars and Were-Jaguars

Olmec rulers were the first in Mesoamerica to portray their dominance in enduring form, in carvings, paintings, and sculptures. Olmec artists used a complex symbolism, including jungle animals of all kinds: birds, caymans, serpents, even spiders. But the jaguar was the dominant image.

The jaguar is the most feared predator in Central and South America, an animal of great physical strength, cunning, and endurance. Jaguars are highly adaptable beasts that flourish on land, in water, and in the "upperworld" of trees. Their hunting behavior resembles that of humans. The jaguar is aggressive and fearsome like a brave warrior, emits a thunderous roar like a violent thunderstorm, and is reputed to have great sexual prowess. And the fact that jaguars hunt at night, crossing boundaries between different environments, links them in the human mind with the power of the shaman. This identification with the jaguar is found throughout tropical America, regardless of culture or ecological zone. It has deep roots in prehistoric times.

In many modern American Indian societies, the jaguar is intimately associated with the notions of rain and fertility. Jaguars prefer watery environments, for such regions offer a great diversity of prey. They frequently hunt caymans and attract fish by tapping the water with their tails. The Olmec homeland, with its many swamps and waterways, abounded with jaguars, an environment where control of water was essential for farming rich river levee soils. Thus, Olmec rulers – whom we may call shaman-kings – may have grafted the age-old ideology of the jaguar onto the need to control water supplies. Under this rubric, a leader who controlled rain and floods did so by his close links to the supernatural jaguar. The Olmec rain-god may have been a half-human, half-animal figure with snarling were-jaguar mouth, but this was one of many combinations of the jaguar, many of them fantastic beasts that came from the hallucinogenic mind rather than from the forest itself. Olmec artists used eagles' feathers and claws to create composite creatures that melded the serpent with the bird and the jaguar. From this melding may have emerged the famous mythical creature Quetzalcoatl, the "Feathered Serpent." Sometimes Quetzalcoatl became even more, a mosaic of jaguar face and fangs, a serpent's body, and bird feathers. He was to become the most enduring of all Mesoamerican deities.

Today, we can obtain only a glimpse of what was once a very complex and rapidly evolving religion. The Olmec took a set of centuries-old tribal beliefs about the spirit world and transformed them into a complex array of beliefs about prestige, success, and control of society that were entirely in tune with American Indian thinking about the nature of the universe. And they, and their successors, ruled with these new beliefs for over 2,500 years.

▲▲

CHAPTER SEVEN

THE GULLET OF THE VISION SERPENT
Discovering the Maya

"Grim and mysterious," John Lloyd Stephens called them, the silent figures that stared him in the face from the walls of Palenque, deep in the tropical rainforest of the Yucatán. Lush foliage entwined the stucco-decorated buildings of the long-abandoned city. The languorous, humid air, the constant rain, the clinging vegetation, and exotic personages peering out at the explorers had a powerful effect on even the most experienced traveler. Stephens had journeyed up the Nile, ventured to the rock-cut city of Petra, and explored the Holy Land. But he had never seen anything like this. He fell under the magic spell of Palenque, yet refused to be beguiled by superficial resemblances to Egyptian art. "We have a conclusion far more interesting and wonderful than that of connecting the builders of these cities with the Egyptians or any other people," he wrote. "It is the spectacle of a people . . . originating and growing up here, without models or masters, having a distinct, separate, indigenous existence; like the plants and fruits of the soil, indigenous." With these words, John Lloyd Stephens founded Maya studies.

Catherwood and Stephens left Palenque with indelible memories. "In the romance of the world's history nothing ever impressed me so forcibly," Stephens wrote, "than the spectacle of this once great and lovely city, overturned, desolate, and lost . . . it did not have even a name to distinguish it . . ." It is only now, 150 years later, that modern scholarship has identified the dynasty of powerful rulers who built and adorned Palenque.

Decipherment

The last remnants of Maya civilization still flickered when Spanish conquistadors explored the Yucatán in the early sixteenth century. They found a densely settled land with vivid memories of powerful cities and great kings. The Maya were a formidable challenge for the missionary zeal of the Franciscan friars. The most zealous was Fray Diego de Landa, a ruthless and efficient prelate, who learned the local Maya dialect and preached to his converts in their own tongue. With one hand he punished the Indians savagely for their perceived idolatries. With the other, he compiled a detailed account of traditional customs with the aid of local informants. He explored the ruins of Chichén Itzá and its mysterious *cenote*, a sacred pool filled with murky water held "in the same veneration as we have for pilgrimages to Jerusalem and Rome." Exotic figures "of nude men, having their loins covered with long girdles," excited his interest at Mayapán. Then there were the mysterious hieroglyphs. "These people also made use of certain characters or letters, with which they wrote in their books ancient matters and their sciences . . . We found a large number of books in these characters and, as they contained nothing in which there were not to be seen superstition and lies of the devil, we burned them all, which they regretted to an amazing degree." Ironically, the burning of these precious codices did not prevent Landa himself from writing a description of the Maya script that has been of considerable use to modern scholars and enabled them to correlate Maya and European dates.

For three centuries, the Maya remained in historical oblivion, their once great cities mantled in thick rainforest. Stephens' brilliant descriptions in the 1830s and 1840s gave a glimpse into this lost world, but the stones were silent, the intricate glyphs unreal. Could they be deciphered, as Egyptian hieroglyphs had been? It was to take a surprisingly long time before scholars truly cracked the Maya code.

Landa's accounts and other sources made it clear that Maya civilization was driven by a complicated calendar. By the end of the nineteenth century, German scholars Eduard Seler and Ernst Forstemann, and American J.T. Goodman, had worked out the basic details of the Maya calendar. By this time, a growing corpus of photographs taken by men like Alfred Maudslay and Teobert Maler provided a priceless archive of inscriptions for the experts to puzzle over. But what did the inscriptions cover? Were they historical records, as a few scholars believed, or were they little more than calendrical and astronomical observations? Thanks to the work of the influential British-born Mayanist J. Eric Thompson, the prevailing view was that "the dates on stelae* surely narrate the stages of the journey of time with a reverence befitting such a solemn theme." Thompson believed that "the endless progress of time [was] the supreme mystery of Maya religion, a subject which pervaded Maya thought to an extent without parallel in the history of mankind."

The calendrical theory dominated scholarly thinking until the 1960s when Harvard Mayanist Tatiana Proskouriakoff proved Thompson wrong. She inventoried thousands of motifs and elements on stelae and artifacts large and small. By using minutely developed classifications, she was able to develop a chronology of Maya stelae. She showed that they treated of individual rulers, the dates of their accessions, conquests, and so on. So thorough were Proskouriakoff's researches that she was able to identify the "name glyphs" of individual rulers and dynasties. She revolutionized the study of Maya civilization when she identified no less than seven successive groups of rulers' monuments at a major center named Piedras Negras in Guatemala's western

---

* The Maya erected large numbers of these carved, freestanding stone monoliths in their cities.

Petén region. Each monument had been erected on the fifth anniversary of the ruler's accession. Far from being merely calendrical markings, Maya glyphs were a priceless source of dynastic history.

Proskouriakoff did not actually decipher Maya glyphs, but her trail-blazing research was one of many breakthroughs that led to decipherment. Back in 1952, Russian epigrapher Yuri Knorosov had proposed that the Maya writing system combined signs that represented entire words with others that merely represented individual syllables. Knorosov's theory was considered highly controversial. Only a handful of epigraphers listened to him. But between 1973 and 1978 a small group of scholars collaborated in combining Knorosov's phonetic approach with Proskouriakoff's historical analyses. As Victorian epigraphers had done with Assyrian cuneiform, they found that a background of constant debate and argument produced a final breakthrough. They assumed that the glyphs were a spoken language, a language with a word order which could be used to determine whether individual glyphs were verbs, nouns, and so on, even if they could not read them. Soon, they could paraphrase inscriptions and treat them as entire texts. This realization provided the broad framework for writing Maya history.

The decipherment of the glyphs has reverberated like a sonic boom through the staid world of Maya archaeology. After years of working in a textless environment, the archaeologists now find themselves confronted with a much more complex historical landscape than they ever suspected. Some archaeologists have embraced the complexities of Maya history with great enthusiasm. Others adopt a wait-and-see attitude, in the belief that many of the dramatic new interpretations go far beyond the permissible limits of scholarly speculation. The most successful researches are those where archaeologists and epigraphers work together in the field, deciphering glyphs literally as they come out of the ground.

Maya writing was extremely complex, to its users far more than mere record-keeping. The glyphs taught history, gave supernatural meaning to the events of daily life. Recorded in beaten bark-paper books, on stelae, tombs, and buildings, Maya literature consists of several genres. There are ritual almanacs, ownership texts, texts that dedicate objects, and narratives. It is the combination of all these that provide modern scholars with a window on the Maya. But, like rulers of many states, Maya lords sought to justify their deeds, their dynasty, and to glorify their victories. Thus, the histories that come down to us on stelae and buildings are "official" narratives, invariably one-sided, always the work of the wealthy, the victorious, and the influential. The challenge is to separate fact from fiction, legend from historical event.

Who were the Maya?

Between 200 BC and AD 900, what archaeologists today call Classic Maya civilization flourished over more than 100,000 square miles (260,000 sq. km)

LEFT *Stela D and its "altar" at the Maya city of Copán. Frederick Catherwood published this magnificent lithograph in 1844. From the glyphs on it we now know that the stela was erected on 26 July AD 736.*

of the Yucatán lowlands. This was a civilization of great lords, a tiny elite who presided over as many as fifty independent states and tens of thousands of humble village farmers. The influence of the Maya extended far from their homeland. They traded with states in the Valley of Oaxaca in the highlands, maintained diplomatic relations with the vast city of Teotihuacan in the Basin of Mexico, perpetuated religious beliefs that took hold over an enormous area of ancient Mesoamerica. Maya leaders were divine kings, quarrelsome rulers obsessed with power and prestige, expert diplomats who were masters of the political marriage. They built great cities and trading centers around palaces, plazas, and pyramids. Grandiose public buildings were adorned with stone and stucco sculptures of deities and mythical creatures, of lords conducting important ceremonies. Maya kings were fanatical about their position in history. They erected intricately carved stelae to commemorate their accessions and their relationships to powerful, mythical ancestors. Everything, however prosaic, unfolded within a wider mythic context and against the background of a rich fountain of epic and legend. Today, we marvel at this complex world. Maya civilization was one of the most sophisticated, exotic, and volatile cultures of ancient America.

The Maya Universe

Like the Olmec, the Maya inhabited a world where the spiritual and physical were closely entwined. The Maya universe was made up of three layers – the Upperworld of the heavens, the Middleworld of humankind, and the murky waters of the Underworld beneath. Not that these layers were separate, for the Maya believed that all layers of existence were interrelated. Linking them was a great tree or World Tree named *Wacah Chan* ("raised up sky"), with its roots in the Underworld, its trunk in the Middleworld, and its branches in the Upperworld. Supernatural beings and souls of the dead could pass from layer to layer via this tree. *Wacah Chan* grew through the center of the Middleworld, the point from which four cardinal directions flowed. These directions were fundamental points of reference, each with their own bird, color, tree, and gods. East, for example, was the principal direction, the direction of the rising sun; its color was red. North, the direction of the ancestral dead, was white.

According to the epigrapher Linda Schele and archaeologist David Freidel – whose book *The Forest of Kings* is the first to attempt to reveal the full story of the Maya from the new decipherments – the Maya believed that the Middleworld through which *Wacah Chan* grew was not located in one specific place, but could be fixed by ritual at any point on the landscape. It was personified by the body of the king, who brought it to existence as he stood in a trance on top of a temple pyramid. The act of communication between the king and the spiritual world – known to the Maya as Xibalba – was the most sacred deed of kingship. Through his trances and by shedding his blood, the

RIGHT *Clay figurine of a Maya lord smoking a cigar, one of many sculptures from Jaina island.* OVERLEAF: LEFT *This painted vase depicts a Maya lord reclining on a miniature canoe, perhaps entering the Underworld.* OVERLEAF: RIGHT *A seated woman dressed much as Yaxchilán queens are, with rich textiles and bloodletting headdress.*

Maya king conjured up the *Wacah Chan* through the center of the temple, opening a doorway into the spiritual world. This was when clouds of incense and smoke rose from the temples and coiled like a serpent around the pyramids high above the onlookers. This was the Vision Serpent, the Feathered Serpent, perhaps the most powerful symbol of Maya kingship, the tortuous path between the natural and supernatural realms.

Bloodletting was the fundamental ritual of Maya life. Every Maya offered blood on ritual occasions, at everything from the birth of a child to marriage and at funerals. The blood could be taken from any part of the body, but the most sacred offerings came from the tongue, or the penis, from cuts made with a sharp obsidian blade or a fish spine. Usually a few drops sufficed, but on occasion major bloodletting formed an important part of great cleansing rituals, when men and women would use finger-thick ropes drawn through the wound to generate copious flows of blood onto sacred papers that were then burnt. The most sacred bloodlettings occurred at major festivals, when the great plazas would fill with thousands of spectators.

These copious blood flows may seem exotic to us, but we should remember that blood has vital symbolic importance in many cultures. Christians, for example, drink blood symbolically at Holy Communion, when they receive the spirit of Christ. Medieval friars drew blood by whipping themselves in abject penitence for their sins. The Maya felt the same way, for they believed that the liquid from their self-inflicted wounds sustained the spiritual world.

Linda Schele and David Freidel believe that what they call "the gullet of the Vision Serpent" was the pathway taken by the gods and the ancestors when they communicated with the king. Once brought into the world of the living, the gods would assume material form, as sacred mountains or other natural features of the landscape, as ritual objects, or even as human shamans. It follows, they argue, that Maya cities were symbolic models of the sacred landscape. Plazas with their upright stelae carved with the images of kings were symbolic forests. The young epigrapher David Stuart discovered that the Maya used the term "tree-stones" to describe the stelae, an apt analogy. Even today, village shamans in Maya country still make models of the natural world with sticks and corn stalks, which they erect at the mouths of caves or at the bases of hills to harness sacred energies.

Sacred Time

All human beings are curious about the past, about times long gone. Today, our linear view of history goes back more than 5,000 years, to the earliest civilizations in the Near East, and far earlier to the very beginnings of human existence more than 2.5 million years ago. The Maya were certainly very interested in recording the passage of time through their system known as the Long Count, as we shall see. But for them time was cyclical, it repeated itself. They perfected the measurement of rotating, and interlocking, cycles of time

LEFT *Greenstone figure probably from the Maya city of Copán. Jade and other greenstones were valued even more highly than gold in pre-Columbian Mesoamerica. About 7 in (18 cm) tall.*

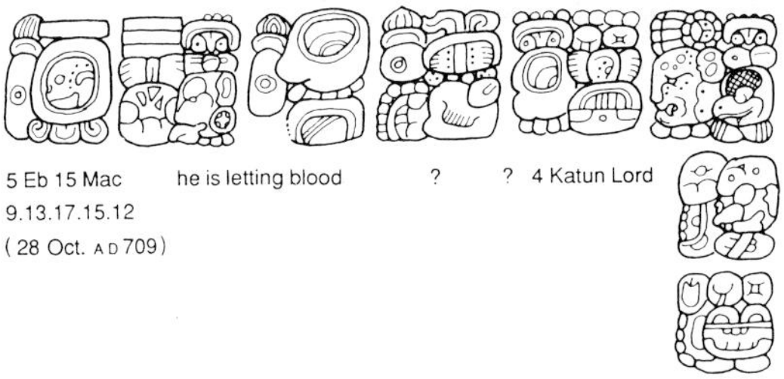

Shield Jaguar
the captor of

5 Eb 15 Mac   he is letting blood   ?   ? 4 Katun Lord
9.13.17.15.12
(28 Oct. AD 709)

Ah Ahaual

Lord of Yaxchilan

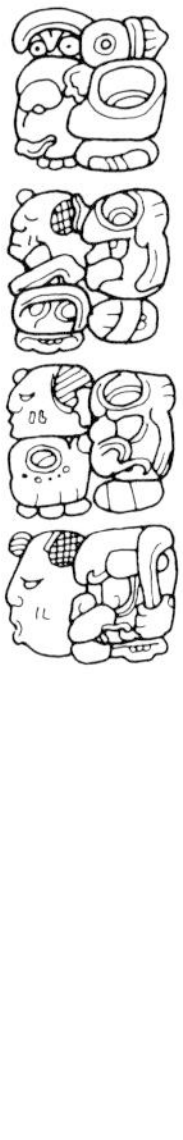

she is
letting blood

name or titles

Lady Xoc

Lady Batab

Lintel 24 from Yaxchilán depicts a bloodletting rite that took place on 28 October AD 709. The ruler, Shield Jaguar, holds a giant torch over the kneeling figure of his wife, Lady Xoc, who pulls a thorn-lined rope through her tongue.

4 Katun Lord

Shield Jaguar   ??   chac   he of fire   his flint shield   he let blood   5 Imix 4 Mac
                                                                     9.12.9.8.1
                                                         (23 Oct. AD 681)

the captor of
Ah Ahaual

Lord of
Yaxchilan
Bacab

she is Lady Maize

title

Lady Xoc   title

??

? Yaxchilan

In Yaxchilán's Lintel 25, marking Shield Jaguar's accession on 23 October AD 681, Lady Xoc witnesses the appearance of the double-headed Vision Serpent, a warrior emerging from the front and a Tlaloc image from the rear.

that tried "to encapsulate historical events in a closed chronological network of time loops," as astroarchaeologist Anthony Aveni puts it.

The ancient Maya did not invent their calendar, for its roots lie thousands of years earlier in prehistory, in the traditional astronomical lore that regulated the planting and harvest of crops. The basic unit in the early Mesoamerican counting system was 20, a number very likely arrived at from the number of fingers and toes in the human body. As early as Olmec times, priests were using a 260-day cycle, which the Maya refined into the *tzolkin*, a combination of 13 numbers and 20 day names. This cycle of sacred days repeated itself endlessly, just as our own weeks do, and was used throughout Mesoamerica. But why 260 days, a duration unique in the ancient world? Anthony Aveni believes the *tzolkin's* 260 days may relate to some other important period of time in Maya life. The average length of the human gestation period is 266 days, and Maya women associate the *tzolkin* with giving birth to this day. Aveni points out that the basic agricultural cycle lasts about the same time as human gestation throughout Maya country, so, perhaps, ancient priests associated the two most fundamental fertility cycles of human life with a period of 260 days.

The Maya also used a 365-day cycle, the *haab*, which was developed somewhat later and consisted of 18 "months" of 20 days each, and one short 5-day month. This was probably a farming calendar, for the names of the months and the symbols associated with them seem to define such activities as planting and harvest. Like the *tzolkin*, the *haab* repeated itself and was not

The interlocking 260-day calendar (left: inner wheel, 13 day numbers; outer wheel, 20 day names) and 365-day calendar (right: 18 months, each of 20 days.

adjusted to the true solar year. Unlike most early civilizations, which broke the year into 12 units, because of the phases of the moon, the Maya stayed with their 20-unit count. As a result, the *haab* gradually went out of alignment with the seasons by a quarter day every four years. It took 1,460 years for the month and day count to return to its original position.

The *tzolkin* was a sacred calendar, the *haab* an agrarian one, two calendars with quite different purposes. Before 2,000 years ago the two cycles were brought together in a unified, interlocking calendar by newly ascendant Maya lords. Joined together, the two time scales formed a cycle of 52 years, 18,980 days, after which name and number combinations were repeated.

By the second century AD, Maya kings had become sufficiently conscious of their status to wish to have it established in the full sweep of history. They expanded cyclical time to encompass not only their own histories, but to take Maya life right back to the creation itself. Their era-based calendar, the famous "Long Count," counted the number of days accumulated since the creation in units of 360-day years, *tuns*. These years combined into ever larger multiples of 20, toward infinity, zero day in the Maya conception being 11 August 3114 BC in our calendar. The Long Count enabled Maya lords to legitimize their actions by melding them with mythological history. They exploited the concept of linear time, but always there was the idea that the cycle would come full circle and that the clock of history would repeat itself.

Cerros Experiments with Kingship

The institution of kingship developed with startling rapidity in many Maya communities. Linda Schele and David Freidel have used the results from recent excavations to document the emergence of the new order in Cerros, for centuries a hamlet of fisherfolk and traders near the New River and close to the Gulf of Mexico. They look at this momentous change in terms not of general trends in society, but as the deeds of actual individuals, even if we do not know their names. As they see it, the scenario was as follows:

In about 50 BC, after centuries of quiet village life, the people of Cerros made a conscious decision to transform their society completely. One of their leaders, probably a prominent patriarch, became a king. We know this because there is abundant archaeological evidence that the people deliberately abandoned their houses in the center of the settlement, carried out the necessary rituals of abandonment in honor of their ancestors, then erected new dwellings around the central area, where they built a temple.

This new temple and plaza were, in a sense, a public stage, where the new lord carried out his shamanistic rituals. Thanks to large-scale excavations, we can imagine the T-shaped temple that stood on a royal pyramid of earth and rock, an artificial mountain like those erected by the Olmec that was part of the symbolic landscape. The pyramid itself was an ancient architectural artifice, but the Maya added a feature of their own – modeled and plastered facades adorned with the political and religious messages that conveyed the essence of Maya kingship. A long stairway ascended from the plaza to the entrance of the shrine, where massive tree trunks set in special post holes formed the carved and painted world trees of the four directions. It was in the stone temple that the king carried out his personal bloodletting and went into the trance that prepared him to meet the gods and ancestors. We can imagine him appearing on the stairway before the people, the red blood showing up vividly on his white cotton raiment. The lower facade of the pyramid bore huge masks of snarling jaguars, representing the Jaguar Sun God, the rising and setting sun, and the Ancestral Twins of Maya legend.

Within a generation, Schele and Freidel tell us, a later lord constructed a much more ambitious temple precinct, more than three times the size of the earlier structure. This time, the builders erected a temple with different viewing levels. The highest raised plaza stood 52 ft (16 m) above the town, making the rituals conducted on it invisible to the populace at large. The new architecture added to the increasing social distinctions that were taking hold.

Not content merely with this elaborate complex, the same ruler erected another temple and plaza directly to the east, facing the rising sun, intending it as a royal tomb. Then he constructed a westward-facing temple to the south, a temple perhaps commemorating war. Two ballcourts were built nearby, places where rituals of war and sacrifice pitted noble captives against one another in symbolic reenactment of the Ancestral Twins' defeat of the Lords of Death in the Underworld.

The unknown ruler never occupied his mortuary temple. Perhaps he was captured in a long-forgotten war or died away from home. His successor began construction of yet another temple. The work was shoddy. In the end, the experiment in kingship failed. The people piled fuel against the masks of their ancestors and kings and set fire to them, smashing ornaments and conducting elaborate termination rituals that effectively desanctified the sacred mountains in their midst. But they did not abandon Cerros, continuing to live close to the ruined temples.

Schele and Freidel cannot tell us why kingship failed at Cerros. Perhaps a weak ruler, or series of kings, or a disputed succession, fatally weakened royal power. In the event, the people seem deliberately to have destroyed the symbolic landscape. We saw the same deliberate vandalism at Olmec San Lorenzo, as if such desanctifications were as old as Mesoamerican civilization itself. Later Maya history is a constant litany of ritual destruction and erasure, as if Maya kings did not wish to be reminded that their predecessors had failed.

The earliest Maya rulers are anonymous figures, but people of enormous significance to Mesoamerican history. It was they who forged the distinctive hierarchical pattern of ancient Maya society, who developed ancient spiritual beliefs into a powerful cosmology that was expressed brilliantly in stone and plaster, and who laid the foundations for the great towns and cities of Classic Maya civilization.

▲▲

CHAPTER EIGHT

MAYA LORDS
Classic Maya Civilization

"Whatever there is that might be is simply not there; only murmurs, ripples, in the dark, in the night. Only the Maker, Modeler alone, Sovereign Plumed Serpent, the Bearers, Begetters are in the water, a glittering light. They are there, they are enclosed in quetzal feathers, in blue-green."

The *Popol Vuh*, the Quiché Maya "Book of Counsel," begins in darkness, in a world inhabited only by gods, continues through the creation of humanity, and ends in the lifetimes of the anonymous nobles who wrote it. At the beginning, the gods are preoccupied with the difficult task of creating humans. At the end, mortals search for evidence of divine intervention in their own deeds. The *Popol Vuh* epitomizes the Maya view of a cosmos in which the divine and the human are inextricably intermingled. The major players in Maya history were those who straddled the boundary between the living and the dead, the great shaman-kings. The new decipherments allow us for the first time to tell their story, and that of their greatest cities.

A Tale of Three Cities: El Mirador, Tikal, and Uaxactún

Seen from an airplane, the rainforest of the Yucatán is like a green blanket stretching to the far horizon. The lush forest mantles all traces of ancient Maya life, except for an occasional artificial mountain, an abandoned pyramid, that pokes through the tree tops. Thus it was that El Mirador, perhaps the greatest early Maya city, came to light, a long forgotten center that lies among the swamps and low hills of the Petén, the central part of the Yucatán. Only the pyramids could be seen. Utah State University archaeologist Ray Matheny literally had to cut his way into the ruins. His excavations have revealed a metropolis that flourished between 150 BC and AD 50 and eventually covered about 6 square miles (16 sq. km). The colossal Danta pyramid at the eastern end of the city rises from a natural hill more than 230 ft (70 m) high. The western face of the hill is sculpted into large platforms covered with buildings and temples. A little over a mile to the west rises the Tigre complex, a pyramid 182 ft (55 m) high surrounded by a plaza, a small temple, and several smaller buildings. The Tigre complex covers an area a little larger than the base of the Pyramid of the Sun at Teotihuacan in the highlands – an enormous artificial mountain by any standards.

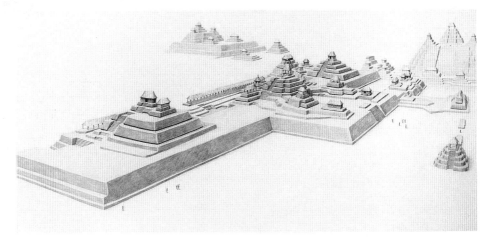

Reconstruction of the ceremonial core at the early Maya city of El Mirador.

El Mirador was a stupendous city, controlled by a highly organized elite, with its own artisans, priests, and engineers, as well as traders. We know nothing of the identity of its rulers, although some of the earliest examples of Maya writing occur at the site. Like its much smaller contemporary, Cerros, El Mirador went into decline in the first century AD, perhaps as a result of changing trade patterns.

A mere 40 miles (64 km) away, two other Maya centers, Tikal and Uaxactún, stepped into the political vacuum left by El Mirador's decline. Tikal lies on a patch of high ground among huge swamps. Today, scholars recognize it as one of the greatest Maya cities, and, as befitted such an important site, a team of archaeologists from the University of Pennsylvania devoted many seasons in the 1960s to its excavation. Such long-term digs, involving not only archaeologists, but epigraphers, architects, and other specialists, are now reconstructing the histories not only of Tikal, but of Quiriguá, Copán, and several other major Maya centers. As early as 600 BC, a small village community flourished here, trading obsidian from the distant highlands and quartzite from northern Belize. By the second century BC, the village had a well-defined central area, delineated by low stone platforms of characteristic Maya design. A century later, the transformation was complete. Large public buildings and royal burial vaults now appear. By this time, Tikal's architects had adorned the central Acropolis of the city with all the flamboyant architectural artifices of Maya kings, including large plaster masks that symbolized the institution of kingship itself. The royal tombs from this period contain the bones of larger and more robust individuals than the average Maya. The nobility were taller and enjoyed a better diet than commoners. ''Burial 85'' contained a headless, thighless corpse of a lord. His incomplete remains lay in a cinnabar-impregnated bundle, with the paraphernalia used for bloodletting. The green fuchsite portrait head tied to the bundle

RIGHT *Green fuchsite mask, 5 in (12.7 cm) tall, with shell-inlaid eyes and teeth, from Burial 85 at Tikal. The headdress design became the crown of Tikal's kings for ten centuries.*

was once his chest pectoral. It wears the headdress that was to be the crown of Tikal's kings for the next ten centuries.

During the third century, Tikal's rulers embarked on an ambitious remodeling of the entire central precinct of their rapidly growing city. This involved not only the remodeling of the North Acropolis, but the leveling and paving of huge plazas where the common people gathered to witness the lord's ritual performances.

Nearby Uaxactún witnessed as dramatic an expansion. The site is remarkable for its six Late Preclassic temples built on a small acropolis, excavated from under later buildings erected at the same sacred location. Here, massive stucco sculptures and masks depict the sacred mountain in the form of a great monster sitting in the primordial waters with vegetation growing from the sides of its head. A similar monster sits at a higher level, perhaps depicting the mountain rising above the waters. The heads of the Vision Serpent peer out on either side.

The great lord who commissioned this scene stands on a gateway, surrounded by the blood scrolls of the Vision Quest. Stucco jaguar masks, symbols of kingship and power, flank the stairways leading to the gateway doors. It is here, at Uaxactún, that we see Maya kings memorializing themselves for the first time.

A Clash of Maya Titans

At the time of El Mirador's demise, Tikal and Uaxactún were equals, the former ruled by a dynasty founded by a lord named Yax Moch Xoc between AD 219 and 238. He was not the first ruler of Tikal, but he must have been sufficiently important to be the ''anchoring ancestor'' for an entire dynasty of great kings. He and his successors portrayed themselves as shamans using complex imagery that reflected not only their royal ancestry but their close relationship to the power of the mysterious jaguar. Here, as with the Olmec, the jaguar appears as the master of the underworld, as the symbol of kingship, of bravery in war, of religious authority. Sometimes, sacrificial victims cower at the monarchs' feet, for warfare and the capture of noble prisoners were an important reflection of royal power, and of the great lord's ability to nourish the gods with noble blood.

The rivalry between Tikal and Uaxactún came to a head during the reign of Great Jaguar Paw, the ninth ruler of Tikal's long-lasting royal dynasty. Great Jaguar Paw waged war against his rival and captured Uaxactún on 16 January AD 378. This was warfare on a new scale and for territorial conquest. We know this was a dramatic departure in Maya life, because the conquering general Smoking Frog is depicted as a warrior, wearing a costume that represents a new and powerful divine partnership in Maya life – Tlaloc (the goggle-eyed god associated in the Maya area with warfare and sacrifice), and a powerful force from Xibalba, Venus.

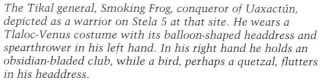

The Tikal general, Smoking Frog, conqueror of Uaxactún, depicted as a warrior on Stela 5 at that site. He wears a Tlaloc-Venus costume with its balloon-shaped headdress and spearthrower in his left hand. In his right hand he holds an obsidian-bladed club, while a bird, perhaps a quetzal, flutters in his headdress.

This departure from earlier military protocol may well have resulted from strong influences from the burgeoning city of Teotihuacan in the Valley of Mexico, whose rise and fall we chronicle in the next chapter. Tlaloc was one of the major deities of Teotihuacan. There had been contact between the Maya and Teotihuacan since at least the first century AD, for the characteristic green obsidian mined near the highland city appears in Late Preclassic Maya sites. By the late fourth century, Teotihuacano artifacts are more common at Tikal. One burial cache contains not only what may be the remains of noble Teotihuacanos but a vase that may depict a diplomatic visit by noble merchants from the highlands to Tikal. These contacts apparently continued. During the fifth century, Teotihuacan forged a trade network that linked hundreds of individual societies throughout the highlands and lowlands. It was along this network that powerful ideals of war and human sacrifice refined in Teotihuacan passed to many other societies.

We know that the new war cults took powerful hold in Maya life, for inscriptions tell us that Tikal's leaders now timed their wars for specific points in the cycle of Venus, the planet associated with war. The Tlaloc-Venus costume became a standard part of the royal regalia, symbolizing the lord as conqueror and brave warrior. The all-powerful ruler not only captured sacrificial victims but imposed his will on his newly conquered subjects. Thus it was that Smoking Frog from Tikal, perhaps the brother of Great Jaguar Paw, became the new lord of Uaxactún. So important was this war of conquest that it was remembered and commemorated by rulers in both cities for centuries afterward. And Tikal dominated the southeastern lowlands for nearly 200 years.

Wars of Conquest

Tikal now entered a period of great prosperity. Generations of kings adorned the city with magnificent temples, pyramids, and plazas, eventually reworking the summit of the North Acropolis into a pattern of eight buildings.

Then, in the mid-sixth century, Lord Water of the rising state of Caracol to the southeast attacked Tikal and overthrew its rulers. The next 130 years saw the rulers of Caracol embark on wars of conquest against other powerful neighbors, but their efforts at empire building were never entirely successful. There was constant rivalry and internecine warfare. To suffer defeat was to suffer the ultimate indignity – capture in war and being offered in sacrifice on a rival's altar.

Maya armies waged war during the dry months between January and May, when the ground was hard underfoot. This is the time of drought, when the farmers burn the forest to clear their lands. The rains come in May and June, at the summer solstice, transforming the arid landscape into a fertile forest that teems with life. The storms can be well spaced and predictable, or inundate the land and flood many acres of gardens. In July and August, they give way to a short dry season before autumn drizzle and cold winter storms bring cooler weather to the lowlands. It is this annual rhythm of drought and heavy rain that created the symbols of power that sustained Maya kings.

In the seventh century, the rulers of Tikal maneuvered to restore the city's ancient greatness in the face of a weakening Caracol. When lord Ah Cacaw ascended to the city's throne on 6 May 682, a new era in Tikal's history began. He embarked immediately on a massive rebuilding program that remodeled the North Acropolis and the Great Plaza that lay at the heart of the ancient city. The buildings that stood there had been desecrated by Lord Water of

Aerial view of the temple-pyramids and plazas at the heart of the city of Tikal.

Caracol. In 695, Ah Cacaw captured Lord King Jaguar Paw of Calakmul in a lightning war. He was tortured and sacrificed in elaborate ceremonies that dedicated a temple (Temple 33) and celebrated the renewal of the great dynasty. Tikal was to enjoy another period of great prosperity, its rulers depicted under the protection of the Jaguar God, the patron deity of the city.

Manipulating History: The Jaguar Kings of Palenque

Writing the political history of the Maya is a task that will consume the energies of many generations of scholars. Each kingdom, large and small, had its own dynasty, its own mythical and material history. These histories are astoundingly complex religious and mythological rationales, as well as vital historical chronicles. Of all these histories, that of the lords of Palenque, carved on limestone monuments, is the most detailed and complete.

Palenque is the most westerly of all Maya cities, set at the foot of a line of rainforest-covered hills, just above the Usumacinta River floodplain. The Otulum River flows right through the site and was canalized to pass under the Palace, a masterpiece of vaults, rooms, and small courts. More of a ceremonial structure than a residence, the Palace is remarkable for its unique four-story tower, which offers commanding views over the surrounding countryside. The nine-level Temple of the Inscriptions stands just to the south, set into the hillside. It covers the tomb of Pacal, the greatest of Palenque's lords.

The Palace at Palenque, most westerly of all Maya cities, with its unique four-story tower.

Palenque's officially recorded history begins with the accession of Bahlum Kuk (Jaguar Quetzal) on 11 March AD 431. The dynasty was to endure until some time after 799. We know of the existence of this ruler from the records of two later kings, Pacal (Shield) and his oldest son Chan Bahlum (Snake Jaguar). Pacal ascended to the throne of Tikal in 615 and was to reign for sixty-seven years. In his seventies, he constructed the famous Temple of the Inscriptions as his mortuary temple. Its corridors display king-lists on stone slabs. His son went even further and extended the list of ancestors back to the founder of the Palenque dynasty, even to the deities who founded the Maya cosmos. In all, the two lords left four king-lists.

Mexican archaeologist Alberto Ruz made one of the most dramatic of all archaeological discoveries when he uncovered a hidden staircase in the heart of the Temple of the Inscriptions in 1952. The stairway descended into the bowels of the pyramid to the undisturbed tomb of the mighty Pacal himself. The great king lay on his back in his red-painted stone sarcophagus, adorned with a jade collar and green headband. A magnificent mosaic mask of jade, shell, and obsidian in a likeness of the king covered Pacal's face. The outside of the sarcophagus depicted Pacal's fall down the World Tree into the Underworld. He is accompanied by an image of the sun in transition between life and death, for the king will rise again in the east, where the sun rises. Pacal's ancestors were carved around his coffin in ascending generations.

Chan Bahlum not only completed his father's temple, but erected another complex of buildings, the so-called Group of the Cross. It was here that the new lord validated his own succession with brilliant images and texts. These buildings – the Temple of the Cross, the Temple of the Foliated Cross, and the Temple of the Sun – bear great plaster reliefs that commemorate the passage of the ruler to the spiritual world and his triumphant return.

The experts have used the rich inscriptions commissioned by Pacal and others to reconstruct a dynasty of twelve kings, with some fascinating discrepancies in the line of succession. These discrepancies account for the obsession with rewriting history that was so remarkable in Pacal and Chan Bahlum's day. Succession was through the male line, yet Pacal, for example, inherited the throne from his mother, Lady Zac-Kuk, who served for a time as ruler. She must have been a remarkable woman, although we know nothing of her. Pacal claimed the throne as her son. In so doing, he had to change the genealogical rules to override the age-old practice of descent through the father. It may have helped that Pacal ascended to the throne at the age of twelve, while his mother was still alive, and that she lived on for a further twenty-five years. The real power may have been in her hands for all those years, for it is only after her death in 640 that Pacal commissioned major inscriptions that justified his own rule.

Eventually, in the ninth century, like other Maya states Palenque faltered and collapsed, its people returning to simple farming around the ruins of their once-great city.

LEFT, ABOVE *Palenque's Temple of the Inscriptions.* LEFT *Deep within the temple, archaeologists found the tomb of Palenque's seventh-century ruler, Pacal. Here, on the sarcophagus lid, Pacal is shown falling down the World Tree into the open jaws of the Underworld.*

Lords of Palenque

ABOVE *The life-size jade mosaic mask of Palenque's ruler, Pacal, found within his sarcophagus (pp. 130–1). The eyes are of shell and obsidian.* RIGHT *Plaster head of an unknown Palenque lord, described by the Maya scholar Linda Schele as "one of the most dramatic and insightful portraits known from Classic Maya art."*

The Lords of Copán

Tikal, Uaxactún, Palenque, Copán – the great centers of Maya civilization were associated with long dynasties of shaman-kings. Copán in modern Honduras was one of the longest lived, a city that lay in the southeast of Maya country. But Copán's critical importance for posterity lies in its hieroglyphic inscriptions and sculpted monuments – more of these have been found here than at any other Maya city. Ever since Stephens and Catherwood first visited the site, generations of leading Maya scholars have studied the city's remains. Today an international team of archaeologists, epigraphers, and other scientists are uncovering new burials, piecing together thousands of sculpture fragments, and deciphering the glyphs.

Copán lies in a magnificent setting of mountains, gently rolling hills and fertile agricultural land. It covers about 30 acres (12 ha), a complex of imposing pyramids built around open plazas adorned with altars and stelae. There were village farmers in the valley as early as 1400 BC. But it was not until about AD 400 that a nucleus of public buildings, including a ballcourt, rose in what became the central core of Copán.

The dynastic line of Copán's sixteen rulers is cast in stone on the four sides of Altar Q, a stone block that lies at the foot of a pyramid-temple on the Acropolis. The founder was Yax K'uk Mo' ("Blue Quetzal Macaw") in about 435. All subsequent kings claimed descent from this lord. Yax K'uk Mo's twelfth successor was Smoke Imix, a ruler of extraordinary ability, even by Maya standards. He ruled for no less than sixty-seven years, from AD 628 to 695, at a time when Copán became a major power in the Maya world. Like Pacal and other great Maya kings, Smoke Imix was adept at manipulating cosmology to his own ends. He erected stelae throughout the city and the surrounding valley, marking the entire area as the gateway to the spiritual world. He forged a kingdom, subduing neighboring centers like Quiriguá.

His successor 18 Rabbit embellished the city with the finest relief carvings in its history. But, after a reign of forty-three years, disaster struck. The ruler of Quiriguá captured 18 Rabbit and beheaded him on 3 May 738. A later king of Copán, Smoke Shell, launched a crusade to restore the prestige of his dynasty. Not only did he marry a noblewoman from influential Palenque, he embarked on an orgy of new construction that culminated in one of the masterpieces of native American architecture, the Hieroglyphic Stairway. His architects designed the ultimate in political statements, a 50-ft (15.2-m) wide staircase of seventy-two steps, constrained between two richly decorated balustrades. The 1250 hieroglyphs on the risers chronicle the dynastic history of Copán from its beginning to 755, when the Stairway was completed. When Smoke Shell dedicated his stairway, he buried a cache of sacred offerings, as archaeologists discovered in 1987: a jade chest ornament, and standing figure, a sacrificial knife and sting-ray spines, and three symbols of kingship, delicately flaked silhouettes of Maya heads executed in translucent chert.

Copán's Monumental Art

BELOW *Reconstruction by Tatiana Proskouriakoff of the eighth-century Hieroglyphic Stairway, one of the masterpieces of pre-Columbian American architecture.* RIGHT *Stela N at Copán, depicts Yax Pac, the last ruler of the city, who died in 820.*

Today, the Hieroglyphic Stairway lies in ruins, but William and Barbara Fash and an expert team of epigraphers are spending years sorting the broken stairs and sculptures, attempting a reconstruction of this stupendous construction, at least on paper.

Smoke Shell's son, Yax Pak ("First Dawn"), reigned until 820, but at his death the kingdom was in decline. Less than a decade later, it had collapsed.

Collapse

During the late eighth and early ninth centuries, political chaos spread across the base of the Yucatán Peninsula. Classic Maya civilization faltered in the southern lowlands, but continued to flourish in the north right up to the Spanish Conquest and for some time beyond. This "Classic Maya Collapse," has generated great controversy. Why this sudden breakdown? Was it due to environmental disaster, to overpopulation, epidemics, or the parasitic behavior of the Maya elite? Most experts believe the collapse resulted from a combination of many factors.

First, there were ecological woes. Between the sixth and eighth centuries, Maya populations increased dramatically. Forest-covered tropical soils lose their fertility quickly, so farmers responded by clearing more land. This strategy worked as long as there was plenty of uncleared forest. But eventually abandoned gardens had to be reused before they could recover their fertility. The inevitable result was a scenario that repeats itself in the tropics again and again in the twentieth century – chronic environmental degradation, frequent crop failure, malnutrition, and starvation. Eighth-century skeletons from Copán display clear signs of stress. The only possible recourse for the victims was to move away, to disperse into unoccupied lands.

Then there were overwhelming political difficulties. Maya kingdoms were always patchwork quilts of ever-shifting alliances. As populations rose and competition intensified, there were constant revolts against central authority. In a society where leadership depended on the political charisma of supreme rulers, on their ability to mount elaborate ritual displays, their real control over land and its products was so weak that long-term stability was impossible. The result was that one kingdom after another rose to brief greatness, only to collapse just as rapidly, then be replaced by an equally volatile rival.

Men like Pacal and Great Jaguar Paw were never able to maintain stable kingdoms, or to forge the alliances necessary to create one large state out of many smaller domains. This was partly because of the social and religious constraints upon them, but also because their lowlying, humid rainforest homeland presented too many insoluble transport and communication problems. The Maya had no draft animals, no wheeled carts, nor the technology or manpower to clear wide roads through the dense forest. They relied on narrow forest trails and dugout canoes, on peoples' backs to carry loads and vital commodities over long distances. These were not the logistics of which stable kingdoms are forged. Then there were the Maya lords themselves, arrogant nobles who claimed to have close kin ties with their subjects, yet preyed on them like parasites.

The southern Maya states collapsed, but the kingdoms of the dry forests of the northern lowlands and coasts, who shared the same language and culture with their southern neighbors, had more contact with outsiders, and maintained both economic and political links that made them less provincial in their outlook and more susceptible to political change. As Maya civilization collapsed in the south, the lords of the north developed a powerful conquest state.

Chichén Itzá and the Itzá Empire

The many cities of the Late Classic north maintained strong ties to the Gulf Coast and the Mexican highlands, ties revealed by architectural similarities and in potsherds. In time, a large Late Classic state developed at Cobá in the northeast, a city with close links with the lords of the southern lowlands. Toward the end of the eighth century, coastal merchant-warriors named the Itzá established strongholds along the northern coast and eventually moved inland to establish a state and capital based on Chichén Itzá, which lay inland of a major salt trading center at Isla Cerritos. Years of grim war ensued. The Itzá battled the forces of Cobá and powerful Puuc Maya cities in the west. When they eventually prevailed, Chichén Itzá became the center of a great and cosmopolitan state that was known throughout the Mesoamerican world.

Chichén Itzá's lords still used public reliefs as a means of making political pronouncements, but, instead of narrative portraits and inscribed texts, they depicted groups of portraits carved on pillars in great colonnades or on the interior walls of their temples. Their inscribed monuments commemorate not dates of accession or personal histories, but rituals of dedication carried out by groups of nobles. Chichén Itzá's chronicles focus on dates, names, and on the relationships between the various lords who participated in these vital rituals. Glyph experts have puzzled over these groupings and have so far failed to identify the names of individual kings. The inscriptions point to groups of lords, who were closely related, who apparently enjoyed equal rank. According to Bishop Diego de Landa, native chronicles declared that Chichén Itzá was once ruled by brothers.

Chichén Itzá is a synthesis of Classic Maya architectural forms and motifs that recall the Toltecs of the highlands – to such an extent that some scholars view the city as a Toltec colony, although others see the influence going the other way. The great four-sided pyramid known as the Castillo stands at the heart of the site, four staircases sweeping up to a vaulted temple with reliefs of sky-god masks and warriors. Nearby lies the Temple of the Warriors, a stepped pyramid very similar to one at the Toltec capital, Tula. One approaches

through rows of square columns adorned with warriors. At the top of the pyramid staircase sits a reclining stone figure known as a "chacmool." Its hands grasp a plate-like dish set over the belly, perhaps to receive human hearts. The interior walls of the sanctuary bear painted scenes of canoe-borne warriors reconnoitering the Maya coastline. Chichén Itzá's ballcourt is the largest in Mesoamerica, with walls 272 ft (82 m) long and 99 ft (30 m) apart, about the size of a modern American football field. A relief under one of the rings shows two teams of seven players opposing one another. In another, the winning team leader has decapitated a losing ballplayer. Above the court's east wall is the Temple of the Jaguars with beautiful frescoes of battle scenes. A long platform near the ballcourt depicts human skulls skewered on stakes – foreshadowing the horrific Aztec skull-rack – and may have supported the heads of sacrificial victims decapitated after losing the game. To the south is the Caracol, an astronomical observatory with a spiral staircase and an observation chamber for observing the movements of the planet Venus.

A 900-ft (274-m) causeway leads from the Great Plaza to perhaps the most famous feature of Chichén Itzá, the Sacred Cenote, a deep pool where, Bishop Diego de Landa tells us: "they have had . . . the custom of throwing men alive as a sacrifice to the gods, in times of drought. . . . They also threw into it a great many other things, like precious stones and things which they prized." Popular nineteenth-century legend had it that the Indians threw not only gold but beautiful young virgins in the dark waters. The eminent Harvard biological anthropologist Ernest Hooton examined about fifty skulls that were dredged up with a great array of gold ornaments, masks, jade items, and other offerings early this century. "All of the individuals involved . . . may have been virgins," he reported, "but the osteological evidence does not permit a determination of this nice point." Many were adult males, others children.

We do not know much about how Chichén Itzá was governed, but the themes of war and human sacrifice were intimately connected with the city. Murals in the Upper Temple of the Jaguars depict warfare with the spearthrower and spear, women fleeing their homes. The gallery of heavily armed warriors on the columns of Chichén Itzá's Northwestern Colonnade and the Temple of the Warriors includes veterans with amputated limbs. There are shamans in full regalia and more battle scenes. A group of captives marches on the columns that lead to the sacrificial stone, the chacmool.

We know little of the rulers who presided over Chichén Itzá, but the many reliefs make it clear they were closely associated with that ancient deity, the Feathered Serpent, known to the later Maya as Kukulcan. He had always been an important god, but he now assumed much greater significance, perhaps because of his associations with an important person who bore the same name. Whatever the association, Kukulcan became a vital, abstract symbol of kingship at Chichén Itzá. He was the Vision Serpent to the southern Maya, Quetzalcoatl to the Toltecs and Aztecs. Kukulcan, the Feathered Serpent, was still an important cult for Maya nobles at the time of the Spanish Conquest.

LEFT, ABOVE *Chichén Itzá's main temple-pyramid, the Castillo, the tallest structure in the city.* LEFT *A reclining chacmool, framed by rattlesnake columns, dominates the summit of the Temple of the Warriors. Compare the Aztec and Toltec chacmools, pp. 21 and 155.*

Mayapán, Can Ek, and Christianity

Chichén Itzá was a great state, the one that was responsible for a strong Maya influence being felt throughout Mesoamerica in the centuries before the Spanish Conquest. But the gravity of political power shifted westward to Mayapán between 1200 and 1400, as Chichén Itzá collapsed in the face of political dissension and rebellion. At Mayapán the Cocom family held sway, legitimizing their rule by claiming to be descended from the ancient lords of Chichén Itzá. Eventually Cocom authority dissolved in factional quarreling.

The last Maya king to reign independently was Can Ek, an Itzá lord who fled the disintegration of Mayapán. One of his successors greeted Hernan Cortés and his conquistadors when they traveled across the Petén in 1525. The Itzá rejected any attempts to convert them to Christianity until 1695, when Fray Andres de Avendano y Layola and two other friars visited Can Ek's capital at Tayasal. Avendano marveled at the pyramids and temples. "And when we caught sight of them clearly, the sun shining on them in full, we took pleasure in seeing them; and we wondered at their height, since without exaggeration it seemed impossible that work could have been by hand, unless it was with the aid of the devil, whom they say they adore there in the form of a noted idol."

Fray Avendano had steeped himself in Maya legend, history, and cosmology. He had read Maya records in the local Yucatec dialect and mastered the intricacies of the indigenous calendar, something the Indians considered impossible for anyone but their priests. "They began to love and fear me at the same time; saying that I was undoubtedly a great personage in the service of my Gods, since I had succeeded in learning the language of their ancestors and their own," Avendano remarked gleefully. He knew that the Maya thought in historical cycles, in terms of symmetrical happenings and parallel events, and of close connections between the actions of kings, the deeds of ancestors, and the doings of gods. The friar's visit fell in the cycle known as Katun 18 Ahau, which was to end on 27 July 1697. So he invoked one of the Mayas' own prophecies from the local *Chilam Balam*, another book of Maya counsel: "The hoof shall burn; the sand by the seashore shall burn. The rock will crack; drought is the change of the katun . . . Holy Christianity will come bringing with it the time when the stupid ones who speak our language badly shall turn from their evil ways. No one shall prevent it; this then is the drought. Sufficient is the word for the Maya priests, the word of God . . ." The next katun, 8 Ahau, was even more ominous, for it spoke of political strife, of religious change. By playing on the ruler's ingrained fatalism, Avendano was able to convince Can Ek that his world was coming to an end, that a new vision of history would soon prevail.

Two years later, after brief and spirited resistance, Tayasal became a minor provincial village of the colony of New Spain. A Christian shrine now adorned the temple where once Itzá warriors had met their sacrificial death.

RIGHT *The East Court of the Palace at Palenque, famous for the carvings of captives seen here flanking the staircase down which Maya lords would have entered the court.*

CHAPTER NINE

BEFORE THE AZTECS
Monte Albán, Teotihuacan, and the Toltecs

"It is told when yet all was in darkness, when yet no sun had shone and no dawn had broken – it is said – the gods gathered themselves together and took counsel among themselves there in Teotihuacan. They spoke; they said among themselves:

"Come hither. Oh gods! Who will carry the burden? Who will take it upon himself to be the sun, to bring the dawn? . . ."

Such was the legendary beginning of the Aztec world, the world of the Fifth Sun, created high on the magnificent, sacred Pyramid of the Sun at Teotihuacan. The ruins of the great highland city in the Valley of Mexico were only about 35 miles (56 km) from the Aztec capital Tenochtitlan – vast, silent, but still deeply revered. It was here that their world had begun, where magnificent, long-forgotten lords had once ruled in a previous existence. Aztec legends and oral traditions cherished a venerated cosmology from the very remote past.

The Origins of Highland Civilization

In fact, the beginnings of civilization in the Mexican highlands go back long before ancient Teotihuacan, to a time when farming villages dotted the uplands and traded green obsidian from the Valley of Mexico for painted pottery, exotic fish spines, and brightly colored tropical bird feathers from Olmec country. The influence of the lowlands was felt most strongly in the warm, semi-arid Valley of Oaxaca, well to the south of Teotihuacan. By 2000 BC, maize and bean agriculture was the staple here of dozens of small communities, hamlets of fifty or sixty people. In time, some of them grew larger, housing more than 500 people and supporting small numbers of non-farmer artisans and priests.

One such settlement, known to archaeologists as San José Mogote, lay at the junction of three side valleys. It soon became a magnet to people from all over the Valley of Oaxaca. In 1350 BC, San José Mogote boasted some simple public buildings, shrines oriented on an angle of 8 degrees west of north, constructed on adobe and earth platforms. A University of Michigan team headed by Kent Flannery found conch shell trumpets and turtle shell drums from the Gulf of Mexico in these buildings, also figurines of dancers wearing

LEFT *Life-size greenstone mask in Teotihuacan style, with obsidian eyes, found buried beneath the Great Temple of the Aztecs in Tenochtitlan. Compare the masks on p. 151.*

costumes and masks. There were fish spines, too, artifacts as we have seen
from the Maya world that were used in personal bloodletting ceremonies.
Some 350 years later the site's central precinct covered nearly 50 acres (20 ha)
and was adorned with high stone platforms and fine temples. Between 600
and 500 BC, the first hieroglyphs and calendar symbols appear. They testify to
profound changes in Oaxacan society.

Only a handful of ritual artifacts like fish spines, figurines, and ceramics
with were-jaguar designs allow us to guess at these changes. All of them were a
legacy from the Olmec, the first Mesoamericans to share common deities not
within the narrow confines of a single community, but over dozens of lowland
villages. Now the powerful influence of this pantheon transcended the
boundaries of the Olmec homeland, for the iconography of the jaguar, of the
feathered serpent, linked people in highlands and lowlands alike.

The First City: Monte Albán

In about 500 BC, a major center, Monte Albán, was established at a strategic
point where three arms of the Valley of Oaxaca meet. The new settlement
grew rapidly, soon housing a population of more than 5,000 people. The
founders of the new city, the earliest in Mesoamerica, literally reworked the
landscape, turning a hilly outcrop overlooking the three valleys into a
humanly made acropolis.

Monte Albán perches high atop an artificially flattened mountain with a
panoramic view across arid mountain ranges and the fertile lands far below.
The serried pyramids and palaces lie around a huge main plaza, an immense
paved area so carefully laid out that it was undoubtedly some form of symbolic
landscape. The hill is without arable land or water, but a strategic location
exposed only on the northern and western sides. Here the rulers built nearly 2
miles (3 km) of stone walls, not apparently as fortifications, but to isolate their
lofty citadel from the valley below. In time, the houses and buildings spilled
over onto neighboring hills that were terraced into distinct neighborhoods.
The setting is magnificent and the view breathtaking, but the choice of this
site for a city does not make economic sense. Why would rulers choose to live
away from the fields that supported them? Archaeologist Richard Blanton
believes that there was such competition between different valley communities that they decided to found a "neutral" city on an infertile hill overlooking
the valley to act as a political capital that provided for defense against
common enemies. The trouble with this argument is that there is no evidence
that Oaxaca was ever threatened by outside attack. More likely, San José
Mogote's leaders decided to build a more imposing capital overlooking their
lands as a tangible symbol of their own power and dominance in the valley
below.

Monte Albán's population rose rapidly, reaching an estimated 15,000 by
200 BC. Experts believe that the founding of the city may be associated with

the Zapotec people, who were certainly present in the Valley after 200 BC. By then, a powerful elite ruled over the Valley of Oaxaca. They surrounded the immense, paved Main Plaza with impressive stone temples and palaces. The famous Temple of the Danzantes was erected between 500 and 200 BC. It contains stone slabs that depict nude male figures in "strange rubbery poses as though they were swimming or dancing in a viscous fluid," as Michael Coe puts it. They have down-turned mouths, much as in the Olmec fashion, and some of them appear to be old men. Originally, experts thought these were dancers, cavorting in long-forgotten rituals, whence the temple name, but the more than 140 bodies are so distorted that they are probably corpses, probably of noble enemies slain by Monte Albán's rulers. Sometimes, scroll motifs flow from their groins, as if they had let blood from their penises. The Danzante figures are thought to be a forthright statement of the power and military prowess of the leaders of Monte Albán. And the connotations of ritual bloodletting provide a strong link to the underlying shamanistic beliefs that fueled and nurtured Mesoamerican civilization.

The city straddled three hills, with elaborate tombs for those of noble birth and no less than fifteen residential subdivisions with their own plazas. The central precincts were where great public dramas unfolded, some of them in the imposing ballcourt with its narrow arena where the ancient ballgame was played. And at the southern end of the Main Plaza lies Mound J, an arrow-shaped, enigmatic structure that points to the southwest and is honeycombed with vaulted tunnels. What was this used for? Some scholars focus on the more than forty carved slabs in the lower walls of the building that display sacrificed corpses. They believe that the undeciphered hieroglyphs with them may record battles, dates, and places, conceivably even the names of conquered towns. On the other hand, astroarchaeologist Anthony Aveni examined the tunnels in Mound J and claims he found one zenith sighting line, that for the bright star Capella, which appears during the solar zenith passage. Perhaps, then, Mound J was a giant chronological marker, an astronomical observatory which measured the passage of time. The two theories – war memorial and observatory – are not necessarily mutually exclusive.

Monte Albán reached the height of its power during the 400 years between 200 BC and AD 200, when it rivaled the expanding state of Teotihuacan to the north. The two cities traded with one another, and there may even have been a residential quarter for Oaxacan merchants at Teotihuacan, for the Valley of Oaxaca was pulled inexorably into its larger neighbor's sphere. Monte Albán's domains did not expand, but it held its own until the eighth century AD, by which time about 25,000 people lived at the Zapotec capital. Then the city declined rapidly, just about the time that its arch-rival Teotihuacan collapsed. The Zapotec leaders of Monte Albán lost their popular support. The city's urban population dispersed into smaller communities, just as so often happened elsewhere in Mesoamerican history.

Monte Albán, Capital of the Zapotecs

ABOVE *The Main Plaza of the hilltop city, looking south, with its imposing stone temple-pyramids.* BELOW AND FAR RIGHT *The enigmatic carvings known as danzantes ("dancers"), now usually interpreted as slain captives, may once have been arranged as indicated here.* LEFT *Masterpiece in jade, a mask representing the bat god found buried with an early Monte Albán ruler, and probably once worn at the waist.* ABOVE LEFT *Clay sculpture, 20 in (51 cm) tall, of Xipe Totec, god of springtime and planting. He carries a stick in one hand and a human head in the other.*

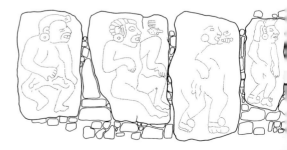

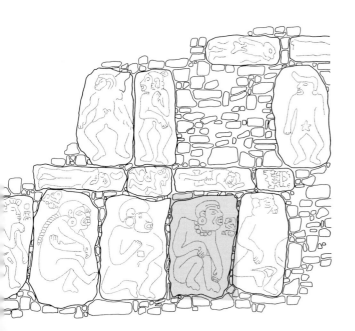

Teotihuacan: a Mesoamerican Metropolis

Like the Oaxacans of 1000 BC, the peoples of the Valley of Mexico to the north had long been in touch with the Olmec, exporting obsidian and other commodities to the lowlands in exchange for exotic tropical products like brightly colored bird feathers and sea shells. The population of the Valley expanded rapidly after 1000 BC, concentrating in two main areas, centered on the city of Cuicuilco in the southwest and at Teotihuacan in a side valley at the northeast corner. Cuicuilco, today under the urban sprawl of Mexico City, had more than 10,000 inhabitants by 300 BC. But the city was living on borrowed time, close to an active volcano. Soon repeated eruptions shook down buildings and weakened the growing city's public buildings. The people watched helplessly as molten lava and ash flowed over their fields and houses. Cuicuilco became a shadow of its former self, its fertile lands buried under sterile rock. It was soon outstripped by its northern neighbor.

Between 300 and 100 BC, Teotihuacan grew to be the dominant force in the Valley of Mexico and soon expanded its influence over a much wider area of the highlands. By the time of Christ, more than 40,000 people were living at Teotihuacan. Some 500 years later, between 100,000 and 200,000 souls dwelt within the precincts of the city. Teotihuacan dwarfed the contemporary London population of a few tens of thousands. In its heyday, it was one of the largest human settlements in the world.

Teotihuacan is, quite simply, immense. Its plazas, pyramids, and avenues overwhelm the visitor with their very scale. Archaeologist René Millon spent years mapping its huge urban sprawl, surveying not only the great public buildings, but dozens of crowded residential compounds and apartment blocks, the places where the common people lived. His team collected samples of potsherds and other artifacts from every building, every room, better to find out what activities took place in the great city. They uncovered not only houses, but entire quarters made up of workshops.

Millon found that, unlike most cities, Teotihuacan did not grow in a haphazard fashion. The city's architects worked to a layout devised early on. This brilliant conception was a symbolic landscape of artificial mountains and foothills separated by open spaces. Generation after generation of Teotihuacanos labored to build 600 pyramids, 500 workshop areas, a great marketplace, 2,000 apartment compounds, and numerous plazas, all laid out on a grid plan anchored by the north-south axis of the 3-mile (5-km) long Street of the Dead. The huge pyramids and buildings that line this famous street are a dramatic expression of the self-confidence, prestige, and unchallenged authority of the city's divine rulers. Even today, the carefully restored central precincts awe the visitor with their scale and sure architectural touch, a statement of human values as impressive as those in any other major world capital.

What provoked this massive building effort? Why did Teotihuacan prove so successful? We know the city rose to prominence in part because of its strategic position in a small side valley close to major obsidian sources. The green obsidian from her outcrops traveled far and wide in Mesoamerica and was much prized by Olmec and Maya stone workers for sacrificial knives, mirrors, and other artifacts. The city also stood astride a major trade route from the Valley of Mexico to the Gulf Coast, and also to the southern highlands. Undoubtedly, trade and tribute helped feed the urban population, and large-scale irrigation agriculture in nearby swamp lands provided huge maize and bean crops, too. But the site of the city was also of great religious significance, so much so that Teotihuacan may have become an important place of pilgrimage from the earliest times.

The great Pyramid of the Sun dominates the city. About 200 ft (61 m) high, the vast, artificial mountain with its five stages and immense staircase lies over a natural cave in volcanic lava, discovered during excavations for installation of a Sound and Light show in 1971. When archaeologists entered the undisturbed cave, they discovered the remains of offerings made in its four chambers centuries before the Pyramid of the Sun was built. The notion of caves as gateways to the spiritual world, the Maya's Xibalba, was deeply ingrained in Mesoamerican belief. Teotihuacan's sacred cave may have been a focus of shamanistic rituals long before the villages nearby coalesced into a city. It was a logical place to build an artificial mountain, a sacred backdrop that depicted the landscape of Teotihuacan's cosmos. The Pyramid of the Sun rose on this sacred spot before AD 150 and was the most sacred edifice at Teotihuacan. It marked the passage of the sun from east to west, and the rising of the Pleiades on the days of the equinox. This association with the forces of the sun, with life and death, were important not only to Teotihuanacos, but to the Aztecs.

A half-century later, the Pyramid of the Moon was constructed at the northern end of the Street of the Dead. It faces an enclosed plaza and is framed by Cerro Gordo, an extinct volcano to the north. The setting is deliberate, for the architects may have tried to place the symbolic, artificial landscape of their city in a compelling natural arena.

The name "Street of the Dead" is a translation of the Aztec word *miccaotli*, perhaps a reference to the ancestral shrines and tombs that once lined it. The avenue is more than an access road, for it changes elevation several times and was carefully built so as to maintain the illusion of visual authority. The southern end skirts the Ciudadela ("Citadel"), where the spectacular Temple of the Feathered Serpent, Quetzalcoatl, stands. Its richly ornamented facade faces west. This beautifully constructed temple is one of the masterpieces of ancient Mesoamerican architecture. Across the Street of the Dead lay a great compound, thought to have been the administrative center of the city.

Except for its pyramids, Teotihuacan is a surprisingly horizontal city. Her engineers built reservoirs and canalized rivers and streams, erected administrative buildings, open air markets, and residential compounds with their own

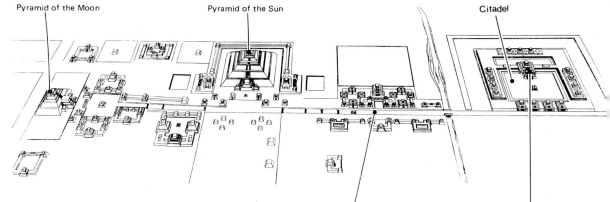

Pyramid of the Moon

Pyramid of the Sun

Citadel

Street of the Dead

Temple of Quetzalcoatl

Teotihuacan, the Pyramid City

LEFT *An airview and perspective sketch show the dominant position of the Pyramid of the Moon (bottom left) and Pyramid of the Sun, but archaeologists have also discovered 600 smaller pyramidal structures, as well as 500 workshop areas and 2,000 apartment compounds.* ABOVE *This giant sculpture – over 10 ft 6 in (3.2 m) tall – of the water goddess Chalchiutlicue, wife of Tlaloc, once stood in the plaza in front of the Pyramid of the Moon.* BELOW *Stone (left) and clay human masks in Classic Teotihuacan style.*

enclosed plazas and shrines. Some of these compounds housed communities of foreigners from Oaxaca and other regions. By AD 500, Teotihuacan was a truly cosmopolitan city covering more than 7 square miles (20 sq. km). Its rulers may not have controlled a vast empire in territorial terms, but their mercantile influence was felt all over Mesoamerica. As we have seen, their militaristic religious beliefs influenced the Maya and other distant peoples.

In many respects, Teotihuacan is now a vast urban skeleton, stripped of its once colorful spiritual context. No intricate glyphs reveal kings' names or genealogies, mark the passage of time, or trumpet great victories. Only artistic traditions survive, public statements about a complex mythological landscape.

Quetzalcoatl and Tlaloc

Teotihuacan was a painted city, a polychrome landscape, for even the surfaces of streets and plazas were painted, the ceremonial precincts predominantly in red and white. Thousands of wall fragments and floors bear signs of whitewash that was polished "with pebbles and very smooth stones; and they looked as well finished and shone as beautifully as a silver plate . . . so smooth and clean that one could eat any morsel off them without a tablecloth, and feel no disgust," wrote Fray Juan de Torquemada of Mexican architecture at the time of the Conquest. Murals in shrines and houses, sculptures, and painted ceramics form a symbolic language that brings Teotihuacan's pantheon to life. The themes often treat of maize and water, two preoccupations in the arid highlands. We can see Quetzalcoatl, the Feathered Serpent, the primeval deity of Mexico. His sculpted image appears on his temple with heads of the Fire Serpent that carried the sun on its daily journey. Tlaloc, the complex god of rain and water (but seemingly of warfare in the Maya area), so important a part of Aztec life in later centuries, now appears in many specific roles – holding forks of lightning, sowing or reaping maize, sprinkling rain drops. Sometimes he scatters largesse, a shower of jade jewels. Jade was always associated with water and with the growth of new vegetation, a symbolic form of rebirth.

The Palace of Tepantitla at Teotihuacan bears murals that depict Tlalocan, the paradise ruled by Tlaloc, where fortunate souls gambol in a world of abundant water, butterflies, and flowers. This patio scene lies below another *tablero* where a single water goddess, perhaps a female shaman, attended by two acolytes gives forth green droplets. What appear to be morning glory plants sprout from her head. Fluttering butterflies and crawling spiders swarm among the foliage. Elsewhere, a giant sculpture of the water goddess Chalchiutlicue, wife of Tlaloc, once stood in the plaza in front of the Pyramid of the Moon. The Sun and Moon Gods were deeply revered, the former nourished with the blood of sacrificial victims, their hearts ripped out in elaborate rituals on the summit of his pyramid.

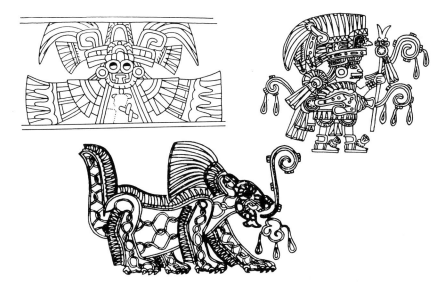

Depictions of gods and felines at Teotihuacan: clockwise from top left, Tlaloc, Quetzalcoatl, and a prowling jaguar.

Jaguars occur again and again at Teotihuacan. "They seem on first acquaintance to perform a whole variety show of trained animal acts, such as straddling corn-grinding tables, wearing flowers and feathered ruffs, blowing on shell trumpets, swimming among waves, and shaking rattles," writes the art historian George Kubler. Far from being a vaudeville act, the jaguar figures form a pattern of ritual and ceremony that centers on a jaguar-serpent-bird icon. This first appears at Teotihuacan, then later at Tula of the Toltecs.

Most of Teotihuacan's jaguar images show humans wearing jaguar costumes. Sometimes the man wears a complete pelt, at others just a headdress. But the jaguar traits are always associated with bird and serpent images. The jaguar-bird-serpent icon occurs only with humans at Teotihuacan, whereas later Toltec and Aztec depictions associate the jaguar with the eagle. The pictorial ancestors of the Teotihuacan jaguars are Olmec jaguars and others found in Oaxaca.

The jaguar and the serpent were inextricably mingled in Mesoamerican belief. The jaguar represented the fertility from earth, the serpent that which comes from water. From this association arose two derivatives of the jaguar cult, those of Quetzalcoatl and of Tlaloc.

Teotihuacan's Downfall

As time went on, the images at Teotihuacan change from purely religious motifs to a great preoccupation with warfare. Armed deities and priests appear with warriors armed with throwing sticks, shields, and spears. This may have had much to do with the worsening fortunes of the city. Between AD 500 and 700, Teotihuacan's power was on the wane. In about 750, the city collapsed and the central precincts were apparently burnt and sacked. Many factors contributed to its demise. Years ago, archaeologist George Vaillant pointed out that thousands of acres were destroyed over the centuries to manufacture the lime for the mortar and stucco that went into the city's buildings. The result may have been environmental degradation, uncontrollable erosion, and the loss of valuable agricultural land. This degradation may have come at a time of drought, a sober warning to modern industrial civilizations which rape and pillage the earth without regard to the long-term consequences of their actions.

In time both drought and ruthless destruction of the landscape may have weakened the authority of Teotihuacan's rulers, already laboring under the pressure of governing an increasingly unwieldy city. The long-powerful state was now vulnerable to invasion by its neighbors, perhaps semi-nomadic groups living just to the north. It may have been they who ravaged the temples and palaces, ushering in a period of political chaos in the Valley of Mexico.

During its heyday, Teotihuacan had acted as a magnet to the rural populations of the highlands, depopulating large areas. Now the process was reversed and other central Mexican cities began to expand. None of them achieved the size and stature of Teotihuacan, and political leadership passed from city to city with bewildering rapidity. But eventually one group achieved partial dominance: the Toltecs.

The Toltecs

As we have seen, Aztec legends recorded after the Spanish Conquest paint the Toltecs in glorious, heroic colors. These were the great conquerors, the brilliant warriors whose achievements served as a blueprint for the Mexica state. The greatest Aztec families claimed to be descended from Toltec ancestors. "The Tolteca were wise. Their works were all good, all perfect, all marvelous . . . in truth they invented all the wonderful, precious, and marvelous things which they made," said one of Bernardino de Sahagún's informants. Aztec oral traditions depict the Toltecs as tall people, who excelled in all the arts and sciences. They invented the calendar and year count, were righteous, wise people in every way. The Toltecs loom larger than life in Aztec history, their rulers the equivalent of the Homeric heroes for the Classical Greeks.

Unfortunately for the Toltecs, the dispassionate eye of the archaeologist paints them in an entirely different light. In 1941, Mexican historian Jimenez Moreno linked the legendary Toltec capital, Tollan, to the archaeological site of Tula in Hidalgo Province. Tula is dwarfed by the vastness of Teotihuacan. At the peak of its power, the city may have had a population of between 30,000 and 60,000.

Tula was a small village in AD 650 and first came into prominence about two-and-a-half centuries later, by which time its leaders controlled the prized green obsidian deposits once exploited by Teotihuacan. During the centuries of political confusion that followed, a new cult of Quetzalcoatl may have emerged in the lowlands, perhaps in coastal Tabasco, before bursting onto the highlands. Quetzalcoatl was instantly popular and emerged as a powerful political force among many Valley peoples, among them the Toltecs.

The semi-legendary ruler of the Toltecs was Mixcoatl, "Cloud Serpent," who later became a hunting god. He and his people first settled at a place called Colhuacan. His son and heir became ruler in about AD 968. He embraced the Quetzalcoatl cult and assumed the name Ce Acatl Topiltzin (or Quetzalcoatl). It was he who transferred the capital to Tula. Topiltzin Quetzalcoatl became a fanatical religious reformer, who soon ran afoul of the powerful warrior class personified by the bloodthirsty war god Tezcatlipoca, "Smoking Mirror." According to legend Tezcatlipoca used his sorcerers to get the sober Topiltzin so drunk that he slept with his sister. These sins ended Tula's golden age. The disgraced Topiltzin Quetzalcoatl fled with his followers. "He looked toward Tula, then wept; as one sobbing he wept . . . And when he had done those things, he went to reach the sea-coast. Then he fashioned a raft of serpents. When he had arranged the raft, there he placed himself as if it were his boat. Then he set off across the sea." Some versions of the legend have Topiltzin setting sail vowing to return in the year 1 Reed to regain his homeland. These legends were to haunt the Aztecs centuries later.

The militaristic faction now controlled Tula. By judicious campaigns of military conquest and diplomacy, the new leaders expanded their domains to encompass the northern parts of the Valley of Mexico and much of Hidalgo Province. Their much vaunted empire was smaller than that of Teotihuacan, although they did maintain trading contacts with the lowlands and other distant regions. Tula engaged not only in conquest, but in extensive irrigation

A fearsome Toltec stone chacmool from Tula, with a sacrificial knife strapped to the upper arm. Compare the similar reclining figures, pp. 21 and 138.

works, settling people in garrisoned areas where they could collect tribute in produce and labor. Thus, the Toltec established precedents of tribute-gathering that were to serve their Aztec successors well.

The ceremonial architecture of Tula epitomizes the militaristic values of this grim civilization. Everywhere, fierce Toltec warriors strut, men carrying feather-decorated atlatls (spearthrowers) in their right hands, bundles of darts in the other. They wear quilted armor, round shields on their backs, hats topped by quetzal feather plumes. Great stone warriors stand atop a six-stepped pyramid. They once supported the roof of the sanctuary on its summit. As at Chichén Itzá, chacmools adorn the temple – reclining figures with round dishes on their bellies, receptacles for the hearts of sacrificial victims captured in war. A great, 131-ft (40-m) long "Serpent Wall" on the north side of the pyramid adds to the effect of militarism, bloodletting, and sacrifice. Serpents consume humans in a bizarre *danse macabre*, their heads reduced to a skull, the flesh partially removed from the limb bones.

At another point on the temple base, a frieze portrays walking jaguars and coyotes on one level. Another level shows pairs of eagles devouring human hearts, images alternating with the effigy of the god Tlahuizcalpantecuhtli, the deity of the planet Venus. His mask emerges from the fangs of a crouched jaguar adorned with feathers and equipped with a forked serpent's tongue. The ardently militaristic themes of Tula are something new, a refinement of much earlier religious beliefs that were forged into a far more aggressive embodiment of conquest and war. They may reflect a new reality in the highlands – intense competition for land, control of trade, and natural resources that erupted during a period of frequent droughts, crop failures, and political uncertainty.

Tula came to a violent end during the reign of a ruler named Huemac, some time in the late twelfth century. The great roof columns were hurled from Quetzalcoatl's pyramid, the city was burned, and the population dispersed. "Everywhere there met the eye,/ everywhere can be seen the remains of clay vessels/ . . . everywhere are their ruins,/ truly the Toltecs once lived there," a Mexica poet wrote centuries later. But the spiritual legacy of the Toltecs survived in many forms, among settled farmers and nomadic Chichimecs who battled for supremacy over the fertile lakeside territory of the Valley of Mexico. The Chichimecs were an essential ingredient in the rags-to-riches history that Aztec rulers concocted as justification for their deeds. "These were the ones who lived far away; they lived in the forests, the grassy plains, the deserts, among the crags. These had their homes nowhere. They only went about traveling, wandering . . ." Among them were a minor group, the Mexica (Aztecs). They wandered into the Valley of Mexico long after all the best agricultural land was in other hands. In about the year 1325, over a century after the fall of Tula, these obscure nomads founded a tiny hamlet in the swamps of Lake Texcoco. Less than a century and a half later, these same people were the masters of much of Mexico.

PART FOUR

CIVILIZATIONS OF THE ANDES

"The Christian God was nothing more than a piece of painted cloth that could not speak; on the contrary, the huacas *made their voices heard to their followers, the Sun and Moon are gods whose existence is visible . . ."*

Manco Inca, c. 1540

Severed head engraved in stone at Cerro Sechin, Peru (compare p. 166).

▲▲▲

CHAPTER TEN

THE CHAVIN CULT
The Rise of Andean Civilization

The sound of rushing water resonates through the narrow galleries like sustained applause, amplified by hidden, stone-walled chambers. It echoes across the sun-drenched plazas and terraces, to the depths of the sunken open-air court of polished and cut stone. The weathered walls of the Old Temple at Chavín de Huantar are mysterious, inaccessible. The watching crowd of worshippers outside in the open-air court waits in dread silence as the building sounds and thunders in the calm morning air. They have fasted for many days, abstained from sexual intercourse, and await the word of the great god who resides inside the temple. A sea shell trumpet blares and everyone looks up. Suddenly, a dancing, masked shaman appears, deep in a hallucinogenic trance, supported by two assistants. He utters incoherent chants, sings, and delivers the pronouncements of the oracle. Then, as quickly as he appeared, the shaman vanishes into the depths of the shrine as drums beat and smoke rises high in the air. As silence falls, the worshippers slowly disperse, while the shaman's aides interpret the messages from the spiritual world.

Chavín de Huantar stands high in the Peruvian Andes, dating back some 2,500 years and therefore one of the most ancient shrines in the Americas. Its U-shaped temple opens east toward the nearby Mosna River and the rising sun. The sacred precinct faces away from the nearby prehistoric settlement, presenting a high, almost menacing, wall to the outside world. The entire effect is one of mystery and hidden power, something quite alien to a Christian visitor. Worshippers entered the sacred precincts by a roundabout route, passing along the temple pyramid to the river, then up some low terraces that led into the heart of the shrine. Here they found themselves in a sacred landscape set against a backdrop of mountains. Ahead of them lay the hidden place where the axis of the world passed from the sky into the underworld, an oracle famous for miles around.

The Celestial River

The sky and the underworld – as in Mesoamerica the layers of the cosmos played a central role in Andean life from the very earliest times, especially in a world of harsh droughts and unpredictable rainfall. Life was especially risky in the mountains, where farming was an endless struggle. It was here that the

RIGHT *View from the summit of Panamarca on Peru's north coast, the southernmost site with major Moche architecture (Chapter Eleven).*

Andean Textiles

Andean weavers created one of the great textile traditions of the world, based on the early domestication of cotton in the fourth millennium BC and on camelid wool. LEFT Alpaca-wool mantle of the coastal Paracas culture, c. 600 BC, embroidered with floating or flying figures carrying a baton or spear in one hand and a fan in the other. ABOVE LEFT AND BELOW The portable backstrap loom, in use today (below) and as depicted on a Moche vase. ABOVE RIGHT A Moche lord attired in a fine cape. RIGHT A Peruvian mantle, 1,000–1,500 years old.

changing seasons assumed great importance, where the movements of heavenly bodies provided a critical barometer for planting and harvest, for the cycles of farming life. For thousands of years, Andean astronomers used the heavens and jagged mountain ridges to measure the endless rhythm of their lives. The Maya used the sun and moon, the Andeans the Milky Way, *Mayu*, the "Celestial River." Their modern descendants use it to this day.

Like astronomers elsewhere in the Americas, the Andeans used sighting lines to track the movements of familiar heavenly bodies. Anthropologist Gary Urton has watched modern Quechua farmers near Cuzco use the corners of buildings and fixed points on mountain peaks to monitor the constellations. The silver tracery of the Milky Way is the fundamental reference point for defining time and space. The Milky Way divides the heavens, slanting from left to right for the first half of the year, in the opposite direction for the second half. The cloudy stream also forms two intersecting axes over a 24-hour period. These NE-SW and SE-NW axes reflect the rotation of the galaxy during the day.

Ancient Andeans, like their twentieth-century descendants, divide the heavens into four quarters – *suyu*. Their astronomers used these four quarters to plot not only stars, planets, and sun and moon, but "dark clouds," the blank darkness between constellations. Even today, some Indian groups believe these are animals – foxes, llamas, snakes, and other creatures. All these phenomena form the basis of both the ancient and modern Andean calendar. The solstices of the Milky Way mark the wet and dry seasons, providing a way of predicting river floods. The movements of the sun and moon help in the planning of planting and harvest. A vast reservoir of astronomical knowledge was integral to Andean agriculture and to religious belief. It was also fundamental to the new beliefs that flowered with the Andean civilizations.

The roots of the religious ideology that centered on Chavín grew deep in Andean soil, among people who lived in harsh, demanding environments, and depended on one another for survival. It was an ideology that borrowed from many sources, from tropical rainforest peoples, from primordial mountain farmers, and from fisherfolk at the mercy of the tides and unpredictable vagaries of the Pacific Ocean.

The first flowerings of these beliefs are lost in the remote past, but we are fortunate that the prehistoric Andeans themselves commemorated them on textiles, in clay, metal, wood, and stone, on artifacts preserved in the arid soils of the desert Peruvian coast. Flying over the desolate landscape, the casual observer would be astonished to learn that this was the cradle of some of prehistoric America's most elaborate and accomplished civilizations, a place where pyramids were first built as early as they appeared along the Nile. How did these remarkable states arise in such an unpromising environment? The answers come not only from the coast itself, but from excavations at archaeological sites high in the Andes inland.

Cotton: The Fabric of Civilization

In 3500 BC, numerous fishing villages flourished along parts of the Peruvian coast. But despite its rich fisheries, the coast was no paradise. Sometimes a warm countercurrent known as El Niño, triggered by complicated pressure changes far offshore in the Pacific, reduced upwelling close inshore so much that anchovies and other fish migrated elsewhere. Even with all the technology of modern weather forecasting, El Niños are very unpredictable and can have a devastating effect on coastal communities. They bring torrential rains and trigger catastrophic flooding inland. Except perhaps locally, the coastal populations of 3500 BC were never large, partly because the fisherfolk lacked cotton for nets and lines and hollow gourds to use as net floats, two critical innovations for fishing on any scale.

Cotton and gourds are not native to the coastal desert. They were introduced in domesticated form around 3500 BC, after many centuries of being grown in moist tropical environments to the north and east. Not that the coastal people were unaware of agriculture, for they grew small amounts of squash, beans, and chile peppers. Over the centuries, they developed strong reciprocal ties with inland communities, supplying them with fish meal and shellfish, also salt, all products essential for farming communities living on predominantly carbohydrate diets. In time, the coast and the highlands became interdependent, not only for food and other staple commodities, but for luxuries such as shiny mountain obsidian and ornamental sea shells. Doubtless, it was these ancient trade networks that brought gourds, and, perhaps most important of all, cotton, to the coast.

Today, we wear cotton, sleep on cotton, use this hard-wearing, yet soft fabric for all manner of day-to-day purposes. We take it for granted, and forget that it was the native Americans who made the world textile revolution possible. Before 1492, cotton was an expensive rarity in the Old World, grown mainly in India and the Near East, used mainly for padding jerkins worn under suits of armor and to make coarse fustian. The Andeans were growing fine quality, long stranded cotton for thousands of years before Columbus, creating fabric sometimes so fine that the Spaniards mistook it for Chinese silk. The dry environment of the Peruvian coast has preserved cotton cloth well over 2,000 years old, much of it dyed in at least 109 hues in seven natural color categories.

The Andeans not only domesticated cotton, but developed many strains that flourished at different altitudes. Such was their breeding expertise that it soon became a staple of coastal society, used for fishing nets and lines, and as a substitute for textiles made of cactus and grass fiber. Cotton could be grown on a large scale in warm, lowland environments, so a lucrative trade in fabric developed with the highlands. This may have been the trigger that opened up large areas of desert valley land on the coast to irrigation, and to large-scale cultivation of cotton. Organized irrigation works perhaps began with many minor projects involving individual families and neighboring villages. Coastal populations rose rapidly. By 2000 BC, some settlements housed between 1,000 and 3,500 people living off a combination of fishing and agriculture.

The simple cotton weaving techniques resulted in symmetrical, angular decorative motifs that were to persist for many centuries, to be copied in clay, metal, and stone. Almost invariably, the weavers used familiar designs from popular ideology: anthropomorphic figures with flowing hair or snakes dangling from the waist, birds-of-prey, snarling felines, and two-headed snakes. Often the weavers would combine the forms of several creatures, such as crabs and snakes, in a single design. When fresh and brightly colored, the cotton textiles recreated familiar myths and spirit creatures that inhabited the cosmos. They were not emblems of rank, of social importance. They were symbols of popular belief in societies where the community came before the individual, where membership in an *ayllu*, the communal institution with its obligations to fellow kin and to the ancestors who controlled land and food resources, was all-important. Judging from the general similarities between early coastal textile designs and later Andean art styles, the same beliefs were very long lived indeed.

Pyramids and a New Social Order

The strong sense of community felt by Andeans as early as 3000 BC expressed itself not only in textiles, but in a remarkable flowering of monumental architecture. More than 1,000 years before the Olmec civilization flourished in Mexico, the people of the Peruvian coast built a series of ritual centers that rank among the most ambitious of all public works undertaken by the prehistoric Americans. One such was El Aspero on the central coast, a large settlement covering nearly 33 acres (13.2 ha), complete with pyramid mounds, residential areas, terraces, and underground storage structures. The largest pyramid, Huaca de los Idolos, is 33 ft (10 m) high, measuring 131 by 98 ft (40 by 30 m) at the base. In about 2000 BC, hundreds of people labored to build the pyramid in stages. During the quiet months of the farming year, teams of *ayllu* members constructed interconnecting room complexes, then filled them with hundreds of tons of rubble dumped in cane, fiber, or reed containers. Perhaps each person fulfilled his labor obligation by carrying a specified number of loads. Such a standard unit of measurement would have been invaluable for working out how many people were needed to build a mound. Once one layer of rooms was full, they built another, then filled that until an artificial mountain rose high above the valley. Then they faced the pyramid with angular basalt blocks brought in from more than half a mile (0.8 km) away. This pyramid building technique was used for more than 2,000 years.

Why should such technologically unsophisticated people build such enormous structures, and who organized these massive public works?

Archaeologist Richard Burger believes that monuments like El Aspero were public displays of prestige and economic power, in the same way that we build ever-taller skyscrapers or send spaceships to the Moon. The individuals who directed these building works were almost certainly descendants of earlier kin leaders who used their wealth and abilities to intercede with the ancestors and the spiritual world to control the labor of hundreds of fellow kin.

Throughout the centuries that followed, power was measured by an individual's ability to marshal large numbers of people for impressive public works in the name of the gods. By this time, too, maize had arrived from the highlands and was doing well in the irrigated lands. The coastal farmers were preadapted to grow it, having already transformed many valley landscapes with major irrigation works. Their highly productive fields often yielded several crops a year, creating large food surpluses that supported a growing population of farmers, artisans, and priests concentrated in villages and occasional large towns.

By 2000 BC, ceremonial architecture on the coast had assumed several forms. There were mounds and pyramids, some, like that at Salinas de Chao on the north coast, more than 80 ft (24 m) high – dwarfed by the 481 ft (146 m) height of Egypt's Great Pyramid, but still a very imposing structure. And there were large circular pits or sunken plazas intended artificially to raise and lower sacred spaces relative to one another, an artifice that anticipates the design of the later shrine at Chavín de Huantar. The worshipper might enter the ceremonial precincts at ground level, then descend into a circular, sunken court, before climbing a rectangular platform mound to the temple on the other side.

Around 1800 BC, at El Paraiso in the Chillon Valley near Lima, ceremonial architecture took another form, a distinctive U-shaped layout of platform structures that circumscribed a large plaza, leaving it open on one side. This vast site consists of at least six huge, square buildings constructed of roughly shaped stone blocks cemented with unfired clay. The builders painted the polished clay-faced walls in brilliant hues. A square building surrounded by tiers of platforms reached by stone and clay staircases dominated each complex. The largest is more than 830 ft (250 m) long and 166 ft (50 m) wide, standing more than 30 ft (20 m) above the plain. Roofs of matting supported by willow posts once covered the interior rooms.

The building of El Paraiso must have taken many years. About 100,000 tons of rock quarried from the nearby hills went into the site. There are few signs of occupation around the major buildings, as if they were shrines and public precincts rather than residential quarters. Why did the architects choose a U-shape? It may be a sacred metaphor for the dual opposing forces of left and right. By building a U-shape, archaeologist Donald Lathrap believes, the priests could focus sacred energy, create a shrine which formed a symbolic vertical axis between the living and spiritual worlds. This axis was to be of fundamental importance in Andean life for many centuries.

El Paraiso was not the largest of the centers that appeared in these centuries. Huaca Florida lies a few miles inland of El Paraiso. Built in about 1700 BC, the great platform is more than 840 ft (252 m) long and towers 100 ft (30 m) above the valley, covering an area nearly as long as three American football fields. Sechin Alto in the Lower Casma Valley covered 1,000 acres (400 ha). A vast, U-shaped main pyramid, built before 1650 BC, looks down over a ceremonial precinct with five large plazas.

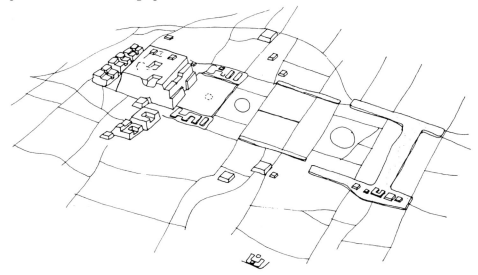

Sketch of Sechin Alto based on aerial photographs, showing the giant main pyramid and five plazas in front of it.

Warriors and figures with severed heads – perhaps sacrificial victims – are depicted on stone monoliths at Cerro Sechin.

We know little or nothing of the religious beliefs of these coastal kingdoms, but the variations in temple architecture hint at a diversity of cults. In the highlands, where people lived off hunting and seasonal agriculture, populations rose more slowly. They built much smaller ceremonial centers at places like Kotosh on the eastern slopes of the Andes, mostly along major trade routes to the coast, places that maintained contacts with the tropical rainforest. Japanese archaeologists working at Kotosh even found the jaw of a voracious piranha fish from the humid Amazon lowlands, apparently prized as a woodworking tool. Highland shrines centered around small chambers where burnt offerings "fed" the gods, as they did in much later times. Although there were many common beliefs, there was, apparently, no pervasive doctrine that unified Andeans of many cultural loyalties. Then, after 900 BC, a flamboyant, shamanistic ideology swept much of the highlands and lowlands, redefining many of the fundamental beliefs of Andean life.

The Chavín Phenomenon

In 1919, Peruvian archaeologist Julio Tello was exploring the remote Pukcha River basin in the foothills of the Andes. To his surprise, he came across the remains of a remarkably sophisticated, stone-built temple pyramid near the small village of Chavín de Huantar. Tello excavated part of the temple. He uncovered carved stelae, monoliths, and many potsherds adorned with a remarkable array of forest animals – felines, birds of prey, lizards, caymans, and mythical creatures, part human, part animal, all executed in a distinctive style. Later that year, Tello recognized the same animal motifs on pottery and goldwork from the north coast of Peru, far from Chavín de Huantar itself.

Like many early archaeologists, Julio Tello was a scholar with wide-ranging interests. Not for him the narrow, specialist approach that is the mark of professional archaeology today. He wandered all over coast and highlands, acquiring an encyclopedic knowledge of sites and artifacts throughout the Andean region. It was during these wanderings that he recognized Chavín-like motifs on the pottery and textiles buried with the dead on the arid Paracas peninsula on the south coast, and at other sites as far south as the shores of Lake Titicaca high in the Andes. But the animals in Chavín art were tropical creatures. From where did this inspiration derive? From the rainforests on the eastern slopes of the Andes was Tello's assessment. Chavín, he said, was the roots and trunk, the "mother culture" of Andean civilization. Today scholars know that those roots go much deeper and earlier than Chavín, but they remain fascinated by the puzzle that is the Chavín Phenomenon.

Chavín de Huantar lies in a small valley 10,000 ft (3,100 m) above sea level, midway between the Pacific coast and tropical rainforest. The local farmers had access to several distinct ecological zones within easy walking distance. There were irrigated maize fields in the valley bottoms, potato gardens on the slopes, and high altitude grasslands for grazing llamas and alpacas. This was

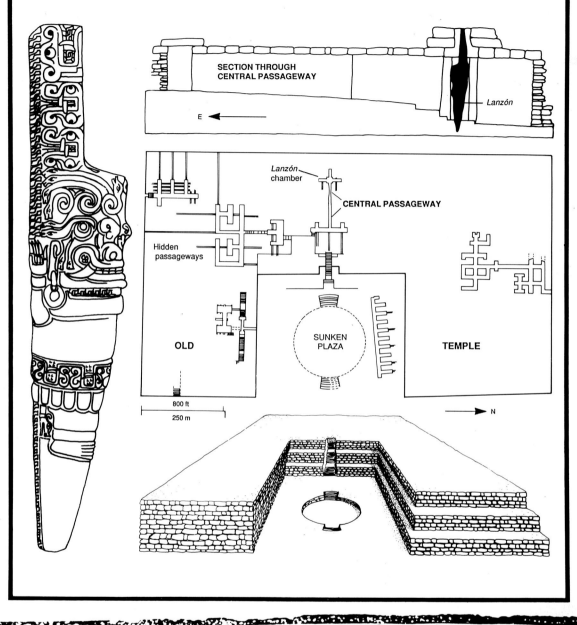

SECTION THROUGH
CENTRAL PASSAGEWAY

E

Lanzón

Lanzón
chamber

CENTRAL PASSAGEWAY

Hidden
passageways

OLD

SUNKEN
PLAZA

TEMPLE

800 ft

250 m

N

Cult and Ritual at Chavín

LEFT *Plan and perspective views of Chavín de Huantar's U-shaped Old Temple, with a cross-section of the central passageway showing the narrow chamber dominated by the Lanzón or Great Cult Image – also seen in an enlargement at far left. The Lanzón represents the "Smiling God," a human body with a feline head and clawed hands and feet.*
ABOVE *One of the many sculpted heads found tenoned into the temple's exterior walls, and perhaps representing shamans being transformed into jaguars.* RIGHT *The "Staff God" from the Raimondi Stone in the temple shows a figure with snarling mouth and serpent headdress grasping two staffs adorned with jaguar mouths.* BELOW *Raptorial bird motifs on a Chavín frieze.*

an environment capable of sustaining hundreds of people and a major ceremonial center.

Between about 850 and 460 BC, Chavín de Huantar was but a small village and shrine, a strategic crossing point for access routes from the Andes to the coast. The entire site is scattered with marine shells, imported pot fragments, and a few bones of puma and jaguar. Richard Burger, a recent excavator of Chavín, believes that these animals were not indigenous to the area, that their bones were imported for making ritual objects. Then, between 460 and 390 BC, the entire population concentrated in the temple area, along the river banks. This may have been a period when Chavín became a major center of pilgrimage, for many exotic objects testify to a myriad contacts with other areas of the Andes. A century later, the town was growing rapidly, and eventually covered about 103 acres (42 ha), four times its previous size, with a resident population of between 2,000 and 3,000 people. By now, Chavín de Huantar was a major religious shrine, probably famous over an enormous area of the Andes and coast, and a highly organized trade and production center where skilled artisans manufactured ceramics and all manner of ritual objects. Some pink *Spondylus* sea shells were of such ritual importance that they had been traded from as far away as the Ecuadorian coast, some 500 miles (800 km) to the north. Some of these shells were decorated with feline motifs, others made into pendants or ornaments for the temple walls.

Chavín de Huantar's Old Temple is a group of rectangular buildings, some standing up to 40 ft (12 m) high. The U-shaped temple, inspired perhaps in outline, by El Paraiso and other ancient architectural traditions of the coast, encloses a rectangular court on three sides, but is open to the east, the direction of sunrise, and of the forest. This original structure was subsequently rebuilt and extended with additional buildings and a new court. Inside, the buildings are a maze of passages, galleries, and small rooms, ventilated with numerous small shafts. Conspicuous, but inaccessible, the Old Temple was a mysterious, and powerful, focus of supernatural forces.

No one knows what rituals unfolded in the innermost sanctum of the Old Temple, in the presence of the white granite monolith in a cruciform chamber near the central axis of the oldest part of the shrine. The lance-like figure (hence its name, the "Lanzón") stands in its original position, perhaps erected before the building was constructed around it. Some 15 ft (4.5 m) high, it depicts an anthropomorphic being. The eyes gaze upward, the feline mouth with its great fangs snarls. The left arm is by the side, the right raised, with claw-like nails. Snarling felines stare in profile from the elaborate headdress. A girdle of small feline heads surrounds the waist.

The Lanzón was built into the floor and ceiling, as if symbolizing the deity's role as a conduit between the underworld, the earth, and the heavens above. Perhaps it was a powerful oracle, for Julio Tello found another, smaller cruciform gallery immediately above the figure, so close that one could reach the top of the monolith by removing a single stone block. Thus, divinations could be so arranged as to evoke responses from the Lanzón itself. There are early historical accounts that describe Chavín de Huantar as an important oracle many centuries after it fell into disrepair.

Chavín art is dramatic, strangely exotic, filled with mythical and living beasts and snarling humans. The imagery is compelling, some of the finest from prehistoric America, an art style with a strong Amazonian flavor. It is as if Chavín ideology has attempted to reconcile the dichotomy between high mountain and humid jungle, melding together primordial beliefs from the forests with those of farmers in remote mountain valleys.

Experts believe there were two major gods at Chavín. The first was the "Smiling God" depicted on the Lanzón stela, a human body with a feline head, clawed hands and feet. The second was a "Staff God," carved in low relief on another granite slab found in the temple. A standing man with downturned, snarling mouth and serpent headdress grasps two staffs adorned with feline heads and jaguar mouths. Both these anthropomorphic deities were supernatural beings, but may represent complex rituals of transformation that took place in the temple according to Richard Burger. There are some clues from other Chavín reliefs. A granite slab from the plaza bears the figure of a jaguar-being resplendent in jaguar and serpent regalia. He grasps a powerful, hallucinogenic San Pedro cactus, a species still used today by tribal shamans peering into the spiritual world. The San Pedro contains mescaline, and has mind-altering effects, producing multicolored visions, shapes, and patterns. This powerful hallucinogen gives the shaman great powers, sends him on flowing journeys through the subconscious, and gives him dramatic insights into the meaning of life. Perhaps the Chavín jaguar-humans represent shamans transformed into fierce, wily jaguars by potent doses of hallucinogenic plants. Such shamanistic rituals, so common in South America to this day, have roots that go back deep into prehistory, to Chavín and probably beyond.

The shaman and the jaguar, and the complex relationship between them, were a powerful catalyst not only in the Andes, but in Mesoamerica as well. This was not because a compelling shaman-jaguar cult developed in, say, Olmec or Chavín society and spread far and wide to become the foundation of all prehistoric American civilization. It was simply because of the deep and abiding symbolic relationship between the human shaman and the animal jaguar in native American society literally wherever jaguars flourished.

Chavín ideology was born of both tropical forest and coastal beliefs, one so powerful that it spawned a lively, exotic art style that spread rapidly over a wide area of the highlands and arid coast. Chavín was the catalyst for many technological advances, among them the painting of textiles, many of which served as wall hangings with their ideological message writ large in vivid colors. These powerful images, in clay, wood, and gold, on textiles and in stone, drew together the institutions and achievements of increasingly sophisticated Andean societies. Such cosmic, shamanistic visions were Chavín's legacy to later Andean civilizations.

▲▲

CHAPTER ELEVEN

THE GOLDEN MOCHE
Lords of Peru's North Coast

The rows of pots grow ever longer, glistening with fresh red and white paint. The Moche potters work quickly, efficiently, fashioning handles, spouts, smoothing long coils of fine clay into bowls, dippers, and goblets. A small group of older artisans sit apart, fashioning more elaborate vessels. One grey-haired, wrinkled man breaks open a well-worn mold. Deftly, he prizes out a pot that is a portrait of a man. Austere, gaunt, with staring eyes, authoritative chin, and ceremonial headdress, the human effigy is a remarkable likeness of the lord who commissioned the vase. The old man carefully cleans off the headdress, dipping his hands into a bowl of liquid clay to smooth the edges. Then he puts the pot aside to dry on a reed mat, next to models of a jaguar, anthropomorphic beings, and another haughty noble.

The faces of Moche lords gaze at us over the centuries, from a time when the Romans ruled over distant western Europe and the Mediterranean world. They presided over one of the most remarkable civilizations of the pre-Columbian world. Tens of thousands of people lived under Moche rule for more than nine centuries, including some of the most talented artisans of ancient America – metalsmiths who could weld, even electroplate gold and copper, expert weavers who created sumptuous masterpieces of clothing and wall hangings, and potters whose clay vessels provide us with a compelling picture of Moche life. The Moche never invented writing, but we have a vivid record of their lives.

What was the nature of Moche society? How did they achieve such artistic and technological success? Any why did their civilization collapse so suddenly in about AD 800? The answers come not only from archaeological excavations and surveys, but from large collections of their fine artifacts, once buried with the dead.

The lords of the Moche never ruled over vast domains. Compared with their successors, the Chimú and the Inca, their kingdom was relatively small. They controlled a strip of some 250 miles (400 km) of desert coastline, probably acquired by conquest, from the Lambayeque Valley in the north to the Nepena Valley in the south. Most of their subjects lived in coastal river valleys that fingered inland no more than about 50 miles (80 km). We do not know who the first Moche rulers were, nor any details of the many campaigns of conquest that led to the subjugation of their narrow kingdom. But we do know that the secret to their success was control of water supplies. The Moche inherited irrigation systems that had been in use for centuries and linked them into ever-larger patchworks of fields and ditches. They built canals along the edges of hills, on embankments, even connecting irrigation systems from neighboring valleys so that every drop of water possible was diverted onto the fields. Many canals were fortified, for the Moche knew full well that they were vulnerable to any enemy who seized their fields and vital water sources. Maintenance and cleaning of the irrigation canals consumed many weeks' work a year with digging stick, hoe, and spade. So did the collecting and spreading of seabird droppings (guano), nitrogenous fertilizer so rich that Peru was to export no less than eleven million tons of it to Europe between 1840 and 1880. According to chronicler Garcilaso de la Vega, the Incas valued guano so highly in later centuries that they executed anyone who approached seabird nesting areas during the breeding season. They allocated small plots of the rich deposits to different groups of farmers, who were only permitted to take as much as they needed for their fields.

The Great Pyramids

The Moche people themselves lived in farming and fishing villages, or clustered around great *huacas*, truncated pyramids that rose high above the river floodplains. The greatest of these was Huaca del Sol, the Pyramid of the Sun, which rises 135 ft (41 m) above the plain. One of the largest such structures ever built in the Americas, it stands two-thirds the height of the Pyramid of the Sun at Teotihuacan. Its summit covers a much larger area than the Teotihuacan pyramid, however, and was carefully laid out with ceremonial plazas and clusters of temples, shrines, and the lavishly painted houses of great lords. Across an arid plain lies a companion pyramid, Huaca de la Luna, the Pyramid of the Moon, a smaller complex of three brick mounds that was probably a temple complex.

How was such an enormous pyramid built? We know something of its construction as a result of a scandalous act of greed and vandalism by seventeenth-century Spanish colonists lusting for gold. A group of them floated a company to search for gold, diverted the nearby Moche River and used its fast-running waters to erode the crumbling adobe. As the flood scoured away the pyramid, workmen grubbed for gold ornaments buried with the dead. The greedy investors melted down hundreds of Moche masterpieces for bullion. At the same time, they washed away at least two thirds of the mound, with one archaeological bonus centuries later – a great vertical slice through the pyramid that reveals no less than eight stages of construction.

Mansfield Hastings and Michael Moseley studied the exposed cross-section. Just the adobe brickmaking alone was a stupendous enterprise, for more than 143 million unfired, sun-dried bricks went into Huaca del Sol and more than 50 million into Huaca de la Luna. Hastings and Moseley examined

dozens of bricks, all made in four-sided rectangular molds open at the top and bottom, mostly from river silt. There the resemblances end, for dozens of teams made them in many sizes, using different quarries. We know there were more than 100 groups involved, because Moseley has counted their symbols stamped into the wet clay, each, apparently, used to distinguish a gang, marks used without change during the century or so it took to build the pyramid.

The architects set up the pyramid plan in four segments, then divided the actual construction into long strips of adobe masonry that lay next to one another but were not bonded together. This simple "segmentation" technique was used by Moche builders whenever they needed to construct a large structure, be it Huaca del Sol, a walled enclosure, or a long canal. They divided the work into carefully delineated parts, then assigned them to different kin groups for completion as part of their *mit'a* obligation to the state. At Huaca del Sol, communities for miles around must have joined in the pyramid building, probably during the quiet months of the farming year, after the harvest.

The sacred pyramids served as temples, as symbolic mountains where Moche lords had their palaces. Here they conducted solemn ceremonies and presided over human sacrifices of prisoners from their many military campaigns. The same leaders supervised the work of skilled craftspeople, who worked in clay, metal, and textiles, and controlled the trade that flowed to the Moche Valley from the highlands and along the coast. It was here, too, that nobles were buried in richly furnished graves under mounds and burial platforms. The eighth-century late Moche pyramid at Pampa Grande in the Lambayeque Valley stood in a magnificent setting, towering high over the densely cultivated and irrigated landscape. Perhaps 10,000 people lived around the 125-ft (38-m) high adobe and rubble structure with its smooth sides, imposing entrance ramp, open ceremonial areas, and clusters of rooms and shrines. Neither Huaca del Sol nor Pampa Grande were densely populated cities like Teotihuacan or Ur in Mesopotamia with their crowded bazaars and packed residential quarters. But they were urban centers nonetheless, their artisans as skilled as any in ancient America.

The Metalworkers

Copper, gold, silver – these metals have always been synonymous with power and prestige. Gold and silver had heightened importance to the Andeans, because their shimmering colors when hammered out in thin sheet were identified with the gods of the sun and moon. Copper and gold ornaments first appeared over a broad area between southern Ecuador and Bolivia between 1500 and 200 BC, but it was Moche metalsmiths who revolutionized metallurgy on the coast. Using only the simplest of tools, they smelted precious metals in small furnaces by blowing on the hot coals through long tubes. They knew the properties of their metals intimately, alloying gold,

LEFT *The ruins of the gigantic Huaca del Sol, or Pyramid of the Sun, in the Moche Valley.*

silver, and copper in different combinations according to need. They used stone hammers to flatten and smooth their metals into fine sheets. From there, they would craft three-dimensional sculptures of animals and create ornaments in low relief. The smiths were masters at crimping and edge welding, at making composite figures.

Many of their techniques came from a related art, that of ceramics, which may have been the inspiration for the complex molds they fashioned to make three-dimensional sculptures. The smith is as adept in soft wax as he is in clay. His practiced hands shape an elegant llama, which he finishes off with deft strokes of a fine spatula to mark the long hair. While the wax model dries, he mixes and kneads fine clay, and then presses the wax llama into the soft matrix. Satisfied there are no flaws, he takes more clay and covers the rest of the half-buried figure to create a complete clay mold with a wax model inside it. After a week's work, he has several molds which he then heats in the embers of a hot fire. As the charcoal burns white, the wax melts and flows out of a hole in the bottom of the mold, leaving an impression of a llama in the hard clay. Now the smith pours molten copper from a bowl into the waiting mold. The copper cools in the clay. Hours later the metalsmith taps the cocoon with a stone hammer and cracks it open gently. A perfect metal llama slides out. This lost-wax technique is a sign of high metallurgical expertise, but it is only the beginning. The smith will now coat the llama in brilliant gold.

The Moche were so obsessed with the color of pure gold that they developed ingenious, and unique, ways of gilding alloyed metals. They would dissolve gold in a solution of salt and corrosive minerals, then add a compound like bicarbonate of soda to achieve a high level of acidity. When dipped in the liquid, a clean copper object became both an anode and a cathode, setting up an electrical current and forming a very thin gold coating on the surface when it was gently boiled. Then the metalsmith would heat the gilded ornament to as high as 1472 deg F. (800 deg. C) to bond the gold to the copper.

The results of this artistry are astounding, not only golden headdresses, face masks and bells, but small earrings, pendants, figures of animals, and ear ornaments. The delicacy of some of the work astonishes modern jewelers, who marvel at the Moche's ability to fashion golden beads with perforations the size of needle holes from two minuscule halves of sheet gold, and at a necklace of gold and lapis peanuts (found with the Lord of Sipán, whom we shall meet later on) so realistic that it copies the ridges on the shells. They were masters at inlaying gold with turquoise and shell, and even adorned some effigy pots with gold nose rings and copper bracelets.

This dazzling technological artistry, with its obsession with golden ornament, carried deep symbolic meaning. Different societies value different materials above all others. The Maya prized lustrous jade for adornment of kings and gods, as did the ancient Chinese, who believed it was a talisman of immortality. The Andeans associated gold with the life-giving sun, the deity that brought warmth and fertility to the soil and to humans. When Moche lords appeared on their pyramids, glittering in all their golden finery, they personified the sun and the ancestors that traveled with it.

America's Finest Potters

Moche potters were true masters of their craft, whose consummate artistry is so much admired today that their products are highly coveted on the international art market. To the collector, they are the American equivalent of the great Classical Greek vase painters. As a result, no burial mound, cemetery, or pyramid is safe from ruthless looters. Most known Moche pots reside in private collections, many of them, alas, away from public view, so studying them requires careful detective work. Peruvian archaeologist Rafael Larco Hoyle and UCLA scholar Christopher Donnan are two experts who have painted a portrait of Moche life by painstaking observation of thousands of their clay vessels in collections all over the world.

To study Moche pots is to enter a totally alien, long-forgotten world. The potters were not only technologically adept, they were expert sculptors, who fashioned naturalistic portraits of noble lords and grotesque anthropomorphic deities, but also realistic scenes of daily life. Working without the potter's wheel, they mass-produced bowls, pots, and bottles painted with red, white, and earth-colored designs. They were the first pot-makers in South America to produce clay objects from molds, a sophisticated technique that enabled an artist to reproduce the same objects again and again.

The most vivid images of Moche life appear on bottles with distinctive stirrup spouts, which curve elegantly from the body of the vessel. There are portraits of great lords adorned with face paint and ceremonial headdresses, depictions so precise they must have been done from life. The artists sculpted not only rulers sitting in high state, but more humble folk, including blind people and the sick, also curers working on their patients. There are anthropomorphic owls, plants, serpents, warriors, musicians, moon gods, humans making love with deities. The list of subjects is almost unending, their facial features often startlingly realistic and individual, bearing expressions of pleasure, serenity, ecstasy, sometimes pain and terror.

The potters portrayed events in the Moche creation and gods in their roles as crabs and other animals. Some of the most interesting scenes depict battles, with warriors charging their enemies with raised clubs. The defenders lift their feather-decked shields in defiance. Another shows a ruler with magnificent feather headdress seated on a pyramid, while a line of naked prisoners passes before him. There are scenes of decapitation and dismemberment as they perish as offerings to the gods.

Why did the potters lavish such care on their products? Christopher Donnan has compiled a comprehensive archive of more than 125,000 Moche art objects, using its many photographs to trace recurring themes running

Masterpieces of Moche Ceramics

Moche potters created one of the finest ceramic traditions of the world. Using clay molds, they fashioned vivid images of lords and humble folk, warriors, gods, plants, and countless animals. LEFT A jaguar attacks a man; c. 8 in (20 cm) tall. BELOW LEFT A stirrup-spouted vase decorated in red and cream slip depicts a deer or deer-priest; c. 9 in (23 cm) tall. BELOW Another stirrup-spouted vase in the shape of a Moche house. RIGHT The timeless gaze of a Moche lord is caught by the anonymous potter in this portrait-vase.

through their art. At first he thought that Moche art was eclectic, that it covered not only rituals, but daily life, too. But as his research progressed, he came to the conclusion that every scene had a ritual or symbolic meaning. What appeared to be a seal hunt was in fact a religious search for the stones swallowed by the animals, which were thought to have powerful curative properties – they are even sought by shamans today. When the artists depicted a man using coca leaves or washing his hair, or a couple having sex, they were recording not humdrum events, but acts with important symbolic meaning in Moche life.

One remarkable pot shows women weaving textiles on looms attached to wooden posts, a reminder that cotton cloth was as important in Moche life as it was in earlier times. Unfortunately, heavy El Niño rains soaked deep into the subsoil and rotted many of the fine textiles buried with the dead, so we know less of the fine work Moche weavers produced. Backstrap looms like those used by the women on the pot are employed in the Andes to this day. Moche weavers used both wild and domesticated cotton, mixed multicolored wool with it, producing fine twill weaves, some of very high quality. And when the ruler appeared at great ceremonies atop the sacred pyramid he sometimes wore a cotton mantle covered with gilded metal plates that shimmered and reflected in the sunlight. The golden sheen of the sun was never far from Moche consciousness.

Felines and War Gods

Moche pots and textiles offer a portrait of a veritable maze of ancient deities. Who were these gods? We can only speculate. According to the American scholar, Elizabeth Benson, the supreme Moche deity, an ancient Sky-God Creator with feline fangs, lived in the mountains. Then there was what Benson calls god-the-son, a more active divine, with feline mouth and jaguar or sunrise headdress, an active god, who came "perhaps from Chavín itself." The Chimú people of later centuries called him Ai Apaec. He was much more concerned with the affairs of humans, with crops and water, for he is often depicted emerging from stands of staple crops.

The same fanged god may also have had associations with the sun, which rose each morning over his mountain homeland, prevailing over the forces of the ocean, then set in the sea to the west, to be reborn next day. He was the protector of the Moche. His wrinkled face, wrinkled from long immersion in the sea, peers at us from pots where he encounters fish monsters with human heads, crab monsters, bivalves, and a marine lizard. But the animal most commonly associated with the god was the jaguar.

Later in Moche times, a new god appears to share power with the fanged deity. He is a warrior, caparisoned in a soldier's costume and warrior headdress, sometimes accompanied by a jaguar. His mouth has fangs, his body radiates snakes' head rays.

Hunters, Warriors, and Gods

RIGHT AND BELOW *Moche vase painted in red on cream with the scene of a warrior hunting.* BOTTOM TWO ROWS *Scenes from another two vases of a battle, and a priest or demon struggling with a fish monster. In the battle scene, warriors carry clubs with pointed-disk mace heads, distinctive emblems of Moche culture.*

The Lords of Sipán

Who were the leaders of Moche society? For years, archaeologists had suspected they were wealthy, but recent discoveries show they were rich beyond conventional imagination. Peruvian archaeologist Walter Alva works at the Bruning Archaeological Museum in Lambayeque, in the heart of Moche country. His is a heartbreaking, demanding job, for he lives in a world of violence and high intrigue, where looters compete for the buried treasure of Moche lords. The sugar-cane farmers of the valley know they have a ready source of cash between harvests – the gold and pottery laden burials deep in the eroding adobe pyramids of their ancient forebears. The *huaqueros* (tomb robbers) work at night, scaling the crumbling pyramids, shoveling and tunneling by dim lantern light. For years, Alva cleared up after the tomb robbers, doing what he could to save a ravaged civilization. Then the local chief of police called him near midnight one evening in February 1987. His men had raided the house of a well-known *huaquero*. Alva arrived at the police station expecting nothing but a few gold castoffs, but was astounded to find thirty-three spectacular objects, including a gold human head with heavily lidded eyes of silver and cobalt pupils. The finds came from a low platform at the foot of the nearby Sipán pyramid. The police heard rumors that a twin of the golden mask was for clandestine sale – for $60,000. Several days later they raided another robber's house. One of the looters was shot, but the fracas led Alva to the richest burial ever found in the Americas.

Alva set out to track down the grave these ornaments came from. He faced stiff competition from the local people, who assaulted the Sipán mound with picks and shovels in spite of police patrols. Relatives of the slain looter shouted threats as Alva and his team camped on the site. Occasionally, the police let off bursts of submachine gun fire to scare off *huaqueros*. After months of careful probing into the honeycombed mound, the archaeologists discovered an undisturbed royal coffin. They used air brushes to waft away fine dust and expose the sepulcher of a man in his early thirties, promptly named "The Lord of Sipán."

The Lord stood about 5 ft 6 in (1.7 m) tall. The magnificence of his clothing took onlookers' breath away. He wore a fine cotton outer shirt adorned with gilded platelets and cone-like tassels over a simple undergarment. He had been laid to rest wearing a pair of gold eyes, a golden nose, and a gold visor over his cheeks and chin. The golden disks at his neck once gleamed like the sun. The turquoise-and-gold-bead bracelets on his forearms were masterpieces. The Lord held a gold rattle and a copper knife. The rattle showed a Moche warrior in full regalia beating an unfortunate prisoner on the head with his war club. Sea shells lay at his feet and he wore ceremonial gold sandals. Another bounty of headdresses and ornaments lay under the body. The entire burial was wrapped in three shrouds, two sewn with gilded copper platelets, fastened with copper straps.

The gold of Sipán: two masterpieces known to have come from this Moche site – above, a tiny gold head with eyes of lapis lazuli and silver; right, a gold necklace.

The Lord of Sipán had not gone to his grave alone. Once he had been laid out in all his splendor, the priests killed two young women each about twenty years old, perhaps concubines or wives of the great lord. They were buried at head and foot, their own heads facing east and west, together with two sacrificed men in their forties, one a warrior, the other with a dog, perhaps the Lord's own pet hound.

Walter Alva was convinced there were more undisturbed royal burials in the Sipán mound. The Moche built the lowest level of the burial structure in about AD 100, adding to it over the next two centuries, laying the Lord of Sipán to rest in about AD 290. Alva probed the lowest level. To his delight, he uncovered the grave of another lord, immediately and inevitably named the

Old Lord of Sipán. The treasures in his tomb exceeded even those of his successor. The Old Lord wore a gilded copper funerary mask, exquisite gold nose ornaments, gold and silver ear spools, and a necklace of ten golden heads of feline figures. There was another necklace of golden spiders sitting in their webs. Most spectacular of all was a nose ornament of a tiny warrior-noble with a fine golden headdress bearing an owl's head. He has turquoise eyes with black stone pupils and a golden nose ornament that actually moves. He carries a war club and shield and is mounted on a silver plate. Few Moche ornaments rival the beauty and intricacy of this masterpiece.

Who were these men of such extraordinary wealth and power? Christopher Donnan pored over photographs of the grave ornaments, visited the site, and compared the finds to the Moche artifacts recorded in his UCLA archive. He believes the two Lords of Sipán were warriors, for the gold and copper backflaps adorning both men were items worn only by soldiers in Moche art. Many of the other artifacts, including the golden rattle, and atlatl darts, have strong warriors associations, too. These were men of very high status indeed, who, Donnan believes, presided over the sacrifices of prisoners after their capture in battle. He bases his theory on scenes of sacrificial ceremonies on vessels in the tomb, where the warrior-priest presiding over the scene wears an identical costume and ornaments to those in the grave.

The warrior-priests may have ordered death by strangulation and decapitation. These are forms of death that cause the penis to become erect, so there may have been a close association between human sacrifice and the idea of creating life, of fertility. It is no coincidence that Moche art is famous for its erotic scenes of men and women making love, of gods copulating with humans, of males with prominent phalli. Life and death were logical, necessary opposites, and the one depended on the other. The eternal cycle of life and death was reflected in the movements of the sun and moon, in the fertility of man and woman. By sacrificing prisoners captured in war, the Moche, like the Teotihuacanos, Toltecs, and Aztecs in distant Mexico, assured the continuity of human existence.

What, then, of the origins of the Moche vision of the world? Undoubtedly, they acquired ideas from many places. Their traders traveled far and wide – to the highlands, of course, and along the Pacific coast in rafts to obtain sea shells from Ecuador and lapis lazuli for jewelry from Chile. Many of the animals depicted on Moche artifacts are animals from distant tropical lowland jungles – jaguars, monkeys, ocelots, and pumas among them. They are combined, like plants, into fantastical designs and strange scenes in which inanimate objects like weapons and helmets have legs, and move of their own volition. Almost certainly, these represent shamans' hallucinogenic visions. The spiritual beliefs and cosmology of the Moche had their roots in very ancient Andean beliefs, elaborated by Chavín shamans and their contemporaries, then refined on the coast to reflect the harsh challenges of a life constantly threatened by floods and the vagaries of the Pacific Ocean.

The Demise of Moche Civilization

In about AD 800, Moche civilization suddenly vanished. One of the great mysteries of Peruvian archaeology for decades was: what happened to the Moche? Were their powerful armies overthrown by upstart invaders from elsewhere, perhaps from the aggressive kingdom of Huari in the highlands, described in the next chapter? Or did internal rebellion tear the kingdom apart? Or, as most archaeologists now suspect, did a series of violent natural disasters spell the end?

The Moche lords exercised considerable control over their patchwork world of river valleys and irrigation canals. But, like all human societies, they were at the mercy of the awesome power of natural forces. They and their people lived in a productive, but violent and unpredictable environment, where sudden earthquakes could collapse mountainsides and divert rivers, while distant atmospheric changes far over the Pacific could bring violent El Niños to the coast. Archaeologist Michael Moseley believes that a series of catastrophes struck the coast in turn. The first may have been a devastating thirty-two-year drought between AD 562 and 594, identified from the growth rings deep in mountain glaciers in the Andes between Cuzco and Lake Titicaca. Crop yields may have fallen as much as 20 percent. Then nature may have struck again. Some time between 650 and 700, a great earthquake rumbled through the Andes, causing landslides and choking rivers with debris. Floodwaters carried the silt downstream where it blocked canals and washed out into the ocean. The sand washed ashore and formed huge dunes propelled by the constant onshore winds. Dense sandstorms blanketed entire villages and mantled hundreds of acres of irrigated lands. People starved, only to be overwhelmed by a severe El Niño that devastated the coastal fisheries. The anchovies virtually disappeared. Torrential rains and violent winds inundated the normally dry coastal plains, turning them into swamps. Raging floodwaters swept canals, houses, even entire villages away. The constant rainfall eroded the imposing adobe of Huaca del Sol, cratering the smooth sides with deep gullies. This was the point at which the southern Moche domains went their own way and the kingdom began to show the strain of constant disaster. But the northerners recovered. The great lords abandoned Huaca del Sol and moved to Pampa Grande in the Lambayeque Valley, over 30 miles (50 km) from the Pacific and close to major irrigation works. But half a century later another El Niño descended on the coast and their civilization collapsed. The residences of the Pampa Grande nobles were burnt and the capital abandoned, perhaps, some experts, believe, as a result of a commoners' revolt against insatiable demands upon them.

No later Andean civilization ever surpassed the artistic and technological brilliance of the Moche, whose achievements rank among the greatest of any native American civilization.

▲▲

CHAPTER TWELVE

BEFORE THE INCAS
Nazca, Tiwanaku, Huari, and Chimor

The men and women work steadily clearing the dark brown rocks from the surface of the Pampa. With deliberate care, they heap hundreds of stones into orderly piles close by, expanding a white line across the trackless, windy expanse of the arid desert. Soon, they will lay out the stones along the sides of the narrow pathway, which forms a long, white line across the desolate landscape. All the workers are fellow kin, from the same *ayllu*, fulfilling their *mi'ta* labor as they clear and sweep the ceremonial route across the plain. The work of clearance goes ahead rapidly, for the lighter subsoil lies close to the surface. The leader of the team sights across the flat lands toward the mounds and temples in the distance, for the white swathe will end at this sacred spot, in the center of the Nazca drainage. There is a feeling of anticipation in the air, for soon the pilgrimage will begin. Everyone will pay homage to the sun, then trot and dance along the newly cleared line to Cahuachi with its sacred huacas and life-giving natural springs.

Cahuachi was a hallowed place to the Nazca people for many centuries, right up to the threshold of Inca times. The Inca empire was created from many cultural strands, from the remnants of commanding states that had dominated the coast and highlands for many centuries, then dissolved in sudden decline as the ever-powerful forces of drought, earthquake, and El Niño changed political and economic equations without warning. Tiwanaku, Huari, Chimor – these great empires and their mighty kings laid the foundations for Tawantinsuyu and the sophisticated strategies used by Inca rulers to subjugate the entire Andes. At the same time, all of them were underpinned by ideologies and sacred geographies like those of the Nazca people on the southern Peruvian coast.

The Mystery of Nazca

The Moche traded with dozens of small states along the central and southern Peruvian coast for sea shells, lapis, and other exotic materials, among them the Nazca, a confederation of minor kingdoms that flourished from the Chincha River south to the Acari Valley. Nazca is celebrated not only for its decorated pots, which reveal a complicated iconography, but for a brilliant textile tradition that incorporated cotton with alpaca wool from the

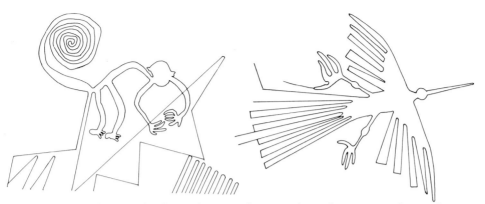

Enigmatic Nazca lines in the desert depict – when seen from above – a monkey with spiral tail, left, and a giant bird, right.

highlands. Nazca populations were never large, for runoff was limited and there were serious water shortages during the droughts of the sixth century. Some Nazca communities responded by digging long tunnels (some more than 1,770 ft (540 m) long) back to aquifers that brought water to specially constructed storage tanks. But above all the Nazca are famous for their desert "lines," one of the great mysteries of American archaeology.

The Nazca lived on the fringes of a desert that had the potential of a giant sketching pad. The Pampa de Ingenio is covered with a layer of fine sand and pebbles that overlies thick white alluvium. By sweeping away the topsoil, the Nazca created a web of white lines – triangles, rectangles, spirals, and zigzags – some mere narrow tracks, others as wide as an airport runway. Some run straight for more than 5 miles (8 km) across valleys and low hills. On the ground the lines make no sense, but high above the desert in a helicopter they coalesce into birds, monkeys, a whale, spiders, even plants. Why would people without airplanes create figures that can only be seen in their entirety from the air? How did they lay out the straight lines and design the figures? What was the meaning behind this web of lines? These are the questions to which German-born mathematician and astronomer Maria Reiche devoted more than forty years.

Reiche fled Germany for Peru in 1932, where she met American archaeologist Paul Kosok, who had just returned from the first scientific examination of the enigmatic lines. By chance, Kosok had observed the sun setting at the end of a line near the village of Palpa, an experience that prompted him to remark that Nazca was "the largest astronomy book in the world." He suggested the young teacher put her astronomical knowledge to good use in the desert. Inspired by his enthusiasm, Reiche traveled to Nazca and became obsessed with the lines. A tough, weathered fieldworker who thought nothing of sleeping outside on the desert floor, Reiche set herself the mammoth task of surveying the lines by herself and became a Peruvian institution in the process. A commonsense, shrewd oberver, she not only spent days on end with her tape measure (she eschewed aerial photographs), but fought to preserve the 100,000 acres (40,000 ha) of the fragile Pampa from the tourists attracted by her work. After all these years, Reiche is convinced the lines point to celestial activity on the distant horizon, that they were built using small models, then lengths of sisal cord to lay them out on the desert floor. The animals are representations of ancient constellations, she believes. Reiche's tenaciously held views have dominated theorizing about Nazca for many years and at times inhibited scientific inquiry.

Until 1963, Reiche worked almost alone. Then the tides of popular culture with its preoccupations with lost mysteries and occult phenomena flooded over the Pampa. First, astronomer Gerald Hawkins of Boston University, famous for his computer calculations at Stonehenge, descended on Nazca to take bearings, so he could calculate the astronomical basis of the lines. To his chagrin, he found only a few alignments that could be linked to the heavens of the centuries when the lines were laid out. Hawkins was followed by the notorious Erich von Däniken, who proclaimed in the early 1970s that the Nazca lines were runways used by ancient spaceships from outer space, a conclusion that garnered a large and enthusiastic following. The enthusiasms of the mystics and amateur astronomers diverted serious attention from the lines for many years.

It was not until the late 1970s that scientists realized that ground drawings like those at Nazca occurred elsewhere in the Andes and were a common part of native American belief. Such "geoglyphs," as experts call them, occur along much of the Peruvian coast. Many depict humans, llamas, or other animals or are merely symbols on hillsides. Armed with aerial photographs and even satellite images, astroarchaeologists have now pored over the Pampa de Ingenio with all the armory of modern science. Their photographs reveal not only geometric figures, but more than 800 miles (1300 km) of straight lines, some as much as 12 miles (20 km) long. Some radiate from hills, hills interconnected by more linear marks, which lead to well-watered areas and may have served as pathways. All the drawings were of transitory importance, for many figures were drawn across earlier ones, as if they were no longer important.

Everyone agrees that the lines played an important, symbolic role in Nazca culture, but the precise significance of the geoglyphs still eludes us. Did they serve as a form of agricultural calendar oriented towards points on the far horizon? Or did the lines and figures form part of the rituals that connected the living and spiritual worlds of the Nazca? Perhaps some animal-human figures, like a famous figure of an Owl Man, may depict shamans in their roles as intermediaries between two realms of the Nazca world.

One hypothesis comes from anthropologist and mountaineer Johan Reinhard, who has examined not only the Nazca lines, but ground drawings all over Latin America. Everywhere throughout the Andes, he points out, mountain gods are believed to protect humans, guard their livestock, and control the weather. They are associated with lakes, rivers, and the ocean – the ultimate source of both water and fertility. Reinhard thinks coastal people like the Nazca shared in some of these beliefs, for local mountains figured prominently in rainmaking rituals, given that they were the source of water for vital irrigation canals. He draws on modern observations in Bolivia, where churches and crosses lie at the ends of long ground lines. And in the Bolivian village of Sabaya, a sacred line leads from the village where headmen make offerings of sea shells and cotton and sacrifice a llama each January to encourage rain.

Reinhard's exciting theory points Nazca detectives in new directions, away from astronomy into the complex realm of ancient iconography and cosmology. Archaeologist Helaine Silverman's recent excavations at Cahuachi in the heart of the Rio Nazca drainage have revealed a unique ceremonial center of mounds, cemeteries, and shrines, which face out toward the Pampa. Several lines point directly at the center. With its natural springs, Cahuachi may have been a sacred place, but it was not a city. It was a location where offerings to the ancestors were made. Nazca art from the site and other locations emphasizes masked ritual performances by priests and many mythical beings. Silverman and others believe many of the rituals at Cahuachi were connected with rain, water, and fertility. There are signs of human heads as valued trophies, too. As for Cahuachi itself, it was what Silverman calls a ''now you see it – now you don't'' city, which mushroomed at times of important pilgrimage, especially during the agriculturally slack summer months, when rain fell in the highlands, rain that would bring floodwaters to the dry Rio Nazca later in the year.

The Nazca lines were political, social, and religious phenomena that were deeply entrenched in the local world, so much so that those who traversed them became transformed into ritual beings as they arrived at the sacred center, a transformation wrought by dance, elaborate costumes and masks, and by shamanistic trance.

Tiwanaku: ''A Hill made by the Hands of Men''

While Moche and Nazca flourished on the coast, other states arose in the mountains. Working in the Peruvian highlands is dangerous, for the government's hold on its remote mountain valleys is precarious at best, and archaeologists work under the threat of guerilla attack. This has meant that research on the predecessors of the Inca has lagged behind that on the Moche. In recent years, however, American and Bolivian archaeologists have made spectacular discoveries at a once glorious city named, according to legend, Taypi Kala, ''The Stone in the Center,'' near the southern shores of Lake Titicaca. This is Tiwanaku, once a city of 50,000 people that flourished while the Moche were at the height of their power on the coast.

Tiwanaku: Highland City

ABOVE *A great sunken court at Tiwanaku.* FAR RIGHT *The Gateway God, from the lintel of the Gateway of the Sun; probably a solar deity, he wears a sunburst headdress ending in puma heads and holds two staffs with condor heads.* NEAR RIGHT *Stone heads tenoned into the walls of the sunken court.* LEFT *The Gateway of the Moon.* ABOVE LEFT *The Ponce monolith, c. 11 ft 6 in (3.5 m) high, one of several freestanding sculptures at Tiwanaku. The figure holds a scepter in one hand and a beaker in the other.*

"Near the buildings there is a hill made by the hands of men, on great foundations of stone," wrote conquistador Cieza de León after a brief visit to Tiwanaku in 1534. "What causes most astonishment are some great doorways of stone, some made out of a single stone." Tiwanaku lies at the southern pole of Andean civilization, about 9 miles (15 km) east of Lake Titicaca, a strategic, river-side site first occupied by village farmers in about 400 BC. Large-scale construction began between AD 100 and 375, reaching its height during the next three centuries. Tiwanaku was contemporary with, but outlasted, Moche, and finally collapsed some time between AD 1000 and 1100, three or four centuries before the Incas carved out their imperial domains.

A visitor in AD 650 would have marveled at a city of palaces, plazas, and brightly colored temples shimmering with gold-covered bas-reliefs. Tiwanaku shone brightly in the rising sun, as its rays reflected off the veritable field of gold on its temple walls. It is an architectural masterpiece, marked by its many gateways and massive masonry buildings. The city's gateways evolved over many centuries, culminating in great monolithic entryways constructed from single slabs of rock. The celebrated Gateway of the Sun is not only the largest gate, but an intricate statement of Tiwanaku iconography. The "Gateway God," probably a solar deity, stands on top of a stepped platform above the doorway. He wears an elaborate headdress like a sunburst, with nineteen projecting rays that end in circles or puma heads. The tunic-and-kilted god wears a fine necklace and holds two staffs with condor heads. Three rows of winged functionaries with human or bird heads attend the deity. They march toward the center of the portal, staffs of office in hand. The iconography behind this prehistoric masterpiece is a closed book, but the Gateway God has been compared to Chavín deities and there is abundant evidence that Tiwanaku religion revolved around human sacrifice.

The so-called Akapana dominates Tiwanaku, a large artificial platform about 650 ft (200 m) along the sides and some 50 ft (15 m) high. It was originally a terraced platform, with massive, stepped retaining walls of sandstone and andesite blocks. The summit boasted a sunken court surrounded by stone buildings where priests lived. During the rainy season, water would cascade out of this court onto the terraces and into the temple repeatedly until it gushed into the great moat that surrounded the ceremonial precincts. Just as at Chavín de Huantar, the effect was a deep roaring sound. Archaeologist Alan Kolata believes the ceremonial precinct was a symbolic island, like the sacred Island of the Sun in Lake Titicaca nearby. It was in the Akapana that Tiwanaku's leaders appeared in all their gold finery on festival days, dressed, so sculptures tell us, like gods with elaborate headdresses, or as condors or pumas. They wore sacrificial knives from their belts alongside the trophy heads of their victims. The Akapana was a most sacred place, for the bodies of a dozen male sacrificial victims were excavated close to the bottom terrace.

A sprawl of unexplored courts, plazas, and buildings surrounds the great platform. These include a sunken court about 100 ft (30 m) square, which lies to the west. Stone heads depicting men and human skulls once adorned its walls. Many stelae formerly stood in the court, among them the famous Bennett monolith, which bears a human figure, perhaps a ruler or a deity, holding a baton and a beaker. By no means all the stelae in the court are in the Tiwanaku style. One throws interesting light on the ways in which the rulers of Tiwanaku controlled subject peoples. Only half the so-called Thunderbolt Stela stood in the court. The other half came to light far away at the north end of the lake. Michael Moseley theorizes that the rulers held subject peoples' revered monuments hostage in the shadow of their own temple.

How did this large city feed itself? Today, the local Aymara Indians eke out a living from arid hillsides, where irregular rainfall and winter frosts regularly decimate the meager potato crops from the thin soil. Many of them also own unproductive lands on the Pampa Koani, the lake floodplain, where boggy conditions and severe frosts alternately rot and freeze growing tubers. Bolivian archaeologist Oswaldo Rivera and his University of Chicago colleague Alan Kolata teamed up some years ago to investigate the thousands of ridges and depressions that covered the floodplain around Tiwanaku. They soon discovered that they were looking at a vast, abandoned agricultural system and persuaded a local farmer to allow them to dig out the silted canals on his land, to recreate the ancient raised fields. Despite vigorous opposition from his fellow villagers, the farmer agreed, with dramatic results. The potato plants grew higher than he had ever seen. When a severe frost descended on the Altiplano, the villagers watched over their fields all night. The crops on the hillside were ruined, but the potatoes on the raised field below were barely damaged. At dawn, a thin, white mist covered the plot, protecting the

Sketches from a modern booklet used to teach Peruvian Indians how to recreate the ancient raised fields.

precious crop, a fog blanket caused by the heat retained by the surrounding canals. The mist soon burnt off in the warm sun, but returned every night the temperature went below zero. Therein lay Tiwanaku's hydrological genius, for her farmers devised a simple, highly successful way of protecting their crops, while planting them in exceptionally well-watered and easily fertilized soil.

Rivera and Kolata found that Tiwanaku's rulers invested vast resources in reclaiming flat altiplano land, especially during and after the great drought of the sixth century AD. These large field systems supported a population of 40,000 to 120,000 people in the 32-square-mile (83-sq. km) Tiwanaku Valley alone. Their productivity may have been as much as 400 percent higher than current yields.

The rediscovery of these ancient farming techniques is paying off handsomely among the Aymara. About 1,200 farmers have now redeveloped raised fields and at least another 50 villages want training in prehistoric agriculture. The local diet is improving dramatically, for fish and ducks in the canals provide protein in a country where over half the children suffer from malnutrition.

The Tiwanaku people obtained some of their protein from the llama. But llamas not only provided food and wool, they served as pack animals for the caravans that wended their way over tortuous paths and roads down the Andes. Well-made Tiwanaku textiles, pottery, wood carvings, and gold objects come from burials hundreds of miles from the Altiplano. All are beautifully made and of lightweight construction, designed so that they could be carried on the backs of llamas.

Tiwanaku carved out a large domain in the south-central Andes, partly by colonization, partly by conquest, and partly by tight control of trading activity, probably through local agents, some of who were buried with the finery of their distant masters. By Andean standards, Tiwanaku's empire was very long lived, surviving 200 or 300 years after Moche had passed into historical oblivion. But, by the eleventh century, the raised fields were in ruins and the great temples deserted. Like so many other Andean states, Tiwanaku succumbed not to enemies or to disease, but to uncontrollable natural forces, this time a severe drought that lasted for decades. Alan Kolata believes the rivers and springs that watered the raised fields dried up, causing widespread starvation. Eventually the central government and the entire agricultural system collapsed. The local people moved to the nearby hillsides and forgot entirely about the potential of the floodplain below them.

The Mountain Farmers of Huari

Tiwanaku was not unique, for other states of lesser size rose to prominence in the highlands at about the same time. As Moche faltered on the coast, a new state, Huari, emerged in the Ayacucho region of the highlands. The capital city of the same name lies on an upland plateau some 15.5 miles (25 km) north of Ayacucho, once a metropolis of some 20,000 to 30,000 people. Huari society was sharply segregated into kin groups, and by social class and occupation. Each urban section was a complex of compounds, houses, and plazas, with some quarters apparently reserved for the elite, others for artisans such as potters and stone toolmakers.

We do not have to look far for the reasons behind Huari's success, remarkable because she flowered while Moche and other kingdoms suffered under severe drought. One secret was reliable water supplies. Huari's rulers were expert irrigation engineers, who knew everything there was to know about high-altitude water conservation. They built and maintained a long canal that linked high-altitude springs and streams with terraced fields on steep slopes. As a result, Huari's farmers could grow maize on these slopes, breeding high-yielding forms of corn that were well adapted to local conditions. Soon, they terraced high mountainsides and created fields that supported many more people than ever before.

Like so many highland centers, Huari was shrewdly located astride main trade routes across the Andes and down to the coast. Her rulers controlled a strategic economic crossroads, and inevitably came in regular contact with their powerful neighbor to the south, Tiwanaku. Huari adopted the Gateway God of the altiplano city and modified him into an agricultural deity, depicted with corn ears sprouting from his headdress. This was no coincidence, for the fledgling kingdom relied on maize farming for her strength. She expanded her domains by moving into unoccupied niches in the highlands, then building long water canals protected by fortified settlements to bring water to new field systems. Over the centuries, Huari's leaders created a string of highland colonies through deliberate colonization and judicious conquest that stretched from near Cuzco in the south through a series of mountain basins for more than 600 miles (1000 km). In each basin, a small group of Huari elite lived and worked with local people, living in administrative centers made up of rectangular enclosures. These held ceremonial precincts, nobles' houses, and accommodation for people working off their *mit'a* tax. Huari did not conquer the lowlands, partly, perhaps, because their terrace agriculture was of little use in coastal desert environments. But they enjoyed longstanding connections with the Ica and Nazca Valleys in the nearby lowlands. Certainly Huari ideology and burial customs spread widely over the coast, perhaps filling the vacuum left by the collapse of Moche to the north.

Huari itself flourished until about 900, when her domains dissolved rapidly into their constituent parts, perhaps as a result of internal revolts. But her legacy was to change history. Huari's aggressive reclamation of mountain slopes for maize farming resulted in rapid population growth and in intense political competition in the highlands. As we saw in Chapter Two, the Inca empire was forged in this volatile crucible of endemic warfare and relentless political infighting. In Inca royal mythology, Viracocha, the supreme deity, came to Tiwanaku to fabricate the world from soft lake clay. The Inca might claim divine inspiration from Tiwanaku, but their imperial kingdom owed much to the agricultural genius of Huari.

Chimor and the Lords of Chan Chan

The collapse of the Moche empire in 800 left a political vacuum on the north coast. Political confusion and fragmentation ensued as lord vied with lord for control of the dismembered kingdom. Eventually, a confederation of small states developed in the Lambayeque Valley, the most densely settled and irrigated area of the former Moche empire. We know little of these rulers or their gods, but they developed a lively art style that often depicted a figure known as the "Sican Lord," a male figure with small wings, a beaked nose, and sometimes talons instead of feet. Occasionally, the Sican Lord flies on top of a two-headed serpent, an ancient Moche motif associated with the sky.

The Sican Lord may be the mythical Naymlap, whose story comes down from ancient traditions. Naymlap arrived at the Lambayeque with many followers, on a flotilla of balsa rafts. He built a great palace at a place called Chot (thought to be the site of Chotuna) and prospered. His sons and followers founded new settlements in the valley under a dynasty of eleven more rulers. Then the final lord, Fempellec, was tempted to move the ancient stone idol brought from afar by Naymlap. Rains, floods, and disease ensued, Fempellec was thrown into the sea, and neighboring Chimor* conquered the valley.

Chotuna may have been Naymlap's ancestral settlement, but the pre-eminent *huaca* was Batán Grande in the Leche Valley, where the public precincts and pyramids cover 1.5 square miles (4 sq. km) alone and where traders from far afield came to exchange their wares. Here, skilled artisans still worked for powerful lords, perpetuating traditions of metalworking that had flourished in the region for many centuries. Copper was now so commonplace and so integral to coastal life that Batán Grande's copper smiths fabricated thousands of *naipes*, small, I-shaped copper objects that were used as a medium for barter transactions as far north as Ecuador and into the northern Andes. So many people were buried at Batán Grande that the site may have had some special ritual significance. Unfortunately, thousands of these burials have been looted, but it is known that those of the elite contained many gold objects, also human sacrificial victims, and silver necklaces.

For two-and-a-half centuries, Batán Grande prospered greatly. Then, almost inevitably in this unpredictable environment, the legend of Fempellec came to pass. Disastrous floods caused by an El Niño swept through the city, causing great damage to houses and to irrigation works throughout the north coast. The elaborate panoply of Batán Grande's lords dissolved in chaos. The inhabitants piled wood and brush against the devastated pyramids and burnt

*Chimor is the name of the state, Chimú the name of the people.

everything down. This was the chance that ambitious neighbors had been waiting for. Chimú armies from the nearby Moche Valley overran Lambayeque and made it their own.

By this time, civilization was more than 1,000 years old in the Moche Valley. The Chimú inherited ancient traditions of kingship and empire and refined them still further. No one knows whence they came, but their rulers were probably the descendants of the once-powerful Moche nobles whose silent *huacas* dotted the sandy coastal plain. Nor do we know how these new lords acquired the reins of power. After the devastation caused by El Niños, they abandoned high pyramids and chose to live at Chan Chan, close to the Pacific, now one of Peru's most famous archaeological sites. As always on the coast, the first priority was a secure food supply. Beginning in about 850, the lords of Chimor invested heavily in an elaborate complex of sunken gardens, which extended upstream from the ocean for 3 miles (5 km), taking advantage of a high water table. They also used *mi'ta* labor to build an enormous network of canals that watered flatlands north and west of the city. Their foresight paid off for many generations and Chan Chan prospered. Then a violent El Niño in 1100 decimated the irrigation system and altered the course of the river. Ever persistent, and perhaps in desperation, the rulers commissioned a 43-mile (70-km) inter-valley canal to irrigate the land above the city with water from the Rio Chicama. The project was never completed, and future urban growth was toward the Pacific where shallow wells could be dug. After 1200, land reclamation near Chan Chan itself was now uneconomic, so Chimor sought to acquire land by conquest. Many military campaigns expanded the empire from the Rio Santa to the Rio Jequetepeque, then to the Lambayeque Valley and beyond, until the lords of Chan Chan controlled more than 700 miles (1126 km) of the north coast.

At the height of its power, Chan Chan's urban sprawl covered 7.7 square miles (20 sq. km). Only nobles, artisans, and other skilled workers lived within the city limits. As many as 26,000 technicians lived in humble dwellings of mud and cane along the southern and western edges of the civic center, expert metalsmiths and weavers for the most part, who were buried in their own cemeteries. Another 3,000 lived close to their royal employers' compounds, and some 6,000 nobles and officials occupied detached adobe brick enclosures nearby.

As for the Chimú lords themselves, they chose to live in dignified seclusion in enormous walled enclosures that served as palaces, with open courts and a mortuary mound where the owner was to dwell in perpetuity. The latest of these royal precincts had walls that towered three stories high, effectively isolating the Lord from his subjects. Only the royal family, some servants, and a few other individuals resided in the compounds. Royal attendants dwelt in the southern sector, while the Lord and his family lived and held court in the central area. Here, a high-walled court protected the royal burial platform, two or three stories high. A central T-shaped burial chamber and small storage

The City of Chan Chan

LEFT *Aerial view of part of the city on Peru's north coast, with its carefully laid out apartment compounds for Chimú lords.* RIGHT *Wooden figure discovered in a niche by Michael Moseley's team at the principal entrance to the so-called Rivero Compound.* BELOW *Plaster frieze from the Huaca del Dragón (dragon pyramid), at the edge of the city, depicting mythical beasts.*

cells held the royal corpse and its rich offerings. Alas, these were looted long ago, but their lavish contents must have rivaled the sepulchers of the Lords of Sipán centuries earlier. Sometimes, important, but lesser, individuals were buried in smaller mounds attached to the royal platform. The northern sector of each compound contained offices and storerooms for precious goods.

According to Spanish sources, there were between nine and eleven rulers of Chimor before the Inca conquered the coast, but we know little of their individual histories. The earlier Chimú lords did not espouse the principle of one ruler, one palace. For several centuries, their compounds housed several generations of leaders. All this changed around 1200, when the lords of the day developed military ambitions. By all accounts, they justified their deeds in the same way that the Aztecs and Inca did – by manipulating history and deifying themselves. Michael Moseley, who excavated Chan Chan, believes that they now demolished some royal compounds that did not fit their image of imperial history and dynastic succession. At the same time, they each built their own grandiloquent compounds. When they died, the compound stood still in time and became a sort of living museum devoted to serving the dead ruler. His successor erected his own, perhaps even grander compound nearby.

The freezing, as it were, of compound architecture may be connected with another important Chimú innovation – that of split inheritance. Conquest required justification, so, in classic Andean fashion, the Lords of Chimor reworked the ancient institution of ancestor worship to accommodate their needs. The Chimor dynasty passed from father to son. The mummified body of the dead Lord was deposited in his mortuary in all its finery, accompanied by lavish possessions and his wives and retainers. The T-shaped burial chamber was never sealed, so that the mummy could be brought out to attend important ceremonies. The rights and duties of the ruler passed to his son, but the palace compound and all the dead Lord's possessions and land went to his secondary family. A small number of family retainers served the king, just as they had in life. The dead man was now a divine ancestor, who continued to live in exactly the same lavish style as he had in life. Meanwhile, the new ruler had to construct his own palace and acquire the land and possessions to support his office. In this it is not too hard to detect the origins of the elaborate royal mummy cult that, as we have seen, was to fuel the expansion of the Inca empire.

By 1350, Chimor was a major player in the Andean geopolitical equation. Her armies now clashed frequently with the expanding Inca war machine. Lord Michancamon was subduing the coast north toward Rio Tumbes in 1370 when he was defeated by the Incas and taken captive to Cuzco. The Incas installed a puppet king, who moved his enclosure to Chiquitoy Viejo on the south side of the Chicama Valley, where he could control the road to Chan Chan. When Francisco Pizarro landed on the Peruvian coast in 1532, Chimor was but a province of Tawantinsuyu, albeit a rebellious one, and the glories of Moche civilization were long forgotten.

PART FIVE

CHIEFDOMS OF NORTH AMERICA

"Who among men and the creatures could live without the Sun-father? For his light brings day, warms and gladdens the Earth-mother with rain which flows forth in the water we drink and that causes the flesh of the Earth-mother to yield abundantly seeds, while these – are they not cooked by the brand of fire which warms us in winter?"

Zuni priest, quoted by Frank Cushing, ''Zuni Breadstuff,'' *The Millstone*, 1884

Mississippian shell gorget depicting a man with headdress and earplugs.

▲▲▲

CHAPTER THIRTEEN

PUEBLOS AND MOUNDBUILDERS
Cultures of the Southwest and East

The Seven Lost Cities of Cibola, legendary cities of gold, perhaps the fabled El
Dorado – the taverns of Mexico City in 1536 buzzed with gossip of a land
overflowing with gold far to the north. There were rumors of huge towns
crowded with "people clothed in gold and silver." Dozens of ambitious
conquistadors marched north with Francisco Vaṣquez de Coronado four years
later. After great sufferings from thirst, the expedition crossed the southern
deserts of the Southwest and reached the upper reaches of the Zuni River.
After a short and furious skirmish, Coronado and his men pillaged the
storerooms of "a little, crowded village, looking as if it had been crumpled all
up together . . . It is a village of about two hundred warriors, in all three and
four stories high, with the houses small, and having only a few rooms and
without a courtyard." Of gold and silver there was no sign. The Seven Lost
Cities of Cibola were in fact Zuni pueblos.

The disgusted conquistadors visited Hopi pueblos, gazed into the Grand
Canyon, and traveled far out on the Great Plains, where they found enormous
herds of "cattle." They were hairy animals with black horns "similar to those
of the *bufalo*" (the Asiatic buffalo or wild ox). But of gold and great
civilizations there was no sign. Coronado returned to New Spain empty
handed, leaving behind him two legacies – smallpox, which decimated the
Pueblo Indians by the thousand, and the horse, which was to revolutionize
life on the Great Plains.

Today, four-and-a-half centuries later, we know that no civilizations of the
sophistication and scale of those in Mesoamerica and the Andes ever
flourished north of Mexico. But in the Southwest and Midwest there were
small towns, and impressive architecture and astronomical alignments and
fine ceramics – all indicative of American Indian ingenuity and perseverance
in environments far less naturally suited to agriculture and civilized life than
the lands that lay to the south.

PUEBLOS OF THE SOUTHWEST

Why did civilizations never develop in North America? The answer can
probably be reduced to two fundamental difficulties the northerners faced:
difficulty in adapting maize to new climates, and difficulty in maintaining

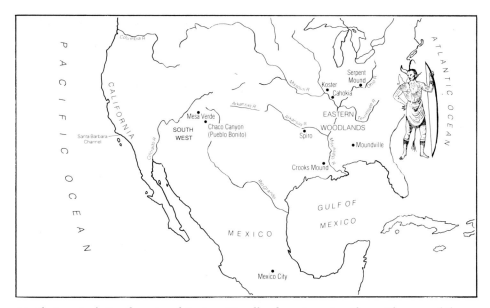

North America's Southwest and Eastern Woodlands regions, together with some of the major sites.

adequate water supplies for people and their crops (a problem even now returning to haunt modern Americans).

As we have seen, maize – the crop above all that underpinned American civilizations – spread into the Southwest in about 1200 BC, thousands of years after its first domestication in Mexico. Here corn was at the northern limits of its range. In its tropical forms, it was intolerant of short growing seasons, weak soils, inadequate rainfall, and strong, cold winds, all environmental conditions endemic to the Southwest. With irregular water supplies, no large lakes or acreages of swamp, any form of raised field farming like Tenochtitlan's *chinampas* or major irrigation works like those of the Moche were impossible. But Southwestern farmers did the best they could. They became experts at selecting the right soils for cultivation – those with good moisture-retaining properties on north- and east-facing slopes that receive little direct sunlight. They favored floodplains and arroyo mouths where the soil was naturally irrigated. And to a limited extent they were able to dig canals that diverted water from streams, springs, or rainfall runoff to irrigate their crops. Even so, they were unable to prevent periodic major calamities brought about by drought.

Many centuries passed before maize and beans became the staples of Southwestern life. By AD 200, corn sustained hundreds of small village communities, usually a few oval or circular pithouses dug into the ground for warmth in winter and occupied over many generations. These were isolated, self-sufficient settlements that had only sporadic contacts with others. Eventually, the inhabitants needed more storage space, so they moved above ground and built combination dwellings and storage areas as multi-room adobe houses. In time, they constructed series of rooms abutting one another, forming pueblos, a thermally efficient way of living above ground in a climate with hot summers and cold winters.

From these humble roots were born the Anasazi people ("the ancient ones"), who inhabited the high desert of the Four Corners region, the Colorado Plateau and the San Juan Basin. This is a majestic land of flat-topped mesas, deep canyons, and wide open sagebrush plains, of some of North America's most famous and oft-visited archaeological sites. The pueblos of Chaco Canyon and Mesa Verde enjoy especially impressive settings.

The Chaco Phenomenon

Chaco Canyon is a dramatic place, set in a stark landscape. The huge canyon cliffs glow yellow-gold in the sun, contrasting with the softer tones of desert sand, sage, and occasional cottonwood trees. Giant shadows are cast across the canyon as the sun sets, the grandiose landscape dwarfing the walls of the great pueblos that are camouflaged naturally beneath the high cliffs. A thousand years ago, flickering fires, barking dogs, and the echoing murmur of human voices would have greeted the evening visitor. Today, the ancient settlements of the Anasazi are silent, an integral part of the arid landscape.

Chaco is an archaeologist's paradise. The 32 square miles (82 sq. km) of the canyon contain not only 13 "towns" and great kivas (ceremonial rooms), but

The Anasazi town of Pueblo Bonito, Chaco Canyon, in a nineteenth-century view.

more than 2,400 other archaeological sites of all kinds. It seems that this has always been a special place, visited by hunters and farmers for more than 8,000 years. The earliest pueblos, built between AD 700 and 900, form small arcs, so laid out that each room was equidistant from a central pithouse. This pithouse soon became a sunken kiva, the focal point of ceremonial life in every Chaco settlement. Kivas were symbolic representations of the primordial underworld from which humans emerged to people the earth. "In the beginning there was only Tokpella, Endless Space . . . Only Tawa, the Sun Spirit, existed, along with some lesser gods. There were no people then, merely insect-like creatures who lived in a dark cave deep in the earth," says a Hopi origin myth. Tawa led the creatures through two levels of the world. Eventually they climbed up a bamboo stalk through the *sipapuni*, the doorway in the sky, into the Upper World. There the gods gave them corn and told them to place a small *sipapuni* in the floor of each kiva. Kivas symbolize the layered Pueblo Indian world. Here, to this day, men discuss the affairs of the community, decide when to plant and harvest crops, plan rituals, and train the young. More than a century ago, anthropologist Frank Cushing was impressed by the kiva ceremony he witnessed, by "the blazes of the splinter-lit fire on the stone altar, sometimes licking the very ladder-poles in their flight upward toward the sky-hole, which served at once as door-way, chimney, and window . . . the shrill calls of the rapidly coming and departing dancers, their wild songs, and the din of the great drum, which fairly jarred the ancient, smoke-blackened rafters . . ."

Sometimes kiva architecture reflects an intimate knowledge of the sun and the stars. The eleventh-century great kiva at Casa Rinconada in Chaco Canyon has a main doorway that faces celestial north. This is the fixed point in the nighttime sky round which all stars seem to revolve. Four huge wooden pillars once defined the cardinal directions, symbolizing the four trees that Earth people once climbed to reach their homeland. At solstice sunrise the sun's rays enter to the right of the doorway and shine into a niche in the northwest wall, marking the northernmost journey of the sun.

The tree rings in Chaco's ancient beams reveal rainfall so uncertain that crops could fail at one end of the canyon and do well at another in the very same season. The Chacoans responded by building three large, semi-circular pueblos at the junctions of major drainages, where they could obtain most benefit from floodwaters – Penasco Blanco, Pueblo Bonito, and Una Vida. The greatest of these small towns was Pueblo Bonito, still remarkably well preserved. More than 800 rooms surrounded the semi-circular plaza at the town's peak, within easy reach of the sacred kivas that were the heart of the settlement. Eventually, at least nine major Chacoan "Great Houses" rose in the canyon during the eleventh century, each a massive undertaking. Archaeologist Stephen Lekson of the National Park Service estimates each room required 40 beams, each from a separate pine or fir tree growing in a forest nearly 40 miles (60 km) away, to say nothing of tons of stone and clay.

Even in good rain years, the soils of the canyon itself would only support at most 2,000 people. Yet experts estimate that the residential rooms in Chaco during the late eleventh century could house some 6,500 souls. How can one account for such a dramatic imbalance? There is only one possible explanation: that large numbers of visitors converged on Chaco at certain times of the year, presumably for important ceremonies.

In the early 1900s, some of the pioneer archaeologists who excavated at Pueblo Bonito and elsewhere noticed what appeared to be the remains of tracks converging on Chaco from outside. It is only in the past twenty years that aerial photographs and satellite imagery have revealed the full extent of the web of more than 400 miles (645 km) of unpaved prehistoric roadways that link Chaco to over thirty outlying settlements. The Chacoans had no wheeled carts or draft animals, yet they constructed wide roads across the desert, shallow tracks up to 40 ft (12.2 m) wide, cut a few inches into the soil, sometimes marked by shallow banks or even low stone walls. The highways run straight for many miles, some of them 40 to 60 miles (64 to 96.5 km) long, connecting as many as half-a-dozen settlements to one another and to Chaco. I followed one road to the north wall of the canyon, then descended the stone-cut staircase to the valley floor. In its way, the Chacoan road system is as imposing as that of the Incas, built three centuries later. Inca roads held together an empire. What was the purpose of the Chacoan roads?

Bright blue turquoise was to Southwesterners what lustrous gold was to the Andeans, and jade to the Maya, a substance with deep symbolic associations, much prized for fine ornaments. Chacoans were major players in the turquoise trade and imported large quantities of the stone from sources near Santa Fe, New Mexico, about 100 miles (160 km) to the east, and may have controlled both sources and exchange of the material over a wide area. Many small Chaco villages contain turquoise workshops and ritual ornaments in all stages of manufacture. At times of important festivals, thousands of people using the Chacoan roads would have converged on Pueblo Bonito and the other large pueblos, many of them bringing loads of turquoise ornaments, baskets of corn, nets full of painted clay vessels, and other goods for barter. Chaco was the hub of the Anasazi world.

What archaeologists call the Chaco Phenomenon encompassed an area of more than 25,000 square miles (64,750 sq. km) of the San Juan Basin and beyond from the Rockies in the north to the Mogollon Mountains in the south, and from the turquoise mines near Santa Fe in the east to the Little Colorado River in the west. There is something symbolic that underlies this entire system, perhaps a series of now forgotten ideological beliefs. They come down to us only in the Chacoans' dramatic use of the natural landscape, of bluffs and canyon walls as natural settings for their settlements. By AD 1115, at least seventy communities dispersed over much of northwest New Mexico and parts of southern Colorado were linked through the social, economic, and ritual networks centered on Chaco Canyon. Judging from other such networks, trade and ritual activities were in the hands of a small number, not of noble lords, but of important kin leaders.

What is remarkable is that Chaco flourished so mightily in such an unpredictable environment. Despite many good rain years, there must have been periodic food shortages. And at least 20,000 pine beams went into the major pueblos, which must have decimated forests over a wide area, to say nothing of the firewood needed not only for cooking and heating, but for firing pots. Did this woodcutting activity strip hillsides of timber and cause widespread soil erosion? Perhaps Chaco communities overextended themselves in the bounty of wet years and rendered themselves unusually vulnerable to the inevitable drought cycle that affected the San Juan Basin for more than a half century after 1100. Stretched to its limits, the Chaco system collapsed and the people moved away from densely populated pueblos into independent, widely dispersed hamlets.

Mesa Verde

On a snowy day in 1888, cowboys Richard Wetherill and Richard Mason were tracking some stray cattle across Mesa Verde in northern Colorado. They walked out on a vantage point that faced a high rock overhang and peered through the snow into the deep canyon below. They gasped in astonishment. A huge cave filled with tier upon tier of houses lay below them. The stray cattle forgotten, they explored what they called the "Cliff Palace." Mesa Verde has been a mecca for archaeologist and casual visitor alike ever since.

There is a paradisal quality about Mesa Verde. It is one of those quiet places where time seems to stand still, where the air is clear, and you feel very close to the people who once lived here. Lush with pinon, juniper, and dense undergrowth, the deep canyons of Mesa Verde are like an oasis in a land of wide horizons and long, dusty summers, close to the fertile Montezuma Valley. Here, Anasazi farmers built compact, sometimes almost inaccessible pueblos in caves and under convenient overhangs, scrambling up precipitous trails to their plateau farmlands on the open mesas.

The Anasazi first appeared at Mesa Verde around AD 600, living in small villages of pithouses with up to 150 residents. Each pithouse sheltered an extended family, three generations descended from one married couple, all cooperating in the daily business of hunting, foraging, farming, and food preparation. By the ninth century, these clusters had come together in much larger villages, clustered around large pithouses that now became kivas. Two centuries later, as many as 30,000 people lived in the nearby Montezuma Valley region, but only about 2,500 of them dwelt in Mesa Verde. Some of the Montezuma towns held more than 1,000 people. The Mesa Verde people lived on a smaller scale, but developed ingenious ways to trap water and divert it to their fields. They built a system of collection ditches that diverted rainwater into an artificial reservoir capable of holding up to a half-million

gallons of water. Another canal carried precious water to terraced gardens built around houses, in ravines, and on mesa tops.

As many as 500 people lived in the Far View village on Mesa Verde in 1100, moving 10 miles (16 km) south to become the nucleus of a much larger community a century later. Between 1150 and 1250, some 600 to 800 people lived in Cliff and Fewkes canyons. They built perhaps 550 rooms and 60 kivas, concentrated in 33 cliff dwellings huddled under high cliffs. The Cliff Palace was by far the largest pueblo, with 220 rooms and 23 kivas. About 10 trails wound up the sandstone cliffs to the mesa farmland high above. The canyon pueblos prospered for several generations. Then, in about 1300, the Anasazi abandoned Mesa Verde for ever.

Why did they desert their canyon home? Was it because of marauding enemies? Or did factional disputes and epidemic diseases decimate the pueblos? More likely, it was because of drought. The Mesa Verde people prospered as long as the climate favored them. If the rains failed in one canyon, the inhabitants would simply move a short distance away, returning, perhaps, the next year or some generations later. But a much more widespread and prolonged drought set in about 1150, the same dry cycle that disrupted life in Chaco Canyon to the south. At first Mesa Verde was somewhat insulated from famine by its ingenious water conservation methods, but eventually the inhabitants had to move away, never to return. In time, the Anasazi of Chaco Canyon and Mesa Verde were absorbed into later Southwestern society, leaving only their artifacts and pueblos as a tangible legacy to the modern world.

Mogollon: The Mimbres Potters

The Mogollon people were highland farmers, who lived in the arid and sometimes mountainous country that is now eastern Arizona and southwestern New Mexico. Like their Anasazi neighbors, they dwelt in pueblos, but these were much smaller than those of Chaco Canyon or Mesa Verde. The Mogollon people are famous for their magnificent painted pottery. And of all Mogollon potters the most expert were the Mimbres people, who lived in villages along the banks of the river of that name in southwestern New Mexico. Each community had its skilled woman potters, who built up thin-walled bowls from long coils of fine river clay. Once dried, the pots were fired and then painted with brushes made of yucca plant fiber. Each potter had her favorite designs, passed down through the generations. One woman might paint her bowl white, then adorn it with a black bat with outstretched wings. Another depicted a bird with black-and-white checkered chest. There are polychrome designs with insects and bighorn sheep, pairs of male and female humans that may represent life and death, and a man spearing exotic fish.

Mimbres pots are the finest of all North American ceramics and are prized so highly by professional looters and collectors that they command

LEFT *Cliff Palace, Mesa Verde, an Anasazi community with some 220 rooms and 23 kivas (circular ceremonial chambers).*

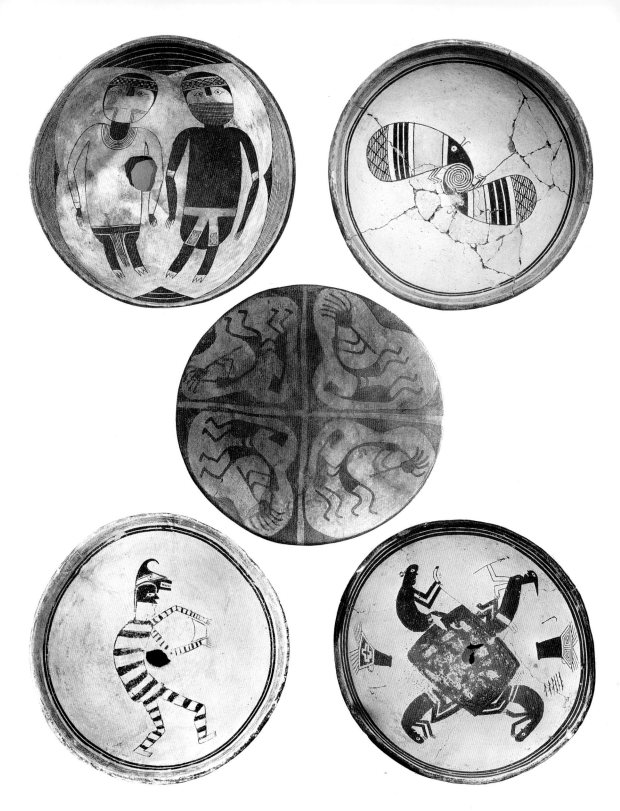

OUTER FOUR *Mimbres painted ceramic bowls, all c. 12 in (30 cm) in diameter, with, from top left, two human figures, an insect, the "guardians of the four directions," and a masked coyote dancer.* CENTER *A Hohokam bowl from Snaketown depicting flute players, c. 10.7 in (27 cm) in diameter.*

astronomical prices on the international art market. Their original owners valued them not necessarily for their artistry, but for their symbolic depictions of clan ancestors, of mythical beings and animals, and took them to their graves. The mourners would lay out the body, then punch holes in the bottoms of the brightly painted bowls, perhaps to release the spirit of the painted figures or symbols.

The Mogollon people were accomplished stoneworkers as well, and traded ritual artifacts and ornaments over long distances. They also imported copper bells from the south, from Mexico – which raises a fascinating question: did artifacts and ideas from contemporary civilizations in Mesoamerica ever penetrate the Southwest? Did merchants from Teotihuacan, the Toltecs, or other Valley of Mexico cities ever reach Anasazi or Mogollon pueblos? Did they manage to cross the hot and dusty southern deserts where the Hohokam lived?

Hohokam – "The Vanished Ones"

The Gila River flows from the eastern mountains of the Southwest into the Colorado River, through mesquite-studded desert landscape. This is semi-arid country with long, intensely hot summers, but the banks of the Gila were like an oasis, with fertile soils and abundant deer, rabbits, and water birds. It was here that University of Arizona archaeologist Emil Haury excavated the undulating mounds of Snaketown (so called after the Pima Indian name Skoaquik: "Place of Snakes"). No pueblo this, but an important lowland town occupied for many centuries, for the entire span of time Anasazi people lived at Mesa Verde, and for a century and a half longer, until 1450. Snaketown prospered because the Hohokam were masters of desert irrigation. They dug a 3-mile (4.8-km) canal to water fields near the Gila River, a canal so efficient it remained in use for the entire lifetime of the settlement.

In its heyday, Snaketown was an untidy scatter of pithouses and above-ground pole and brush dwellings. These many houses lay outside a central plaza, itself surrounded by low mounds up to 50 ft (15.2 m) across and up to 3 ft (1 m) high, this time capped with thick clay, which turned them into platforms for large houses or shrines. Nearby lay two ballcourts, with floors about 130 ft long and 100 ft wide (40 m by 30 m). The builders piled up the sand on either side and brought in more soil to fashion the sloping sides. The architecture of mounds, plazas, and ballcourts seemed almost Mexican to Haury, who wondered whether the Hohokam were migrants from the south, who brought new ideas with them. Archaeologists have debated the issue for decades. The current fashion is to play down the likelihood of migrations. Certainly Snaketown's ballcourts are smaller and much less elaborate than those from Mexico. There are no signs of human sacrifice or of any of the other gruesome rituals associated with the ballcourts at, say, Copán or Chichén Itzá. The idea of a ballgame may have come from Mexico, but the ceremonies associated with it must have been very different. They may even have been arenas used for major dances and other public ceremonies, even for markets. As for the trade goods found at Snaketown, they are almost all of Southwestern origin, and if not from there, from the Pacific Coast or the Gulf of Mexico. Only the brilliant macaw feathers used for dance costumes strike an alien note, for they may well have come from humid, tropical forests. Yet even macaws could be bred in captivity in northern Mexico, witness the caged macaw skeletons found at the fourteenth-century Casas Grandes trading center over the border.

Some pervasive ideas undoubtedly drifted northward from Mexico, but what is striking about the Anasazi, Mogollon, and Hohokam is that they are indigenous cultures, forged from local roots. Theirs was not an environment in which civilizations and cities could easily flourish, for the forces of nature compelled constant adjustments to cycles of drought and sometimes plentiful rainfall. But the towns with "crumpled houses" seen by Coronado and his conquistadors were, in their own way, an impressive response to surroundings far harsher than those of the Valley of Mexico or the Yucatán.

MOUNDBUILDERS OF THE MIDWEST

The ancient earthen mounds of Ohio and the Midwest are as well known a part of the North American heritage as the pueblos of the Southwest. The late eighteenth- and early nineteenth-century European settlers who first came across these great earthworks refused to believe that native Americans were capable of constructing such large structures. A "vanished race" had once settled in the Midwest, they believed, a white civilization that had flourished by the banks of the Mississippi long before Columbus. Inevitably, popular writers got in on the act. "Armies, equal to those of Cyrus, of Alexander the Great, might have flourished their trumpets and marched to battle, over these extensive plains," speculated writer Josiah Priest in 1833. In its more bizarre forms, the Myth of the Moundbuilders, with a capital M, became a Victorian equivalent of the Cecil B. DeMille movie epic. There was, for example, Behemoth, a huge, mammoth-like beast, who ravaged moundbuilder settlements and trampled over entire armies. But a great hero named Bokulla outwitted the huge animal by devious cunning, and the moundbuilders triumphed . . .

Great civilizations, teeming cities, and warrior hosts – the heady and romantic ingredients of the Myth of the Moundbuilders did not survive the cool, dispassionate eye of science. Late nineteenth-century archaeologists like Cyrus Thomas of the Bureau of American Ethnology dug into more than 2,000 mounds between Wisconsin and Florida. All "which have been examined and carefully studied are to be attributed to the indigenous tribes found inhabiting this region and their ancestors," declared Thomas roundly in 1894.

Adena and Hopewell

Who, then, were the builders of the mounds? Much earlier explorers than the Ohio colonists actually met some of them. By all accounts, conquistador Hernando de Soto was an imperious and thoroughly unpleasant man, who had made a fortune in Mexico and Peru. He marched from Florida to the Mississippi Valley in 1539–42 through a land ruled by chiefs who lived in settlements with earthen burial mounds. At the town of Cofitachiqui in South Carolina, his men plundered charnel houses on such tumuli filled with bone chests, freshwater pearls, bundles of raiment, and copper-bladed weapons. The frustrated conquistadors found no gold, de Soto died of fever by the banks of the Mississippi, and the survivors of the expedition returned empty-handed. Their eye-witness accounts of mounds and charnel houses were forgotten until the nineteenth century.

In 1720, French explorer Le Page du Pratz visited Chief Tattooed-Serpent of the Natchez, a group of about 4,000 people in seven villages built around a large mound. The chief died suddenly, so du Pratz was able to witness his funeral. Tattooed-Serpent lay in state, dressed in his finest regalia, his face painted, wearing a "crown of white feathers mingled with red." His arms and ceremonial pipes lay by his side. At the temple, his two wives and six other sacrificial victims knelt on mats. Their heads were covered with skins as they chewed on tobacco pellets to stupefy them. Swiftly, the executioners strangled them. Then, after the funeral, the temple was completely burned to the ground.

These kinds of burial cult began humbly enough in about 2000 BC, when some communities started to bury their dead in low, natural ridges often overlooking river valleys. Even to build such modest earthworks required thousands of basketfuls of loose earth. From the very beginning, burial mounds all the way from the western Appalachians to the Mississippi Valley and north into Michigan and Wisconsin were places strongly associated with mythical and human ancestors, and were used for many generations by people from several communities.

Between 300 and 500 such "Adena" mounds come from the Ohio Valley alone. At first each kin group started with a small earthwork, which covered the grave of a single individual. As more and more burials were added to the tumulus, so it grew in size. Eventually, about the time of Christ, simple graves gave way to large burial chambers that contained one or two people, lying on, or under, circular houses. Perhaps, believe local archaeologists, the dead were exposed in these huts before their bones were buried in the mound. By now, copper bracelets, mica, marine shells, wooden masks, and finely carved pipes appear in the graves.

Who were these important individuals? Judging from the mica sheets, copper ornaments, and carved pipes that proclaim their importance from the grave, they were important clan leaders and shamans, the people who organized work parties when needed – to erect burial mounds, construct earthworks, and carry out other communal tasks. They also organized major planting and harvest rituals, and bartered exotic raw materials and fine ornaments from fellow kin leaders elsewhere.

By the early centuries AD, successor "Hopewell" peoples (named after an Ohio town) enjoyed great prestige and were buried in high state in finery made from materials gathered from literally every corner of North America. Their artisans used native copper from the Lake Superior region, silver from the same place, and from Ohio. Mica, quartz crystal, and chlorite came from the southern Appalachians. These precious materials passed along thousands of narrow trails that connected village after village all the way from the Great Lakes to Florida. These well-trodden paths took kin to the next settlement for a wedding, carried small parties of heavily laden men carrying skins full of sea shells from the distant Gulf of Mexico, brought chiefs calling on their neighbors with formal gifts of shiny obsidian knives from rock that came from as far away as the Yellowstone area of the Rocky Mountains. Months later, the recipient would arrive on his return visit with a fine carved soapstone pipe to mark a relationship that had existed for generations.

The Hopewell people sometimes created entire mortuary landscapes of mounds and enclosures. At Mound City, Ohio, for example, an enclosure covering 13 acres (5.2 ha) protects 24 tumuli. The burial mounds at Newark, Ohio, are linked by a network of circles, squares, and octagons joined by avenues. The symbolism behind these landscapes eludes us. Like the Nazca lines in Peru, the only way for their builders to have appreciated them fully in their pristine condition would have been from a helicopter. The average Ohio Hopewell mound is about 30 ft (9 m) high and 100 ft (30 m) across, with a volume of about 500,000 cu. ft (14,000 cu. m). Each would have taken at least 200,000 hours of earthmoving with simple stone tools and baskets to complete. Perhaps most spectacular of all is the Great Serpent Mound, where a snake modeled in earth lies with coiled tail and sinuous body atop a low ridge, its mouth wide open to gobble up an oval burial mound in its jaws.

Hundreds of people were cremated and buried in Hopewell earthworks. Their leaders and shamans received much more elaborate treatment. They lay in log-lined tombs, sometimes inside special burial houses. Judging from the motifs on buried ceremonial artifacts, there were close links between Hopewell kin groups and game animals and birds of prey, perhaps the mythical ancestors of clans and lineages.

A Landscape Transformed

For all their elaborate burial customs and energetic moundbuilding, the Hopewell people lived in small villages and subsisted almost entirely off hunting and wild plant foods. Their hamlets contrast dramatically with the vast mounds and palisaded enclosures of succeeding centuries. How did

Hopewell Traders and Builders

RIGHT, ABOVE *A raven or crow, 15 in (38 cm) long, made in the Ohio region from imported native sheet copper. The bird's eye is of freshwater pearl.* RIGHT, CENTER *A superb Hopewell ornament, cut from sheet mica and 11 in (28 cm) in length, depicts the claws of a bird of prey.* BELOW *The Great Serpent mound, constructed some 2,000 years ago by Hopewell builders, crowns an Ohio hilltop.*

villages become great centers? The catalysts as elsewhere were maize and beans. Maize spread into eastern North America across the Plains from the Southwest during the first millennium AD when Teotihuacan in Mexico reached its apogee and Europe was in the Dark Ages. But it did not become a major crop until both beans and hardier, higher-yielding strains arrived in about AD 1000. Within a remarkably short time, perhaps only a few generations, maize and bean agriculture swept the Midwest and Southeast.

The most spectacular result was Cahokia, the largest town and ceremonial center ever built in prehistoric North America. Today, the remains of Cahokia lie under the urban sprawl of East Saint Louis. Its imposing earthworks seem incongruous, rising out of this modern landscape, but, nine centuries ago, more than 30,000 people lived here. Cahokia lies in the heart of the American Bottom, a pocket of low-lying floodplain that extends south for about 25 miles (40 km) from the confluence of the Illinois River Valley and the Mississippi. At the height of its power, between AD 1050 and 1250, Cahokia extended over an area of more than 5 square miles (13 sq. km), a tangle of thatched houses, earthen mounds, and small plazas built along a north-south ridge, the highest and driest ground. Here lay Monk's Mound, the largest earthwork ever constructed by prehistoric North Americans. It rises in four terraces to a height of 100 ft (30 m) and covers 16 acres (6.4 ha), relatively small by Mexican standards at half the height of the Pyramid of the Sun at Teotihuacan, but still an impressive artificial hill in this flat country. Monk's Mound is more than twice the size of any other tumulus at Cahokia, so the large temple that once stood on its summit must have been the focus of the entire community. The plaza at its foot, and the associated platform mounds, charnel houses, and burial places, were surrounded by a high wooden palisade that effectively isolated the 200-acre (80-ha) central precincts from the outside world. Close by stood a circle of 48 wooden poles, 410 ft (125 m) across with a central observation point for observing the positions of sunrise at the equinoxes and solstices.

Cahokia's chiefs lived in the heart of the sprawling complex, but their identities are a mystery. University of Wisconsin archaeologist Melvin Fowler found the burial of one such individual. He lay on a platform of 20,000 shell beads and was accompanied by three high-status men and women buried nearby. About 800 arrowheads, copper and mica sheets, and 15 polished stone disks used in a spear-throwing game lay near these skeletons, perhaps the bodies of close relatives sacrificed at the funeral. Nearby were the remains of four decapitated men with their hands lopped off. More than 50 young women aged between 18 and 23 lay in a pit close by. Fowler suspects they were strangled to death at the funeral.

An imposing ceremonial precinct with temple mounds, a great plaza, and prominent burial places: Cahokia was a unique and very important place, the hub of economic, political, and religious life for thousands of people. She presided over a network of 9 large settlements with their own chiefs and burial mounds and at least 40 small, palisaded hamlets and farmsteads within the narrow compass of the American Bottom alone. Her artisans' copper ornaments, masks, and fine pots with effigies of humans and animals were known to shamans and chiefs hundreds of miles away.

Archaeologists group Cahokia and many other contemporary centers into the "Mississippian culture," a culture that extended from the Mississippi Valley far into Alabama, Georgia, and Florida and flourished in various forms from about AD 900 to European contact. One of the largest chiefdoms within this cultural complex was at Moundville on the banks of the Black Warrior River near what is now Tuscaloosa, Alabama. In AD 1000 merely a small village lay on a bluff overlooking the river. It soon grew into a small center, marked by a few mounds. Between 1250 and 1400, Moundville reached the height of its power. The central focus was a group of 20 large platform mounds built around a rectangular plaza that covered no less than 79 acres (32 ha). The largest mound rose 60 ft (18 m) above the river and straddled over an acre. Much smaller than Cahokia, and a village compared with Tenochtitlan or Teotihuacan, Moundville supported about 3,000 people living inside the bastioned palisade that protected the central precincts on three sides. The fourth side was open to the river.

Archaeologist Chris Peebles of Indiana University has created a portrait of Moundville society from more than 3,000 burials. He estimates that about five percent of the population were a hereditary, privileged group. It was they who lived in larger residences atop platform mounds overlooking the central plaza. When they died, their bones were stored in special charnel houses before eventual interment, resplendent with their badges of privilege and rank, with fine ceremonial stone axes, masks, and delicately engraved shell ornaments. The rest of the population, the commoners, were buried in their villages outside the northern boundary.

How centrally organized were Cahokia and Moundville? Were they incipient states, divided into social classes, or merely complex chiefdoms? Mississippian societies in general seem to have been a far cry from the hierarchical Aztec empire with its thousands of artisans, merchants, and priests. In the Midwest, every household, even that of the chief, probably farmed land and fished for bass. There were few full-time craftspeople, although every village and small town had its experts at making stone hoes, masks, and ceremonial pots. In these respects, the Mississippians may not have differed greatly from their Hopewell predecessors. But Cahokia and Moundville do seem to have had a tribute-paying hinterland, indicative of considerable power in their own particular regions. The areas from which they collected tribute were nevertheless small by, say Aztec standards. Archaeologist Vincas Steponaitis examined the tribute found at Moundville. He calculates that large-scale tribute-gathering was only effective over a distance of about 9 miles (14.5 km). Without organized caravans of porters or pack animals, and an army for enforcement – strategies used in both the Andes and

Cahokia and the Southern Cult

MAIN PICTURE *An artist's reconstruction of the Mississippian town of Cahokia, the largest urban and ceremonial center ever built in pre-Columbian North America. Visible here are the giant Monk's Mound, with its subsidiary mounds in the palisaded central core, and, at the left, the circle of wooden posts used for astronomical observations.* RIGHT *Weeping eyes are two common Mississippian Southern Cult motifs seen on both this tiny shell head, and the shell gorget incised with the figure of a flying shaman, a death's head in one hand and a ceremonial mace in the other.* LEFT AND BELOW LEFT *Weeping eyes feature prominently too on these effigy vases, perhaps suggesting an association between tears, rain, and fertility in Mississippian belief.*

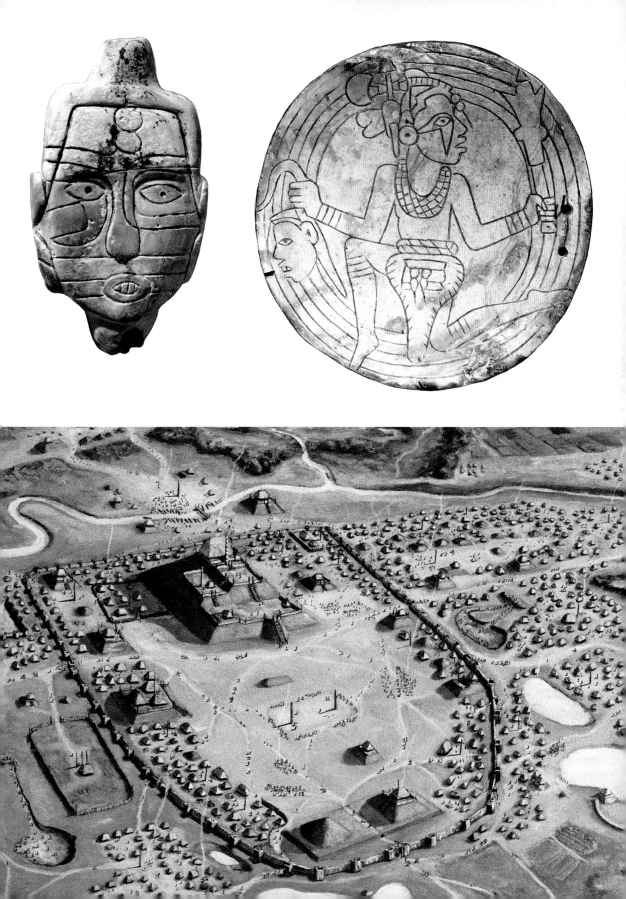

Mesoamerica – the chiefs of Moundville could only compel tribute payment from nearby communities. They did, however, draw some allegiance from local centers and villages up to 45 miles (72 km) away.

Trading and tribute were vital to the chief's survival. The magnificent artifacts of copper, mica, and shell they obtained from afar became symbols of their legitimacy, of their special relationship to the spiritual world. In the same vein of thinking, they used their control over the local people to erect great earthworks clustered around imposing plazas as symbols of their world, and of their authority. These were the settings in which they performed the important planting and harvest rituals that assured the fertility of the land.

Mexicans and Mississippians

All of this bears an eerie, if superficial, resemblance to Mesoamerican civilization. Did the Mississippians inherit their religious beliefs and architecture from Mexico? The issue is just as hotly debated today among archaeologists as the question of Mexican contacts with the Southwest – and the answers are just as inconclusive. Generations ago, Mississippian experts identified what they called a "Southern Cult," a set of religious beliefs reflected in ceremonial artifacts found from the Atlantic and Gulf Coasts as far inland as the Ohio Valley. Originally, they thought these showed strong Mexican influence, but closer scrutiny seems to have thrown up more differences than parallels. Finely made pots and shell cups depict long-nose gods still commemorated as ancestral figures by nineteenth-century Midwestern tribes. There are weeping eyes, striped poles, and a constant preoccupation with wind, fire, sun, and human sacrifice, motifs associated with the perpetual movements of the heavens. We can only guess at the meaning of these symbols, but many of them are connected with war. They commemorate the rising and setting sun, the movements of stars in the northern sky. These indigenous beliefs, which originated long before the Mississippian, were shared by people living all over the Midwest and Southeast. Mississippian chiefs may have ruled as semi-divine representatives of the sun, even if they were not living gods on earth like Moctezuma or the Sapa Inca. Standing on their great mounds they would rekindle new fire during a ritual renewal of the world, perhaps during ceremonies honoring growing, green corn in summer. Perhaps ideas filtered in from Mexico many centuries earlier, for many of the ceremonies, such as those surrounding maize, may have arrived with the new crops.

The Mississippian flourished in a temperate environment where year-round farming and large-scale irrigation were impossibilities for people using only Stone Age technologies. The chiefs of Cahokia and other great Mississippian centers presided over powerful, even complex societies. But the harsh realities of long winters and sharp frosts could not support the dense populations of the cradles of native American civilization.

CHAPTER FOURTEEN

EPILOG

"To these quiet Lambs, endowed with such blessed qualities, came the Spaniards like most cruel Tygres, Wolves, and Lions, enrag'd with a sharp and tedious hunger; for these forty years past, minding nothing else but the slaughter of these unfortunate wretches . . . of three millions of people which Hispaniola it self did contain, there are left remaining alive scarce three hundred persons. And as for the Island of Cuba, which contains as much ground in length . . . it lies wholly desert, until'd and ruin'd . . ." Bartolomé de las Casas arrived in the Indies in the early days and became a wealthy landowner in Cuba. He suffered a crisis of conscience about the treatment of the Indians, became a Dominican and a passionate advocate for the native Americans. In tract after tract, the "Apostle of the Indies" thundered against injustice and exploitation, against war, torture, and punishment. In 1542, his *A Very Brief Account of the Destruction of the Indies* claimed that millions of Indians had died at the hands of Christians, who "made gold their ultimate aim, seeking to load themselves with riches in the shortest possible time." Bartolomé de las Casas was vilified and abused for his pains, but he was right. The Admiral of the Ocean Sea's momentous voyage in search of new lands rumbled like a thunderclap across the Americas, bringing death and destruction to countless human societies that had lived in complete isolation for more than 14,000 years.

"People Began to Die . . ."

The real killers were exotic European diseases. In 1519, a Spanish conquistador infected with smallpox landed at Vera Cruz, Mexico. The Indians had no immunity and the disease spread like wildfire, reaching Tenochtitlan in 1520. The statistics, reconstructed from Spanish parish records and censuses, are devastating. At the time of the Spanish Conquest in 1521, about 11 million Indians lived in central Mexico. Only some 6.4 million remained in 1540, a decline of nearly 50 percent. By 1607 the aboriginal population was less than one-fifth of that of a century earlier. "This most fertile and rich land, together with its capital Mexico, has suffered many calamities and has declined with the loss of its grandeur and excellence and the great men who once inhabited it," lamented missionary historian Diego

Duran soon after the Conquest. In Peru, smallpox landed with the very first conquistadorial excursion ashore in the northern part of Inca domains. The mysterious disease swept across lowlands and highlands within months, wiping out entire villages long before any Spaniard set foot in Cuzco. It was a severely weakened empire that fell to Pizarro's unscrupulous adventurers.

Similar massive demographic catastrophes hit North America. Smallpox and other diseases spread across the Southeastern interior soon after Spanish ships visited the Florida coast. English settlers at Roanoke in the colony of Virginia soon infected the local people. "Within a few days after our departure from everies such towns, people began to die very fast, and many in short space," wrote Thomas Hariot, the same writer who wrote enviously of the Indians: "They are very sober in their eating and trinkinge, and consequently verye longe lived because they doe not opresse nature . . . I would to God we would followe their example." The epidemics spread inland, sometimes killing up to 90 percent of village populations. The survivors probably suffered from starvation, especially if the epidemics struck during planting or harvest. "Not a month has elapsed since they had rid themselves of smallpox, which had carried off most of them. In the village are now nothing but graves, in which they were buried two together, and we estimated not a hundred men were left," wrote a visitor to the Arkansas people in 1698.

In many areas, the depopulation was so rapid and devastating that ancestral traditions and much indigenous culture vanished in a few short months. Even in the most literate American Indian societies, priceless knowledge had been passed orally from generation to generation, information on genealogy, on astronomy, on ritual, on cosmology. The older people who were the repositories of such knowledge were among the most vulnerable to the new diseases. Without this critical lore, the survivors were crippled in their efforts to adjust to and understand the entirely alien culture of the newcomers.

Millions of native Americans perished from European diseases long before they came into contact with colonists, explorers, and missionaries. Enormous areas of the Ohio Valley and Midwest were almost depopulated by the time white settlers swarmed over the Appalachians in the late eighteenth century. The statistics become even more daunting after colonization. For example, more than 310,000 Indians lived in California at the time of Spanish colonization in 1769. There were only 20,000 California Indians in 1900.

The Great Diversity

The appearance of Europeans and their exotic diseases cut across thousands of years of independent native American history with a mind-numbing finality. That history had begun more than 14,000 years ago, when a handful of late Ice Age hunters crossed from Siberia to Alaska. Their descendants moved south into a vast, virgin continent inhabited only by a multiplicity of game animals. A new chapter began about 11,000 years ago when the great Ice Age animals – the megafauna – that had sustained the pioneers vanished in the face of inexorable global warming, and, very likely, overhunting by human predators. The Paleo-Indians of later generations lived in a biologically impoverished America, almost devoid of large mammals, except for the bison, and without potentially domesticable animals like the wild goat or ox. As a result, they developed an out-of-the ordinary expertise with wild plants of every kind. This botanical proficiency was to have momentous consequences for the course of world history after 1492.

Many people think of prehistoric hunters and foragers as being impoverished, and always on the verge of starvation. Nothing could be further from the truth in the Americas. Some of the most sophisticated hunter-gatherer societies in the world developed along the Pacific Northwest Coast. Further south, off southern California and Peru, cold water upwellings close offshore created some of the richest fisheries on earth. The Chumash Indians of the Santa Barbara Channel in southern California used fine plank canoes to voyage to nearby islands and to fish offshore. Some of them lived in permanent communities with more than 1,000 inhabitants. And coastal Peru is the only region of the globe where fishing and sea mammal hunting helped create more than 4,000 years of civilization.

If the extinction of big-game animals was the first watershed in native American history, the second was the domestication of plants. In the Andes, people were transplanting squashes, beans, and other indigenous plants from one mountain valley to the next as early as 8000 BC. And in highland Mexico, some 3,000 years later, hunter-gatherers began experimenting with a wild grass named teosinte and turned it into a staff of life – maize. The new staples spread far and wide over the Americas after 2500 BC, to the Amazon Basin and the Andes, into the Southwest by 1200 BC, and across the southern Plains to eastern North America in the first millennium AD. They transformed not only the landscape, but the whole shape of native American society.

Maize and bean agriculture, indeed any form of farming, is a communal activity, especially where the farmer has to cope with unreliable rainfall, irrigation, or large-scale land clearance. Corn fostered the sense of community, and the cyclical nature of human life. The cycles of birth, life, and death, of planting, growth, and harvest, became all-important, marked by communal rituals. "The Rain Boy with the dark cloud feet, He arises facing me . . . The Rain Girl with the dark fog feet, She arises facing me," goes a Navajo chant for rain. Everything reinforced not the individual but the community, a community in which land was owned by kin groups, where everyone had obligations to everyone else.

To fix and perpetuate these cycles, American Indian societies now began to develop calendars and elaborate religious rites. The sun, above all, became the focus of worship – the sun whose passage across the heavens marked the changing seasons, the sun whose warmth ensured a successful harvest. In the civilizations that grew up in Mesoamerica and the Andes after 2000 BC great

temple pyramids became the focal point for astronomical observations and
sun worship. On temple summits shaman-priests and shaman-kings enacted
rites of propitiation, rites to feed the sun and the other gods and thus ensure
the continuation of the universe. Of the many offerings made to sustain the
gods, the greatest was also the most terrible: human blood.

Human sacrifice was commonplace not only among the Aztecs and their
predecessors, but in Moche, Chimú, and other Andean civilizations.
Mississippian chiefs were accompanied to the other world by human victims.
The Aztecs were explicit in their belief that the blood of sacrificial victims and
of warriors killed in battle nourished the sun on its journey across the
heavens:

> "There is nothing like death in war,
> nothing like the flowery death
> so precious to the Giver of Life:
> Far off I see it: my heart yearns for it!"

proclaims an Aztec poem. The fact that human sacrifice was an integral part
of native American life should not surprise us. Sixteenth-century friar Diego
Durán, who wrote a detailed account of Aztec history, was led to remark
"how cleverly this devilish rite imitates that of our Holy Church, which
orders us to receive the True Body and Blood of our Lord Jesus Christ."

Why are there many common features in Andean and Mesoamerican
civilizations, some of which appear to be common, also, to North American
societies like the Mississippian? Human sacrifice, sun worship, a concern for
ancestors, the construction of mounds and pyramids, a preoccupation with
jaguars and with supreme power – these are but some of the commonalities
among ancient American civilizations. Were such societies in direct touch
with one another? Or can one explain common features by looking for a
dominant and unifying influence of voyagers from Asia or Europe who may
have crossed to the New World long before Columbus? Despite attempts to
connect Egyptian pyramids with Maya monuments, and claims that Japanese
clay pots bear decorative motifs that resemble those from Ecuador, there is no
good evidence whatsoever for long-distance voyaging across the Atlantic or
Pacific by ancient Egyptians or anyone else before the Vikings of the tenth
century AD. And in any case, why seek outside influences when there is such
abundant evidence indicating the indigenous development of civilizations in
the Americas? The building of mounds and pyramids in Egypt and the
Americas, and indeed in Mesopotamia, southeast Asia and elsewhere,
suggests not some worldwide influence of one civilization, but a much more
interesting and challenging theme – the universality of the human desire to
reach up to the gods and the heavens by erecting sacred mountains.

Such parallel cultural evolution must also be the explanation for many of
the similarities between civilizations within the Americas as well. For
Andean and Mesoamerican civilizations, and the more complex societies of

The ballgame, one of the unifying cultural attributes of Mesoamerica. LEFT *Aztec ballplayers.* BELOW *Zapotec ballcourt at Monte Albán.*

North America, seem to have developed largely independently of one another. We can be sure that many innovations and ideas traveled far and wide, such as maize and bean farming and certain religious beliefs. That there was also some physical contact between Andeans and Mesoamericans seems certain, but it was limited to sporadic long-distance trading by sea. The Moche and their successors traded along many miles of the Peruvian coast and far beyond for metals and shells. Some of the balsa rafts that carried this trade sailed much further north, to the Isthmus of Panama and beyond. The crews included skilled metalsmiths, who practiced their craft while waiting out the hurricane season in safe Mexican havens. It was then, during the first millennium AD, that the arts of copper and gold working seem to have spread into Mesoamerica. But these contacts can have been fleeting at best, for the number of rafts engaged in the trade and the distances involved militated against sustained intercourse.

Many of the similarities between these societies arose because all native Americans, whether hunters, farmers, or subjects of mighty lords, shared a common ancestry and adaptations to often similar environments. The power of the jaguar and the cayman, observations of the sun journeying across the heavens, the marking of summer and winter solstices, notions about mounds and caves, about death and rebirth, and the intricate symbolism behind such phenomena, all of them originated, ultimately, in primordial beliefs that were thousands of years old.

Pyramids in the Americas: Diffusion or Independent Invention?

Temple-pyramids and mounds are found wherever there is monumental architecture in the Americas – and indeed in many other hearths of civilization, such as Egypt, Mesopotamia, and southeast Asia. Their very universality suggests not the dominant influence of one all-powerful culture, but the common well-springs of the human imagination, and the common engineering solutions discovered by trial and error in the desire to build monumental structures on a massive scale. LEFT *Mesoamerican pyramids: above, Teotihuacan's Pyramid of the Sun, echoing the shape of the mountain range behind; below, a temple at Monte Albán.* BELOW *Andean pyramids: above, the Huaca del Sol (Pyramid of the Sun) in the Moche Valley; below, another Moche pyramid complex.*

Feeding the World

The native Americans of 1492 were the most expert plant breeders in the world, with a vast knowledge of different species and pharmacology. They discovered the curative properties of quinine, the unique anesthetizing qualities of coca, and dozens of plant drugs that are now the foundations of modern medicine. But the ultimate defeat of their societies was so overwhelming, and seemingly so final, that we forget their legacy to humanity.

Long before Columbus landed in the Bahamas, American Indians had domesticated hundreds of varieties of corn, cassava, and peanuts, also the humble potato. At least 3,000 varieties of the potato alone grew in the Andes in Pizarro's day, and it was grown in Mexico and by the Navajo in the Southwest. (Only some 250 varieties are now harvested in the United States.) Native Americans gave the world more than three-fifths of the crops cultivated around the world today, crops that have improved diets, caused massive population growth, and changed nations.

Maize and potatoes – these were the miracle crops. At first, Europeans treated potatoes with suspicion, for they were used to eating bread or oatmeal made from cereal grains. The exotic tubers were considered tasteless, even to cause leprosy. Only the Irish grew them on a large scale, until the eighteenth century, when Frederick the Great of Prussia and Catherine the Great of Russia forced their peasantries to plant potatoes or starve. The result was a revolution in European diet. Cereal consumption in Belgium and Holland alone dropped by 40 percent. Populations climbed rapidly throughout northern Europe, which soon outstripped the south in political and economic might. Potatoes brought about a miracle – the virtual elimination of episodic famine. Had European peasants followed the Andean example and planted many different forms of potato, they would have eliminated the danger of blight, which caused catastrophic problems in nineteenth-century Ireland and a wave of emigration to the United States.

Maize became a vital animal food in Europe that increased the output of cheese, meat, milk, and other dairy products. The Africans embraced corn and cassava, the Chinese maize and sweet potatoes. Asians now cultivate more amaranth than do the Americans. Apart from a wealth of calories and new crops, American foods and spices also revolutionized national and local cuisines everywhere. They soon found their way into Indian curries, and especially into Italian pastas – tomatoes of all sizes and colors, sweet peppers of many shapes and hues, also zucchini and beans. And in America itself, Europeans grafted Indian foods onto their own cereal and meat diet, to produce the great variety of regional dishes we enjoy today.

In 1492, European medicine had advanced little beyond witchcraft and alchemy. The American Indian pharmacopeia was highly sophisticated and included not only deadly poisons like curare, but hallucinogenic drugs, also ointments to aid healing of flesh wounds and many medicines. In 1535

French explorer Jacques Cartier visited the Huron village of Hochelaga, on the modern site of Montreal. He built a winter camp, but his men gradually succumbed to scurvy. The Indians also suffered from scurvy but invariably recovered. Cartier was astonished when they showed him how to make a tonic from a hemlock or pine tree that cured his men within a week. (The tonic contained huge doses of vitamin C.) It was not until 1795 that the British Admiralty supplied all its ships with lime juice for the same purpose.

Goldlust

The crops and drugs developed by American Indians improved agriculture and medicine. They made possible the world population explosion of recent centuries. But it was the European hunger for gold that fueled the conquest and exploration of the Americas. "They thirsted mightily for gold; they stuffed themselves with it; they starved for it; they lusted for it like pigs," said one of Bernardino de Sahagún's Aztec informants. The conquistadors acquired amazing quantities of the yellow metal from what were, truly, kingdoms of gold. Between 1500 and 1650, between 180 and 200 tons of gold and vast quantities of silver flowed from the Americas into European hands, into banks, church coffers, and government treasuries. Hitherto, European monarchs had obtained two-thirds of their gold from Mali, Ghana, and other West African kingdoms, carried in caravans across the Sahara. Timbuktu was famous as a golden city. Now a flood of precious metal put gold and silver from mines worked by Indian slaves into the hands of private merchants and the common people. Europe changed rapidly to a true money economy based on plentiful silver coinage for everyday transactions.

In 1492, Europe possessed about $200 million worth of gold and silver. By 1600, the amount had increased eightfold. The "large amount of gold, of pure silver in bullion and hand-wrought," which flowed into Antwerp and other European ports provided new measures of wealth other than land and created new classes of merchants and businessmen. These riches created new economic opportunities and Europe expanded into an international market system. The silver flowed to Asia, too, but demand for West African gold declined. Only one commodity was exported to the New World – slaves, who fueled the new and booming Atlantic trade in sugar and spices grown with African slave labor on Caribbean islands.

The sixteenth century saw the birth of the era of the powerful nation-state that prospered off American gold and silver, off tropical products from the West Indies, and off the remarkable agricultural expertise of the native American. The five centuries since Columbus encountered his "guileless, unwarlike people" in the Indies have seen the same states circle the globe, conquering, exploiting, exploring, and colonizing, creating the foundations for the world economy of today. It is an irony of history that in so many ways we owe the existence of this same world economy to the Americans of 1492.

FURTHER READING

The bibliographical commentary that follows makes no pretense to being complete, and mentions but some of the sources I consulted in writing this book. These references will steer you through the complicated academic and general literature on this enormous subject. For the most part, I have confined myself to book sources.

Introduction   THE ENCHANTED VISION
No one interested in American Indian society in 1492 should fail to read Bernal Díaz del Castillo's immortal account of the Spanish Conquest of Mexico: *The Conquest of New Spain*, trans. J.M. Cohen (Pelican Books, Harmondsworth & Baltimore, 1963). A good account of Columbus' voyages is Robert H. Fuson, *The Log of Christopher Columbus* (International Marine Publishing Company, Camden, Maine, 1987). Hugh Honor, *The New Golden Land: European Images of America* (Putnam, New York, 1975) is a classic essay on stereotypical images of native Americans in European art. John Hemming, *The Conquest of the Incas* (Penguin Books, Harmondsworth & Baltimore, 2nd ed., 1983), provides a superb summary of the Pizarro expedition and its aftermath. There are few good general accounts of native American societies at European contact. Philip Kopper, *The Smithsonian Book of North American Indians* (Smithsonian Books, Washington DC, 1986) is a lavishly illustrated account. Alvin Josephy, *The American Heritage Book of the American Indian* (American Heritage, New York, 1968) is also informative. More serious readers can find much of interest in the weighty and authoritative *Handbooks of North American, Middle American, and South American Indians*; published by the Smithsonian Institution, they are a mine of information on a myriad American Indian societies and can usually be found in larger academic libraries. Peter Nabokov and Robert Easton's *Native American Architecture* (Oxford University Press, Oxford, 1989) is one of those volumes that is truly hard to put down. Mario Vargas Llosa's *A Writer's Reality* (Syracuse University Press, Syracuse, NY, 1990) contains a masterly essay on the Spanish Conquest.

Chapter 1   THE WORLD OF THE FIFTH SUN
Benjamin Keen, *The Aztec Image in Western Thought* (Rutgers University Press, New Brunswick, NJ, 1971) is an authoritative essay on European perceptions of Aztec civilization. My own *The Aztecs* (W.H. Freeman, New York, 1984) gives a general summary of the rise, apogee, and fall of the Aztecs, based on historical, archaeological, and ethnohistorical sources. So does Francis Berdan, *The Aztecs of Central Mexico: An Imperial Society* (Holt, Rinehart, and Winston, New York, 1982). Nigel Davies, *The Aztecs: A History* (University of Oklahoma Press, Norman, 1973) covers the rise and fall of the Aztecs from a historical perspective. Geoffrey W. Conrad and Arthur A. Demarest,

Religion and Empire (Cambridge University Press, Cambridge, 1984), gives an authoritative and provocative comparison of Aztec and Inca civilization. Bernardino de Sahagún's *General History of the Things of New Spain* has been ably translated by Charles E. Dibble and Arthur O. Anderson in *Florentine Codex: General History of the Things of New Spain* (University of Utah Press, Salt Lake City, 12 vols, 1950–1975). For Aztec archaeology, see Muriel Porter Weaver, *The Aztecs, Maya, and Their Predecessors* (Academic Press, New York, 2nd ed., 1981), also Eduardo Matos Moctezuma, *The Great Temple of the Aztecs: Treasures of Tenochtitlan* (Thames & Hudson, London & New York, 1988). No one should miss Patricia Anawalt's *Indian Clothing Before Columbus* (University of Oklahoma Press, Norman, 1981), a superbly illustrated essay on Mexican sumptuary customs.

Chapter 2   THE LAND OF THE FOUR QUARTERS
John Hemming's *The Conquest of the Incas* (Penguin Books, Harmondsworth & Baltimore, 1983) is an excellent starting point for the general reader and is well referenced. Conrad and Demarest's *Religion and Empire*, already referred to, provides a useful analysis of the royal mummy cult. Michael Moseley, *The Incas and Their Ancestors* (Thames & Hudson, London & New York, 1992), Luis G. Lumbreras, *The Peoples and Cultures of Ancient Peru* (Smithsonian Institution Press, Washington DC, 1974) and George Bankes, *Peru Before Pizarro* (Phaidon, Oxford, 1977) place the Inca in a wider archaeological and historical context. John Rowe's *Inca Culture at the Time of the Spanish Conquest* (Handbook of South American Indians, Smithsonian Institution, Washington DC, vol. 2, 1946) is still authoritative and widely quoted in the literature. For Inca buildings and settlements, see Graziano Gasperini and Luise Margolies, *Inca Architecture* (Indiana University Press, Bloomington, IN, 1980). John Hyslop's *The Inka Road System* (Academic Press, New York, 1984) and *Inka Settlement Patterns* (University of Texas Press, Austin, 1990) are authoritative. Garcilaso de la Vega (El Inca)'s *Royal Commentaries of the Inca* have been ably translated by Harold V. Livermore (University of Texas Press, Austin, 2 vols, 1966). Victor W. von Hagen, *The Incas of Pedro de Cieza de León (1553)* (University of Oklahoma Press, Norman, 1959) and Ronald Hamilton, *History of the Inca Empire: An Account of the Indians' Customs and Their Origin . . . (1653)* (University of Texas Press, Austin, 1979) provide translations of Cieza de León and Bernabé Cobo's works respectively.

Chapter 3   THE BIG-GAME HUNTERS
The literature is enormous, controversial, and sometimes polemical. My recent summary, *The Great Journey* (Thames & Hudson, London & New York, 1987) reviews the controversies and makes a case for relatively late settlement. More recently, I have

outlined the global background to the human settlement of the Americas in *The Journey from Eden* (Thames & Hudson, London & New York, 1990). A special issue of *Prehistoric Mongoloid Dispersals*, No.7 (University of Tokyo, 1990) summarizes the most recent theories on human colonization of Beringia, the latest archaeological findings, and linguistic evidence, in a series of well argued general essays. The Bering Land Bridge is well summarized in David Hopkins and others (eds.), *Paleoecology of Beringia* (Academic Press, New York, 1982). David Meltzer, "Why Don't We Know When the First People Came to America?" *American Antiquity* 54 (1989): 471–490 is a useful discussion of first settlement. The controversial early Latin American sites are discussed by Thomas Lynch, "Glacial Age Man in South America? A Critical Review," *American Antiquity* 55 (1990):12–36 in a paper that is provoking lively discussion. For linguistics, see Joseph Greenberg, *Language in the Americas* (Stanford University Press, Stanford, 1987).The Clovis tradition is Vance Haynes' specialty: "Elephant Hunting in North America," *Scientific American* 214(6) (1966):104–112 is a popular essay on the subject. For megafaunal extinctions, read Paul Martin and Henry Wright (eds.), *Pleistocene Extinctions: Search for a Cause* (Yale University Press, New Haven, 1967) and Paul Martin and Richard Klein (eds.), *A Pleistocene Revolution* (University of Arizona Press, Tucson, 1984), where the controversies are well aired. See also James Mead and David Meltzer (eds.), *Environments and Extinctions: Man in Late Glacial North America* (Center for the Study of Early Man, University of Maine, Orono, 1985).

For the bison hunters, George Frison's *Prehistoric Hunters of the High Plains* (Academic Press, New York, 1978) is seminal. For a magnificent study of a Paleo-Indian kill site, see Joe Ben Wheat, "The Olsen-Chubbock-Site: A Paleo-Indian Bison Kill," *Memoirs of the Society for American Archaeology* 26 (1972). John Speth's *Bison Kills and Bone Counts* (University of Chicago Press, Chicago, 1983) is a model of sophisticated archaeological research into bison hunting.

Chapter 4   THE FISHERFOLK
No one has ever written a book on prehistoric fishing, foraging, and hunting in the Americas, so the non-specialist reader has to rely on monographs and scientific papers. I summarized North American archaeology in *Ancient North America: The Archaeology of a Continent* (Thames & Hudson, London & New York, 1991), but this is, perforce, a general account. Michael Moseley's volume, *The Incas and Their Ancestors*, already cited, provides a useful summary of early coastal societies, as does his *Maritime Foundations of Andean Civilization* (Cummings, Menlo Park, CA, 1975). Jeffrey Quilter, *Life and Death at Paloma* (University of Iowa Press, Iowa City, 1989) describes this important site and its fascinating mortuary customs. The Chumash Indians

were studied by the famous but eccentric anthropologist John Harrington. His notes are a rich lode of ethnographic information for modern scholars. Travis Hudson and Tom Blackburn, *Material Culture of the Chumash Interaction Sphere* (Ballena Press, Socorro, NM, 1983) is a fundamental source, while the same authors and others describe the reconstruction of a Chumash canoe in *Tomol: Chumash watercraft as described in the ethnographic notes of John Harrington* (Ballena Press, Socorro, NM, 1978). For a general summary of this remarkable culture, try L.C. Landberg, *The Chumash Indians of Southern California* (Southwestern Museum, Los Angeles, 1965). For the vision quest, Richard Applegate, *Atishwin: The Dream Helper in South-Central California* (Ballena Press, Socorro, NM, 1978). The Northwest Coast is summarized by Roy Carlson, *Indian Art Traditions of the Northwest Coast* (Simon Fraser University, Burnaby, BC, 1983). For Ozette, see Ruth Kirk, *Hunters of the Whale* (Morrow, New York, 1975). The Thule are discussed by Don Dumond in *The Eskimos and Aleuts* (Thames and Hudson, London, 2nd ed., 1987). Robert McGhee's *Canadian Arctic Prehistory* (National Museums of Canada, Ottawa, 1978) is also useful.

Chapter 5   THE FARMERS
The botanical evidence appears in Richard Ford (ed.), *Prehistoric Food Production in North America* (Museum of Anthropology, University of Michigan, Ann Arbor, 1985). Superb articles by Walter Galinet and others on maize can also be found in this volume. Jack Weatherford, *The Indian Givers* (Fawcett Columbine, New York, 1988) summarizes the agricultural legacy of the native Americans. Guitarrero was excavated by Thomas Lynch (ed.), *Guitarrero Cave* (Academic Press, New York, 1980). For early agriculture in Central America, the interested reader should study Kent Flannery's provocative monograph *Guila Naquitz* (Academic Press, New York, 1985), which describes the life of a small Valley of Oaxaca population in Mexico just as food production began. Richard MacNeish outlines Tehuacan in *The Science of Archaeology?* (Duxbury Press, North Scituate, Mass., 1978). His edited *The Prehistory of the Tehuacan Valley* (University of Texas Press, Austin, 1970) is an informative monograph. The Ford volume on *Prehistoric Food Production in North America* cited above, carries excellent and authoritative essays on maize. The best popular account of the Amazon sites is by Anna Roosevelt, "Lost Civilizations of the Lower Amazon," *Natural History* 2 (1989):74–83. The same author's definitive monograph *Moundbuilders of Marajo* (Academic Press, New York, 1991) was not available for the writing of this book.

Chapter 6   THE JAGUAR AND THE SHAMAN
John Lloyd Stephens and Frederick Catherwood are among the immortals of archaeology and their own writings are still worth an evening's read. Stephens' *Incidents of Travel in Central America, Chiapas and*

the Yucatan (Harpers, New York, 1841) describes Copán, and this and his second book *Incidents of Travel in Yucatan* (Harpers, New York, 1843) give his conclusions on the Maya. Michael Coe's *America's First Civilization: Discovering the Olmec* (American Heritage, New York, 1968) outlines the discovery of the Olmec, as does Nick Saunders' *People of the Jaguar* (Souvenir Press, London, 1989), a source I drew on heavily here, remarkable for its thoughtful analysis of shamanism. Ignacio Bernal, *The Olmec World* (University of California Press, Berkeley, 1969) is a classic. Michael Coe and Richard Diehl, *In the Land of the Olmec* (University of Texas Press, London, 1980), describe important excavations. David Grove, *Chalcatzingo* (Thames & Hudson, London & New York, 1984) outlines this fascinating site on the Olmec periphery. P.D. Joralemon, *A Study of Olmec Iconography* (Dumbarton Oaks, Washington DC, 1971) and E.P. Benson (ed.), *The Cult of the Feline* (Dumbarton Oaks, Washington DC, 1972) are essential reading on Olmec religious beliefs.

Chapter 7   THE GULLET OF THE VISION SERPENT
Chapter 8   MAYA LORDS
The literature is complex, diffuse, and obscure except to the specialist. Fortunately, there are some excellent summaries. A fundamental source for these chapters was Linda Schele and David Freidel, *A Forest of Kings* (Morrow, New York, 1990), a remarkable popular account of the rise and fall of Maya civilization that draws on both glyphs and archaeological sources. This is a vivid, often almost visionary, book that sometimes stretches the evidence. But it stands as a unique synthesis of the complex make-up of ancient Maya civilization. Linda Schele and Mary E. Miller, *The Blood of Kings* (University of Texas, Austin, 1986) is another seminal work on glyph research. For the archaeology, Jeremy A. Sabloff's *The Cities of Ancient Mexico* (Thames & Hudson, London & New York, 1989) and the same author's *The New Archaeology and the Ancient Maya* (Scientific American Library, New York, 1990) are fundamental. Also, Michael Coe, *Mexico* (Thames & Hudson, London & New York, 3rd ed., 1984) and *The Maya* (Thames & Hudson, London & New York, 4th ed., 1987). Norman Hammond, *Ancient Maya Civilization* (Rutgers University Press, New Brunswick, NJ, 1982) is an excellent summary. References to specific sites will be found in these publications. For art and architecture, George Kubler, *Art and Architecture of Ancient America* (Pelican Books, Harmondsworth & Baltimore, 3rd ed., 1984) and Mary Ellen Miller's *The Art of Mesoamerica* (Thames & Hudson, London & New York, 1986) are excellent. Also Doris Heyden and Paul Gendrop, *Pre-Columbian Architecture of Mesoamerica* (Electa Rizzoli, New York, 1980). For Mesoamerican calendars and time generally, Anthony Aveni, *Empires of Time* (Basic Books, New York, 1989) provides a sophisticated perspective. The Popol Vuh has been brilliantly translated by Dennis

Tedlock, *Popol Vuh: The Mayan Book of the Dawn of Life* (Simon and Schuster, New York, 1985). The Itza and Spanish contacts are discussed by Philip Ainsworth Means, *History of the Spanish Conquest of Yucatan and of the Itzas* (Peabody Museum Papers VII, Cambridge, Mass., 1917) and Alfred M. Tozzer, *Landa's Relacion de Las Cosas de Yucatan* (Peabody Museum Papers XVIII, Cambridge, Mass., 1941).

Chapter 9   BEFORE THE AZTECS
The Valley of Oaxaca is a classic area of Mesoamerican archaeology. Kent Flannery (ed.), *The Early Mesoamerican Village* (Academic Press, New York, 1976) ranks among the most insightful books on archaeology ever written, and is hilariously funny in parts, as well as an excellent piece of research that describes San José Mogote and other early Oaxacan settlements. Richard Blanton (ed.), *Monte Alban: Settlement Patterns at the Ancient Zapotec Capital* (Academic Press, New York, 1978) analyzes later developments. René Millon, R.B. Drewitt, and George Cowgill, *Urbanization at Teotihuacan* (University of Texas Press, Austin, 1974) offers a comprehensive view of this remarkable metropolis. See also Arthur Miller, *Mural Painting of Teotihuacan* (Dumbarton Oaks, Washington DC, 1973). A seminal and complex piece of research is William Sanders, Jeffrey Parsons, and Robert Santley, *The Basin of Mexico* (Academic Press, New York, 1979), one of the largest scale archaeological surveys ever undertaken, which places both Teotihuacan and the Aztec civilization in a broad perspective. Nigel Davies has written two books that analyze the complex history of the Toltec civilization: *The Toltecs Until the Fall of Tula* (University of Oklahoma Press, Norman, 1977) and *The Toltec Heritage From the Fall of Tula to the Rise of Tenochtitlan* (University of Oklahoma Press, Norman, 1980). By far the best archaeological description is by Richard Diehl, *Tula, the Toltec Capital of Ancient Mexico* (Thames & Hudson, London & New York, 1983). Richard Blanton and others, *Ancient Mesoamerica* (Cambridge University Press, Cambridge, 1981) also has useful insights.

Chapter 10   THE CHAVÍN CULT
Michael Moseley, *The Incas and Their Ancestors* (Thames & Hudson, London & New York, 1992), George Bankes, *Peru before Pizarro* (Phaidon, Oxford, 1977) and Luis Lumbreras, *The Peoples and Cultures of Ancient Peru*, already cited, are good basic sources. Richard Keatinge (ed.), *Peruvian Prehistory* (Cambridge University Press, Cambridge, 1988) contains helpful essays. For the origins of Andean civilization, Michael Moseley, *The Maritime Foundations of Andean Civilization* (Cummings, Menlo Park, CA, 1975) is provocative and authoritative. Christopher Donnan (ed.), *Early Ceremonial Architecture in the Andes* (Dumbarton Oaks, Washington DC, 1985) brings together a series of articles on ceremonial centers on the coast and in the highlands. Richard Burger, *The Prehistoric Occupation of Chavin de Huantar, Peru* (University of

California Press, Publications in Anthropology, Berkeley, 1984) is the most valuable source on this important site. Elizabeth Benson (ed.), *Dumbarton Oaks Conference on Chavin* (Dumbarton Oaks, Washington DC, 1971) and the same author's *The Cult of the Feline* (Dumbarton Oaks, Washington DC, 1972) are important. Nick Saunders, *The People of the Jaguar*, already cited, gives an intelligent and thoughtful summary of Chavín which I drew on here. Anyone studying Andean religion ignores Lawrence E. Sullivan's *Icanchu's Drum* (Macmillan, New York, 1988) at their peril. This long and extraordinarily scholarly work is a heavy read, but a mine of information and insights into this most complex of subjects. The chapters on shamanism are absolutely fundamental. Gary Urton, *At the Crossroads of the Earth and the Sky* (University of Texas Press, Austin, 1981) is a compelling first-hand study of Andean astronomy.

Chapter 11 THE GOLDEN MOCHE
For the basics, see Christopher Donnan and Donna McClelland, *The Burial Theme in Moche Iconography* (Dumbarton Oaks, Washington DC, 1987), and Elizabeth Benson, *The Mochica* (Thames & Hudson, London, 1972). Also: Elizabeth Benson (ed.), *Death and the Afterlife in Pre-Columbian America* (Dumbarton Oaks, Washington DC, 1975). The National Geographic has run a series of superbly illustrated descriptions of Moche civilization and of the Lords of Sipán in recent years. For example, see Walter Alva, "Discovering the New World's Richest Unlooted Tomb," *National Geographic Magazine* 174(4) (1989):510–548 and "New Royal Tomb Unearthed," *National Geographic Magazine* 177(6) (1990):2–16.

Chapter 12 BEFORE THE INCAS
The Nazca lines and Maria Reiche are sympathetically covered by Tony Morrison, *The Mystery of the Nasca Lines* (Nonesuch Expeditions, Woodbridge, Suffolk, England, 1987). See also Johan Reinhard, *The Nasca Lines: A New Perspective on their Origin and Meaning* (Editorial Los Pinos, Lima, Peru, 1987). For Cahuachi, see Helaine Silverman, "The Early Nasca Pilgrimage Center of Cahuachi and the Nazca Lines: Anthropological and Archaeological Perspectives," *in* Anthony Aveni (ed.), *The Lines of Nazca* (American Philosophical Society, Philadelphia 1990), pp. 209–244. Chan Chan and the Chimú: Michael Moseley and C. Kent Day (eds.), *Chan Chan: Andean Desert City* (University of New Mexico Press, Albuquerque, 1982). Tiwanaku: Alan Kolata, "Tiwanaku: Portrait of an Andean Civilization," *Field Museum of Natural History Bulletin* 53(8) (1982):13–28. Also, the same author's "The Agricultural Foundations of the Tiwanaku State," *American Antiquity* 51(4) (1986):748–762. Huari: William Isbell and Katharina Schreiber, "Was Huari a State?" *American Antiquity* 43 (1978):372–389.

Chapter 13 PUEBLOS AND MOUNDBUILDERS
Linda Cordell's *Prehistory of the Southwest*

(Academic Press, New York, 1984) is a fundamental source on the Southwest for the serious reader. My *Elusive Treasure* (Charles Scribners, New York, 1977) tells the story of the Seven Cities of Cibola. Frank Cushing, *Zuni* (University of Nebraska Press, Lincoln, 1979) contains a selection of this pioneer anthropologist's writings and an essay on his life by Jesse Green. David Noble (ed.), *New Light on Chaco Canyon* (School of American Research, Santa Fe, NM, 1984) and *Mesa Verde National Park* (School of American Research, Santa Fe, NM, 1985) are two admirable summaries for the lay reader. Emil Haury, *The Hohokam, desert farmers and craftsmen: excavations at Snaketown 1964–1965* (University of Arizona Press, Tucson, 1976) describes the Hohokam tradition.

The Moundbuilders: Robert Silverberg's *Moundbuilders of Ancient America: the Archaeology of a Myth* (New York Graphic Society, New York, 1968) remains the classic work on the famous moundbuilder controversies. For Adena and Hopewell, see David Brose and No'mi Greber (eds.), *Hopewellian Archaeology* (Kent State University Press, Kent, OH, 1979). W.S. Webb and R.S. Baby, *The Adena People* (University of Tennessee Press, Knoxville, 1957) is still a fundamental source on Adena. Mark Seeman, *The Hopewell Interaction Sphere: the Evidence for Interregional Trade and Structural Complexity* (Indiana University Press, Indianapolis, 1979) is very useful, as is the same author's "Feasting of the Dead," in the Brose and Greber volume already mentioned. The Mississippian appears in a multitude of publications, mainly highly technical. See Bruce Smith (ed.), *Mississippian Settlement Patterns* (Academic Press, New York, 1978) and the same author's masterly synthesis: "The Archaeology of the Southeastern United States: From Dalton to de Soto, 10,500 to 500 BP," *Advances in World Prehistory* 5 (1986):1–92. Cahokia: Melvin Fowler, *Cahokia: Ancient Capital of the Midwest* (Addison-Wesley, Reading, Mass., 1974). Moundville: Vincent Steponaitis, *Ceramics, chronology, and community patterns: an archaeological study at Moundville* (Academic Press, New York, 1983). Patricia Galloway (ed.), *The Southeastern Ceremonial Complex: Artifacts and Analysis* (University of Nebraska Press, Lincoln, 1989) discusses the iconography and significance of the Southeastern Complex.

Chapter 14 EPILOG
The events of the Spanish Conquest and later European contact lie outside the scope of this book, but the following works are of interest: Eric Wolf, *Europe and the People without History* (University of California Press, Berkeley, 1984) is a monumental synthesis of the closely interconnected world of the Age of Discovery and, later, of the notion of "world systems." My *Clash of Cultures* (W.H. Freeman, New York, 1984) is a more popular account, which covers Spanish reactions to the American Indian. Ann Ramenovsky, *Vectors of Death* (University of New

Mexico Press, Albuquerque, 1987) analyzes the impact of smallpox and other epidemics on native American populations. Kirkpatrick Sale, *The Conquest of Paradise: Christopher Columbus and the Columbus Legacy* (Knopf, New York, 1990) is a general account of Columbus and his legacy. Charles Gibson, *The Aztecs under Spanish Rule* (Stanford University Press, Palo Alto, 1964) and Nancy Farris, *The Maya Under Colonial Rule* (Princeton University

Press, 1984) both describe Indian reactions to Spanish colonialism in all their subtlety. Jack Weatherford, *Indian Givers* (Fawcett Columbine, New York, 1988) is a perceptive essay on the legacy of the American Indian based on wide reading and travel. I have drawn on his fascinating observations here. See also Ferdinand Braudel, *Civilization and Capitalism, 15th to 18th Century* (Collins, London, Harper and Row, New York, 1982–84).

ILLUSTRATION AND TEXT CREDITS

Abbreviations: a = above; b = below; c = center; l = left; r = right; t = top; IGK = Irmgard Groth-Kimball; MEM = Mary Ellen Miller; MNA = Museo Nacional de Antropologia, Mexico; NJS = Nicholas J. Saunders.

Color Plates

p.9 Photo Eduardo Matos Moctezuma and the Great Temple Project, Mexico City. **10** Bibliothèque de l'Assemblée Nationale, Paris. **11** Vatican Library, Rome. **12** Museum für Völkerkunde, Vienna. **21–22** Photos Eduardo Matos Moctezuma and the Great Temple Project. **39** Photo M. Yamamoto, Tokyo. **40** Photo Michael E. Moseley. **113–116** Photos Francis Robicsek. **141** Photo MEM. **142** Photo Eduardo Matos Moctezuma and the Great Temple Project. **159** Photo Michael E. Moseley. **160** Photo M. Yamamoto, Tokyo.

Monochrome Illustrations

Frontispiece MNA. Photo IGR. **p.17** Courtesy Great Temple Project, Mexico City. **24** After Matos Moctezuma 1988. **27a** Photo NJS. **27b** Codex Magliabecchi (facsimile), British Museum; photo John Freeman. **29** MNA; photo IGK. **30–31** Photos Great Temple Project, Mexico City. **30b, 30–31b, 31br** Photos Salvador Guilliem Arroyo. **30–31t** Reconstruction by Marquina; Instituto Nacional de Antropologia e Historia, Mexico. **34t, 35t** Codex Mendoza; Curators of the Bodleian Library, Oxford. **34b, 35bl** Museum für Völkerkunde, Vienna. **35cr, 35br** Sahagún, *Historia de las Cosas de Nueva España* (Codex Florentino). **43** Photo Hans Mann. **46t** University Museum of Archaeology and Anthropology, Cambridge. **46b, 46–47, 47t, 47b** Photos NJS. **51** Guaman Poma de Ayala, *Nueva Coronica, c.1610.* **52** National Gallery of Art, Washington DC. **55** Courtesy the Centre for American and Commonwealth Studies, Exeter. **60t** Drawn by Simon S.S. Driver. **60b** After J. Wymer, *The Palaeolithic Age* (1982). **65** Arizona State Museum, University of Arizona; photo E.B. Sayles. **69** Smithsonian Institution, Washington DC, National Anthropological Archives, neg. no. 205 60. **73** Photo Hans Mann. **77t** Hutchings, *California Scenes*; © California Historical Society. **77c** Santa Barbara Museum of Natural History; photo Peter

Howorth. **77b** Santa Barbara Museum of Natural History; photo William D. Hyder. **78** Drawn by Simon S.S. Driver. **80l** Photo C.F. Feest. **80b** Photo Richard D. Daugherty. **80–81** Photo NJS. **81t** Royal British Columbia Museum, Victoria, BC. **81b** Photo Werner Forman. **84** National Museums of Canada, Canadian Museum of Civilization, neg. no. 51166. **85bl** From W.W. Fitzhugh and Aron Crowell (eds.), *Crossroads of Continents* (1988); courtesy Smithsonian Institution Press (drawing by Jo Ann Moore). **86t** Smithsonian Institution, Washington DC, National Anthropological Archives, neg. no. 73 – 10872. **86bl** National Museum of Man, Ottawa; photo Werner Forman. **86br** National Museums of Canada. **93t** Sahagún, *Historia de las Cosas de Nueva España* (Codex Florentino). **93c** Guaman Poma de Ayala, *Nueva Coronica, c.1610.* **95** Photo George Holton. **97** From W.L. Fash, *Scribes, Warriors and Kings* (1991); drawing by Barbara W. Fash. **100t** Photo MEM. **100bl, 101** MNA; photos IGK. **100br** Photo IGK. **102** From Michael D. Coe, *Mexico* (1984). **104tl** Courtesy the National Geographic Society. **104bl, 104tr** MNA; photos IGK. **104–105** From David C. Grove, *Chalcatzingo* (1984). **105tl** British Museum; photo Werner Forman. **105tr** Photo Leonard Lee Rue III. **106** From Michael D. Coe, *Mexico* (1984). **110** Lithograph by Frederick Catherwood, 1844. **118, 119** Trustees of the British Museum. **120** After J.E.S. Thompson. **124** Reconstruction by Terry Rutledge, courtesy Ray T. Matheny. **125** University Museum, Philadelphia. **127** Drawn by Geoff Penna, after Schele and Friedel (1990). **128** Photo MEM. **129** Photo Alberto Ruz L. **130t** Photo J.A. Sabloff. **130b** Photo Alberto Ruz L. **132** Photo Alberto Ruz L. **133** MNA. **135t** Trustees of the British Museum. **135** Reconstruction by Tatiana Proskouriakoff; courtesy Peabody Museum, Harvard University (photo Hillel Burger). **138t** Photo MEM. **138b** Photo J.A. Sabloff. **146tl, 146bl** MNA; photo IGK. **146–147** Photo MEM. **146–147b** Tracy Wellman, after Marcus 1983. **147b** Photo J.A. Sabloff. **150–151** Photo © René Millon. **150b** After G. Kubler. **151t** MNA; photo IGK. **151bl** Instituto Nacional de Antropologia e Historia, Mexico. **151br** MNA; photo IGK. **153** After L. Séjourné, *Burning Water* (1956). **155** MNA; photo IGK. **157** Photo Hans Mann. **161c** The Brooklyn Museum, New York. **161b** Photo NJS. **166t** Courtesy

Carlos Williams Léon. **166bl**, **166br** Photos Hans
Mann. **168t** Drawings by Annick Boothe. **168–169**
Abraham Guillén. **169tl** Photo R.B. Welsh. **169r** After
Anton, *The Art of Ancient Peru* (1972). **174** Photo
Shippee-Johnson. **178t** University Museum of
Archaeology and Anthropology, Cambridge. **178bl**
Photo Edwin Smith. **178br** Courtesy of the Linden
Museum, Stuttgart. **179** Museum für Völkerkunde,
Munich. **181t** Ethnographical Museum, Berlin. **181c**
After G. Kutscher, *Nordperuanische Keramik* (1954).
181b From Anton, *The Art of Ancient Peru* (1972).
183t, **183c** Photos Michael E. Moseley. **187** After
Michael E. Moseley. **190tl** Photo Bunny Stafford.
190bl, **190–191**, **191bl** Photos NJS. **191br** After
Anton, *The Art of Ancient Peru* (1972). **193** Drawing
by Annick Boothe, after Jesus Raymundo. **198**, **199t**
Photos Michael E. Moseley. **199b** Photo Ferdinand
Anton, Munich. **201** Museum of the American
Indian; photo Werner Forman. **203** Drawn by Simon
S.S. Driver. **204** From Morgan, *Houses and House Life
of the American Aborigines*, 1881. **208** Photo Werner
Forman. **210tl**, **210tr**, **210c**, **210br** Photos Werner
Forman. **210bl** Colorado Springs Fine Art Center –
Taylor Museum Collection. **215t**, **215c** Photos
Werner Forman. **215b** Ohio Historical Society. **218t**,
218b, **219tl**, **219tr** Photos Werner Forman. **218–219**
Cahokia Mounds State Historic Site. Painting by
William R. Iseminger. **225t** Sketch by Karl Weiditz,
1528. **225b** Photo J.A. Sabloff. **226t** Photo R.B.
Welsh. **226b** Photo MEM. **227t** Courtesy Professor
Hermann Trimborn. **227b** Photo courtesy the
Wenner-Gren Foundation.

Sources of Quotations

p.7 Bernal Díaz, *The Conquest of New Spain*, trans.
J.H. Cohen. Pelican Books, 1963, p. 214. **18** ibid., pp.
386–387. **20** Arthur Anderson and Charles Dibble,
The Florentine Codex. University of Utah Press, vol.
10, pp. 171–172. **33** Anderson and Dibble, op. cit.,
vol. 9, p. 18. **36** (line 3ff) ibid., p. 47. **36** (line 12ff)
Díaz, op. cit., p. 232. **36–37** All quotes for the
Spanish Conquest unless otherwise stated are from
Anderson and Dibble, op. cit., vol. 12. **38** (line 1ff)
William Prescott, *Conquest of Peru*. Lippincott, New
York, 1874, p. 413. **38** (line 14ff) ibid., p. 419. **38**
(line 26ff) Quoted by John Hemming, *The Conquest
of the Incas*. Harcourt, Brace, Jovanovich, New York,
1970. **41** Garcilaso de la Vega, *Royal Commentaries
of the Inca*, trans. Harold V. Livermore. University of
Texas Press, Austin, 1966, p. 64. **44** Victor W. von
Hagen, *The Incas of Pedro de Cieza de León* (1553).
University of Oklahoma Press, Norman, 1959, p.
144. **48** Pedro Pizarro, *Relation of the Discovery and
Conquest of the Kingdom of Peru*, trans. Philip A.
Means. The Cortés Society, New York, 1921, p. 203.
50 Quoted by John Hyslop, *The Inka Road System*.
Academic Press, New York, 1984, p. 343. **53**
Prescott, op. cit., p. 245. **66** Paul Mehringer, "Clovis
Cache Found: Weapons of the Ancient Americans,"
National Geographic Magazine 174(4) (1988):503.
67–68 Merwyn Garbarino, *Native American Heritage*.
Little, Brown, Boston, 1976, p. 164. **68** (line 11ff)

ibid., pp. 248–249. **68** (line 16ff) Alexander Henry,
Travels and Adventures in the Years 1760–1776. R.R.
Donnelly, 1971, p. 135. **69–70** Paul Kane,
*Wanderings of an artist among the Indians of North
America*. C.E. Tuttle, Rutland, 1971, p. 55. **71**
Hilary Stewart, *Indian Fishing*. University of
Washington, Seattle, 1977, p. 163. **79** James
Beaglehole, *Life of Captain James Cook*. Stanford
University Press, Palo Alto, 1976, p. 586. **88** Gordon
Brotherston, *Image of the New World*. Thames and
Hudson, London, 1979, p. 214. **89** Edward Tylor,
Anthropology. Appleton, New York, 1883, p. 214. **90**
Frank Cushing, *Zuni*, Jesse Green (ed.). University of
Nebraska Press, Lincoln, 1979, p. 366. **93** Anna
Roosevelt, "Lost Civilizations of the Lower
Amazon," *Natural History* 2 (1989):77. **94** Cushing,
op. cit., p. 346. **96** (line 3ff) John Lloyd Stephens,
*Incidents of Travel in Central America, Chiapas and
Yucatan*. Harpers, New York, 1841, p. 272. **96** (line
17ff) John Lloyd Stephens, *Incidents of Travel in
Yucatan*. Harpers, New York, 1843, p. 344. **97** F.
Blom and Oliver La Farge, *Tribes and Temples*.
Tulane University Press, New Orleans, 1926, p. 77.
108 John Lloyd Stephens 1983, op. cit., p. 277. **109**
(line 28ff) Alfred Tozzer, "Landa's Relacion de las
Cosas de Yucatan," *Papers of the Peabody Museum
of American Archaeology and Ethnology* vol. 18,
Cambridge, Mass., 1941. **109** J.E.S. Thompson, *Maya
Hieroglyphic Writing: An Introduction*. Carnegie
Institution of Washington DC, Publication 589,
1950, p. 155. **123** Dennis Tedlock, *Popol Vuh*.
Touchstone Books, New York, 1985, p. 72. **139**
Tozzer, op. cit. **140** Philip Ainsworth Means,
"History of the Spanish Conquest of Yucatan and of
the Itzas," *Papers of the Peabody Museum of
American Archaeology and Ethnology* vol. 7,
Cambridge, Mass., 1917, pp. 128–129. **143** Anderson
and Dibble, op. cit., vol. 7, p. 4. **152** Juan de
Torquemada, *Monarquia Indiana*. Madrid, 1616, p.
36. **153** George Kubler, "The iconography of the art
of Teotihuacan," *Dumbarton Oaks Studies in Pre-
Columbian Art and Archaeology* 4, Dumbarton Oaks,
Washington DC, 1967, p. 74. **154** Anderson and
Dibble, op. cit., vol. 10, pp. 165–166. **156** ibid., p.
167. **192** Cieza de León, *The Incas of Cieza de León*
(1553), trans. Harriet de Onis. University of
Oklahoma Press, Norman, 1959, p. 223. **202** (line 9)
Brian Fagan, *Elusive Treasure*. Scribners, New York,
1977, p. 66. **202** (line 16) Garbarino, op. cit., p. 211.
212 Josiah Priest, *American Antiquities and
Discoveries in the West*. New York, 1833, p. 57. **212**
Cyrus Thomas, *Report of the Mound Explorations of
the Bureau of Ethnology*. Washington DC, 1894, p.
36. **221** Bartolomé de las Casas, *A Very Brief Account
of the Destruction of the Indies*. Seville, 1542. **221**
Diego Duran, *The Aztecs: The History of the Indies
of New Spain*, trans. Doris Heyden and Fernando
Horcasitas. University of Oklahoma Press, Norman,
1964, p. 214. **223** Thomas Hariot, *A Briefe and True
Account of the New Found Land of Virginia*. Dover
Press, New York, p. 111. **224** Michael Coe, *Mexico*.
Thames and Hudson, London, 1962, p. 168.

INDEX